RULING CANADA

Corporate Cohesion and Democracy

Jamie Brownlee

Fernwood Publishing • Halifax

Editing: Judith Kearns and Brian Turner
Printed and bound in Canada by: Hignell Printing Limited

A publication of:
Fernwood Publishing
Site 2A, Box 5 8422 St. Margaret's Bay Road
Black Point, Nova Scotia, B0J 1B0
and 324 Clare Avenue
Winnipeg, Manitoba, R3L 1S3
www.fernwoodbooks.ca

Canadian   Patrimoine   The Canada Council for the Arts   NOVA SCOTIA
Heritage   canadien   Le Conseil des Arts du Canada   Tourism and Culture

Fernwood Publishing Company Limited gratefully acknowledges
the financial support of the Department of Canadian Heritage,
the Nova Scotia Department of Tourism and Culture
and the Canada Council for the Arts for our publishing program.

Library and Archives Canada Cataloguing in Publication

Brownlee, Jamie
Ruling Canada : corporate cohesion and democracy / Jamie Brownlee.

Includes bibliographical references.
ISBN 1-55266-156-3

1. Corporate power--Canada. 2. Business and politics--Canada. 3.
Elite (Social sciences)--Canada. 4. Democracy--Canada. I. Title.

HD3616.C32B78 2005   322'.3'0971   C2005-900927-6

CONTENTS

ACKNOWLEDGEMENTS

The process of writing this book was for me a thoroughly rewarding experience, but the final result is the product of many hands. The time, the effort and the expertise put into these pages constitute a truly collective undertaking. The research on which the book is based formed part of my MA thesis work. I would like to acknowledge my advisor, Dr. Gregg Olsen, in the Department of Sociology at the University of Manitoba. Gregg first encouraged me to pursue this project in a graduate class, and he subsequently helped me to develop the theoretical and empirical approach. Many thanks also to Rod Kueneman for his unquenchable gusto and keen interest in the material, and to Stephen Brickey and Fletcher Baragar for their assistance and input throughout the process. I would also like to acknowledge the work of William Carroll, Wallace Clement and Murray Dobbin, whose sharp examinations of Canadian political economy were an inspiration from the outset.

It is an honour to work with a publishing company like Fernwood. I deeply admire the Fernwood crew for their steadfast commitment to political activism and to social justice. From the very first day of consultation, I was encouraged by the enthusiasm of Wayne Antony. Wayne provided a welcome source of moral support, and his critical commentary greatly improved the work. As part of the writing process, the book manuscript was read by two anonymous reviewers. I thank them both for their insightful commentaries on how to develop particular sections. As well, thanks to Judith Kearns and Brian Turner who carefully and skilfully copy edited the final draft of the book. The production folk at Fernwood were also an integral part of this book: Thanks to Beverley Rach for production layout and cover design, to Debbie Mathers for typing the final manuscript and to Brenda Conroy for proofreading.

I would also like to thank my family for their assistance and encouragement, especially my parents Dale and Rod. Like many of the opportunities and privileges I have enjoyed, my education was made possible largely through their efforts. Lastly, sincerest thanks to my partner Salena for her caring and patience—and her gifts for editing and writing.

INTRODUCTION

Throughout the course of the last two decades, Canada has experienced unparalleled levels of economic and social decline. Indeed, many would argue that—other than the depression era of the 1930s—the 1990s was Canada's worst economic decade of the century, one which continues to resonate into the present. The ongoing effect of this decline is evidenced by many markers, including Canada's drop from first place on the United Nations Human Development Index between 1995 and 2001, to third place in 2002, to eighth place in 2003. Moreover, social inequality is now greater in Canada than in most other developed nations.

Currently, Canada spends just under 19 percent of its Gross Domestic Product on social programs, which is 15 percent less than a decade ago (Barlow 2004: 7). Not surprisingly, these changes to the social infrastructure have had devastating impacts on the lives of many Canadians, especially those most dependent on social support. Since the late 1980s, the number of homeless people in Canada has markedly increased. Likewise, the number of people who receive emergency groceries from food banks has doubled between 1989 and 2000, with over 760,000 now relying on such subsidies to make ends meet (Barlow 2004: 7). Though the Canadian parliament unanimously voted in 1989 to "end child poverty" by the end of the century, the number of poor children in Canada increased 60 percent in the ten years following the promise. At the same time, the number of children in families with incomes less than $20,000 grew by 65 percent and the number of children in families on social assistance increased by 51 percent (Barlow and Clarke 2001: 119–120). Canada's approach to and record in dealing with poverty, among adults and children alike, have been attacked by international agencies whose mandate it is to track poverty levels throughout the world.

In 1999, for the first time in Canadian history, the country spent less on supporting the elderly and the unemployed than did the U.S. (Barlow and Clarke 2001: 120). Significant reductions in employment insurance (formerly unemployment insurance) benefits in the last decade has meant that only about one-third of unemployed workers presently receive employment benefits, compared to 75 percent in 1990 (Economic Policy Institute 2001: 28). Those who work for wages have also been adversely affected by recent changes. Specifically, there has been an increase in the number of contingency workers, those who work part-time or are self-employed and do not receive job security, pensions or benefits. The market incomes of the bottom 10 percent of families with children fell 84 percent from 1990 to 1996; those of the next 10 percent fell by 31 percent (Economic Policy Institute 2001: 24). And for many, the 40-hour work week has become a thing of the past. In fact, working conditions have become so onerous that thousands of Canadians have been forced to delay starting a family, this at a time when corporate salaries grew at an average rate of 15 percent per year and the number of Canadian millionaires tripled (Barlow and Clarke 2001: 120). With the decline of their social protections, Canadians have become more reliant on the private labour market than at any time in the past four decades.

In Canada, as in most industrialized nations, the gap between the rich and the poor is becoming increasingly pronounced. In 2000, this disparity was greater than at any point in the previous thirty years. By the end of 2001, Canada's 100 wealthiest citizens were worth approximately $120 billion, which equals the combined wealth of 5.4 million Canadian families at the other end of the spectrum (Hurtig 2002: 271). In 1999, "an almost unbelievable" 94.4 percent of the wealth was controlled by the wealthiest 50 percent of family units, leaving only 5.6 percent of the wealth for the bottom 50 percent of families (Kerstetter 2003: 4). Put another way, there are "millions of families and individuals living on the brink of financial disaster, while others have managed to accumulate huge slices of the wealth pie" (Kerstetter 2003: 9). If the extent of such disparity is surprising, the fact of its existence is not. Recent opinion polls indicate public awareness of the growing problem: "Canadians believe that in recent years Canada and its corporations have been doing well, but Canadians have not" (Environics poll cited in Barlow and Clarke 2001: 121).

How can we explain these changes? What accounts for increasing levels of economic and social inequality?

This book is not about the tens of thousands of Canadian citizens who have suffered the brunt of these dramatic changes. Rather, it critically examines Canada's "economic elite"—a collection of the country's richest and most powerful individuals, many of whom preside over Canada's largest corporations. The argument advanced here is that the economic elite in Canada is, increasingly, a unified and class conscious group. As a direct result of the elite's solid organizational unity and coordinated lobbying efforts, numerous policies and programs have been either cut or implemented to the benefit of this elite group—and at the expense of the majority of Canadian citizens. Specifically, this book focuses on a number of key questions. To what extent do the Canadian economic elite constitute a unified group? What mechanisms facilitate the unity of this elite? Has globalization affected the nature or extent of elite unity? What are the consequences of the unity of this group? What does their unprecedented access to power and resources mean for the majority of Canadian citizens? Put very simply: does Canada have a ruling class? If so, how does it rule?

An analysis of this kind can inform our understanding of the nature of corporate domination. Indeed, this type of class-based analysis may be more critical today than at any point in history. Corporate power has reached unprecedented levels and has taken hold of the state and public spheres, influencing decisions about who governs and how, the production process, the distribution of resources, the nature and generosity of social programs, the quality and quantity of jobs, the extent of environmental pollution and the content of media and communication systems. In short, corporations have gained an alarming degree of control over the most important aspects of our lives. What is more, corporate control has become so pervasive that these issues are now regularly treated as problems of the market, and therefore as outside the sphere of democratic politics.

An informed understanding of elite organization is also a necessary first step to understanding how economic supremacy is translated into political domination. There has been relatively little analysis done on the political influence of modern corporations, the power they exercise over governments, or the implications this has for democracy. The extent to which the elite is unified directly impacts its ability to pursue—and achieve—a common policy consensus. In other words, to be a leading social and political force, the economic elite must achieve and maintain a certain social cohesiveness as a business community with a shared perspective on what is to be done.

The wealthy and powerful have always figured prominently in this country's social and economic affairs. What is new today, however, is that economic elites appear to be increasingly politically aware and sophisticated in their dealings with government and the public. Speaking of corporate power, Tony Clarke (1997: 113) says that in recent times "big business has become much more strategic and dominant in its political activities ... corporations have begun to think and act, both individually and collectively, as a 'political machine.' ... [They] have learned how they can more effectively translate their considerable assets into political clout."

An accurate assessment of the organizational capacity and political workings of large corporations also helps to illustrate the extensive degree of class consciousness and political awareness among the elite. Many people believe that business leaders are concerned with only the short-term profit interests of their own firms. This is a false and dangerous misconception. In reality, some business leaders are highly class conscious and motivated to defend the interests of the entire class. They recognize, correctly, that they are engaged in an ongoing class struggle, and that protecting "the system" in which they thrive is crucial to maintaining their positions of power and privilege. This may be especially true in Canada because, as Thomas d'Aquino, head of the Canadian Council of Chief Executives (CCCE), tells us, "no business community in the world at the CEO level has taken such an active interest in politics" (cited in Newman 1998: 159-160). The same structures and organizations that facilitate elite unity also directly facilitate class consciousness and, subsequently, unified political action.

CLASS AND THE ECONOMIC ELITE

If you asked a typical Canadian about the range of social classes in Canada, he or she would probably speak in terms of an upper, middle and lower class, with the characteristics of each being associated with some combination of income, occupation and education. Most often, families and individuals are grouped together on the basis of income. Those with the highest incomes are said to constitute the upper class, those with the lowest incomes represent the lower class, and most other workers combine to form the middle class. While these differences are meaningful, differences in income (as well as occupation and education) are more reflective of a person's socio-economic status than their class position. In the social sciences, class is usually understood in terms of one's specific relationship to the current economic system. Drawing on Marxist terminology, this perspective assumes that the attributes noted above matter less than does a person's location within the structure of capitalism.

At its most basic level, capitalism is a mode of production (or way of producing and distributing goods) consisting of two major classes. The dominant class owns and controls the principal means of material production and is usually referred to as the capitalist or owning class. Because productive activity is central to human existence, owning the means of production is a source of enormous economic and political power. The subordinate class is represented by those who work for wages. This class is commonly referred to as the working class because its members own no significant means of production. In economic terms, the owning class is sometimes referred to as capital, while the working class is referred to as labour. Most members of the working class must sell their labour power to capitalists (who "own" the jobs) in exchange for a salary or wage. Capitalists buy labour power in the same way they purchase other commodities: the lower the purchase price, the better able the employer is to secure profits. Given that the structure of capitalism presumes an inherent power differential between capital and labour, the relationship between these two classes is characterized by class conflict and exploitation.

In recent times, the corporation has emerged as the most powerful organizational unit of capital. A major historical trend in the Canadian capitalist structure (and those of other countries) has been the increasing concentration of capital in a relatively small number of dominant corporations. In Canada, and to varying degrees in nations throughout the world, the economy, state and political systems are now heavily influenced by these vast institutions.

While it sometimes makes sense to restrict class membership to the two broad classes noted above, doing so can often inhibit meaningful analysis. A person's position in the labour process is certainly important, but it does not strictly coincide with a person's class position. Class, status and power are distinct but entangled in very complex ways. The subtleties involved in defining class membership extend to all members of society, including those people who occupy the most powerful positions. Individuals who own the means of production (or the majority of shares in major corporations) often stand in similar relation to capital as those who operate corporations on their behalf. Thus, some researchers have found the term "economic elite" more accurately characterizes class and power in modern society.

In Canada today, there exists an economic elite that controls the country's major industrial, financial, and commercial companies and utilities. The elite consists of two major groupings: the capitalist class—large shareholders in major corporations—and the senior executives of business management. The inclusion of these two groups in one category—the economic elite—generated considerable criticism and debate in previous writings. Two of the most prominent writers, C. Wright Mills (1956) and Ralph Miliband (1969), argued that these different groups should not form distinct analytical categories, as they are united by their interest in the ownership of big business. Both stressed the fact that professional managers and executives are often among the largest shareholders, regularly buying shares through preferential purchasing schemes. Furthermore, they argued, even those top executives who do not become major shareholders are easily assimilated by the elite and have similar goals, motivations and commitments.

In the upper echelons of corporate power there is another group, many members of which are included within high management, active in corporate governance. This group Gramsci (1971) calls "organic intellectuals"; they may be lawyers, academics, consultants and other professionals. Gramsci did not view capitalists and organic intellectuals as mutually exclusive categories; rather, he recognized a considerable convergence of the two groups. Indeed, because of their social position, the needs and interests of organic intellectuals harmonize with those of major shareholders.

Other scholars have criticized the alleged unity between capitalists and their high managers. For example, Jorge Niosi (1982) points out that upper-level managers and advisors often hold few shares and are not typically assimilated into the world of major shareholders. Accordingly, a clear distinction must be made between these two groups. The term "economic elite" tends to blur this distinction, leading to theoretical and empirical errors. In this view, the power of managers and advisors is ultimately derived from that of the capitalist class; they were hired and can be fired, holding on to their positions only through satisfactory performance. In other words, high-level managers and advisors do not own the means of production. Therefore, they cannot belong to the economic elite. Other analysts, such as Nicos Poulantzas (1969, 1975b), go further and argue that any focus on elite individuals warrants theoretical concern because it is the structure of capitalism that is "all-determining." In other words, it is the positions that have power, not individuals, who are replaceable.

Even with these contrary perspectives in mind, it seems appropriate to see the economic elite as including the capitalist class and its upper-level managers and advisors. Insofar as the latter group does possess and exercise considerable power—power that is derived from ownership but also rooted in organizational position—it makes sense for the two groups to be considered together in an analysis of corporate power. Moreover, the relative power of each group cannot be easily or obviously distinguished. Does a high executive with few shares, for example, have less than, the same as or more power than a major shareholder who is not involved in the control of his or her company? Put simply, the relationship between investors, directors and managers in the structure of power is a very close one. Each group relates to the corporation and derives its power from that relationship.

UNDERSTANDING THE ECONOMIC ELITE

The debate about economic elites includes theoretical disagreements. "Unity theorists" claim there is strong social cohesion and political solidarity among corporations and their elite members. In contrast, "disunity theorists" argue that different segments of the business community do not form a cohesive whole and routinely oppose one another on political issues. Individual corporations or fractions of capital, disunity theorists maintain, are far too concerned with their own particular goals and interests to come together as a united force. Chapter One explains this theoretical debate and talks about some of the economic and political changes in the world since the early 1970s.

Part Two of the book begins to show how the ruling class rules. Chapter Two focuses on concentrated economic ownership. In general, through corporate mergers and acquisitions, diversification patterns and intercorporate ownership, increasing levels of concentration have resulted in fewer competing interests in the domestic market, which, in turn, has resulted in greater economic cooperation among elites. Further, these processes have expanded the range of economic sectors and activities that corporate executives are involved in, broadening their focus and tying them together in pursuit of common goals. Canada's mass media is given special attention in Chapter Two because of the role it can play in setting agendas of public debate. Chapter Three defines and explores the Canadian network of interlocking directorates. The boards of dominant corporations serve to integrate the elite and establish a broad, class-based outlook among corporate executives.

In Part Three, the discussion turns to three important—and often overlooked—organizational sources of unification: intersectoral policy organizations, advocacy think tanks and free-enterprise foundations. Together, they comprise the "policy formation network." Policy organizations and think tanks (Chapters Four and Five) both provide a setting for members of the elite to establish a common policy outlook and a set of strategic initiatives that help put policy consensus into action. Chapter Six outlines how foundations provide a key source of funding for think tanks and enable the elite to direct vast sums of money towards particular political projects. The organizations of the policy formation network are heavily interlocked with each other and with the corporate community. Together, these organizations unify the elite by helping to clarify their political agenda and by giving the veneer of objectivity to the political interests of the ruling class.

Part Four of the book discusses the mechanisms that tie Canada's economic elite to the state and political systems. These ties play a key role in establishing a common policy perspective within the state elite, as well as among capital, the state and political parties. In Chapter Seven, the focus is on overlapping interpersonal ties between capital and the state, the social class backgrounds of elites, and the connections between Canada's major political parties and their corporate benefactors. These ties are important because some degree of continuity and cohesion between the major systems of power is needed for a united business class to assert its dominance effectively. From this perspective, the networks of elite relations detailed in Part Four are unifying mechanisms in their own right.

The concluding chapter shifts the focus from elite unity and business power to the ways in which Canadians and citizens around the world have started to resist corporate domination. If Canada's economic elite is indeed the cohesive and powerful political force suggested here, the implication is that challenging such power will not be easy. Citizens who wish to promote progressive social change must realize that the odds are not in our favour. This is made clear by Tom D'Acquino, head of the CCCE. He states:

> If you ask yourself, in which period since 1900 has Canada's business community had the most influence on public policy, I would say it was in the last 20 years. Look at what we stand for and look at what all the governments, all the major parties... have done, and what they want to do. They have adopted the agendas we've been fighting for in the past few decades. (cited in Newman 1998: 151)

Only a highly organized business community, effectively unified around key public policy issues, would have been able to achieve what D'Acquino describes. Because social and economic policy is largely the product of organized and conscious effort on the part of business leaders, what this actually makes clear is that there is nothing remotely inevitable about the current situation. That is to say, a great deal of potential exists for citizens to alter current economic arrangements to realize the interests of the vast majority. Collective social action could change the public policy consensus. If the goal is genuine democracy—in which the economy serves the needs of the general population—the current conditions of corporate rule must be challenged.

The overall purpose of this book, then, is not only to illuminate some of the critical aspects of power relations in Canadian society and around the globe, but also to emphasize that these relations are not inevitable, that they could be modified through networks of social activism and unified resistance. An essential pre-requisite to opposing corporate rule is to understand how the elite is able to dominate economic, social and political life. To confront this stark political reality, people must become conscious of it. It is hoped that this book makes a small contribution to such an understanding. Today, given the intensive corporate efforts to undermine the significant gains that have been won through decades of popular struggle, in the West and elsewhere, these issues could not be more important. If people become aware of the present reality, construct alternatives and implement the necessary mechanisms to realize those alternatives, corporate power could be seriously challenged in the years ahead. Society's energies may then be devoted to genuine and urgent human needs.

1. THE ELITE UNITY DEBATE

The extent to which elites constitute a unified group is a central issue in discussions about business power and the opportunities for a properly functioning democracy. This controversy centres on whether or not elites— particularly the owners and managers of business firms—can achieve unity and solidarity around key issues of public policy and promote a common agenda. It makes a great deal of theoretical and practical difference if the economic elite is, in fact, internally cohesive and integrated. When unified, the vast resources of the corporate world are typically able to overwhelm the resources of all other social groups. Under these conditions, the prospects become increasingly remote for other citizens, especially marginalized sectors of the population, to participate meaningfully in the political arena. Thus, the mechanisms of social cohesion available to the business community have far-reaching implications for the exercise of political power.

ELITE UNITY AND ITS DISCONTENTS

Some social theorists are skeptical of the possibilities for unity within the economic elite. One of the most vocal on the subject has been Nicos Poulantzas (1969, 1975a and 1975b)—a "structural" Marxist—who argues that the elite should not be considered a homogeneous ruling class, as though it had an unambiguous class-wide interest. Rather, business leaders are a highly fractionalized group with divergent interests at both the economic and political levels. In his debates with Ralph Miliband in the late 1960s and early 1970s,[1] Poulantzas (1969) criticized him for under-emphasizing the importance of sectoral cleavages, such as between industrial and financial capital, within the capitalist class. According to Poulantzas (1975a: 297–298), this division of the bourgeois class into antagonistic fractions generates powerful conflicts of interest, which means that the economic elite are "incapable (through their own organizational means) of transforming their specific interest into the political interest." Left to themselves, the economic elite are "not only exhausted by internal conflicts but, more often than not, founder in contradictions which make them incapable of governing politically."

Structuralists, like Poulantzas, maintain that corporate managers are typically concerned not with class loyalties or commitments but only with the specific interests of their own firms. They contend that most business leaders are simply too narrow minded to cooperate on behalf of their common class interests. As a result, those policies which are designed to preserve the long-term collective interests of big business are not given much consideration in the corporate world. Conflicting priorities ensure that the economic elite is incapable, by itself, of achieving political unity and acting collectively (Mizruchi 1992: 23). Therefore, structuralists argue that the state must do for business what it is unable to do for itself—mediate and transcend the individual interests of particular elites and class fractions. It is here where the "relative autonomy" of the state becomes important. The state is "autonomous" because state policy is independent of the narrow pursuits of individual capitalists, but this autonomy is only "relative" because ultimately the whole societal system, including the political system, is dependent on the economy. Because state autonomy always remains relative, it can only be used to implement policies that are in the overall, long-term interests of the capitalist class (even though particular members of this group may fail to recognize it). For example, according to some structuralist accounts, the introduction of factory legislation to protect women in the late 1800s did not result from the efforts and sacrifices of women's groups and other social activists. Rather, it was more about the state preserving capitalism by ensuring the reproduction of a future labour force (O'Connor and Olsen 1998: 23). Put simply, the state is the key unifying mechanism. Poulantzas insisted that business itself had no mechanisms that enabled it to generate unity and, further, that business leaders were too divided to engage in organized political action.

Yet such a formulation cannot explain the fact that business elites do form many kinds of associations to organize their members, plan policy and engage the political process. A few of these organizations, like the Canadian Council of Chief Executives (formerly the Business Council on National Issues), have as their express purpose the unification of the business community. Some of the theoretical challenges presented by these organizations have been met with "softer" versions of structuralism.

In a capitalist economy, corporate officials decide on their rate of investment on the basis of a variety of specific variables, including size of the market, taxation rates, labour costs and unionization levels. The sum of these evaluations about the political/economic climate leads to a particular level of business confidence. Capitalists, in their collective role as investors, can exercise a "veto" over state policies through their failure or unwillingness to invest at adequate levels, which can create political problems for state managers in the form of declining economic growth, rising unemployment and increased public opposition (see, for example,

Block 1977). State managers, discouraged by these possibilities from taking actions that might seriously decrease business confidence, have a direct interest in using their own power to facilitate it.[2] Appeasing business is important not only for attracting business investment but for keeping it. As long as capitalists have advanced warning that they face a threat, they will be able to launch a capital strike or engage in capital flight. The state, therefore, seeks economic stability not only because of structural forces but because of self-interest on the part of bureaucrats and politicians. In short, maintaining a favourable investment climate will keep business confidence strong, investment levels high and state officials employed.

On the other hand, the structural power generated by investment decisions is just a signaling device. It can help set the political agenda and define alternatives, but it cannot tell governments what to do. If state managers are to know what is needed to maintain or restore business confidence, there must be some institutionalized mechanisms for business to communicate those needs to policy-makers. To explain this, soft structuralists acknowledge campaign contributions, lobbying activities and so forth as techniques of increasing the state's receptiveness to business interests (Block 1977: 13). Included in these channels of influence is the recruitment of business elites directly into the state system, as well their participation in policy organizations. Moreover, these direct pressures from business assume a more important role during "exceptional periods," such as wars, depressions and postwar reconstruction. In these periods the economic context changes, allowing state managers a greater degree of freedom in relation to capitalists, including the leeway to implement more stringent economic controls (Block 1980: 232). Because the loss of business confidence and the threat of capital flight are not as critical in these periods, business efforts are stepped up to employ direct lobbying initiatives.

The notion that business leaders are able to coordinate a strike quickly when faced with threat, or that they can immediately alter political strategies and tactics in response to varying degrees of structural dominance, seems to suggest high levels of business unity and political awareness among elites. Yet Block, for example, rejects such a suggestion, arguing that a division of labour exists between corporate leaders and state managers. State managers are the ones who protect the system by maintaining economic and political stability. Block maintains, like Poulantzas, that investors do not make subtle evaluations as to whether a government is serving the long-term interests of business; firms look out for their own immediate economic interests and the process unfolds without any members of the elite consciously deciding to act politically against the government. Much of the structuralist theoretical model rests on the premise of divided and narrowly focused elites. Structuralists tend to deduce the behaviour of elites from the supposed constraints of the system.

Coming from a very different political position, pluralists also reject the possibility of unity within the elite class (see Dahl 1958, 1961, 1967 and Rose 1967). Specifically, pluralists argue that different segments of the business community do not form a cohesive whole and that they routinely oppose one another on political issues. For pluralists, power is diffuse, and business represents merely one of society's many competing interest groups. The state, pluralists contend, is a neutral arbitrator of conflict, receiving "direction" from many different centres of social power. Because one centre of "power is set against another, power is tamed, civilized, controlled, and limited to decent human purposes, while coercion, the most evil form of power, [is] reduced to a minimum" (Dahl 1967: 24). While particular interest groups can emerge victorious on specific issues, no single group has its interests realized on a regular basis. Put another way, pluralists conceptualize power relations as a game in which "you win some and you lose some"; the outcome of policy formation does not systematically favour any one group (Knuttila and Kubik 2000: 79).

Along the same lines, pluralism proposes a model of power that fundamentally separates the political from the economic. Each individual interest group is said to have roughly the same opportunity to influence the political process. This is because—regardless of a person's class or status—everyone in a democracy has the same right to make his/her opinions known to decision-makers. Some social classes may have more political resources than others, but pluralists see this inequality as being counterbalanced by the voting system (one person, one vote) and the capacity of marginalized groups to influence political elites. In other words, the system is relatively open to all people who are interested in political issues and there are many points of access for their participation. Pluralist assumptions are prominent within academia and—though they are rarely equated with pluralism per se—among the general population as well. On the basis of these assumptions, some have characterized pluralism as the "official ideology of capitalist democracies" (Olsen 2002: 117).

But do all citizens or groups really have similar opportunities to organize and influence the state and the political process? Are there, over time, no consistent winners and losers resulting from social inequalities and power differentials? How can pluralists reconcile these assumptions with the evidence of systematic attacks on the general population by elite groups over the last few decades?

On the issue of elite unity, then, pluralists take exception to theoretical depictions of business as a cohesive and integrated group. Networks of elite power, they say, are divided and have increasingly become so in capitalist societies. Furthermore, pluralists contend that the sources of elite unity identified by its critics—such as interlocking directorates, con-centrated ownership networks and policy organizations—are ineffective; that is, they do not facilitate class cohesion. However, pluralists temper this conviction by pointing out that they *would* lead to unity if they were effective (Mizruchi 1992: 31). In fact, Dahl (1958: 465) even concedes that the "political effectiveness" of any group depends upon its "potential for unity." By claiming that elite unity never arises, pluralists avert concerns regarding the possible consequences of a unified business class. As Mark Smith (2000: 7) points out, "if firms do not exhibit solidarity in practice, [pluralists] need not worry about the hypothetical likelihood that unity would lead to business power so strong as to subvert representative democracy." Of course, pluralist arguments and those based on structural Marxism depart quite radically in the implications they draw from presumed business disunity. For pluralists, the implication is that the economic elite is too divided to be politically dominant, and the state acts as a neutral umpire in interest group disputes. For structural Marxists, the argument is framed in terms of the state's having to assume the role of protecting the common interests of the elite because the business elite is not unified enough to do this for itself.

Critics of the unity perspective are not limited to pluralism and structuralism. Jorge Niosi (1982: Chapter 3), for example, questions elite unity as well, arguing that the inequality of power within large corporations divides the elite. Focusing on Canada, Niosi (1985: 58) speaks of a "deeply divided" economic elite, arising from the regional character of the economy, linguistic and ethnic differences and the high number of foreign multinational corporations operating in the country.[3]

A common thread appears to run through many of these critiques— that the economic elite is inherently incapable of articulating and advancing its own long-term interests. This claim, however, is highly suspect and often simply taken for granted. Clyde Barrow (1993: 47) summarizes, "after all is said and done, methodological decrees do not answer to historical evidence supporting the claim that [the economic elite does] manage to articulate a class-wide interest in the policy-formation process." Indeed, the issue in many ways is empirical. Is the elite unified? Is it politically effective? The remainder of the book addresses these questions.

THE CHALLENGE OF UNITY THEORISTS

In contrast to structuralism and pluralism, power elite theorists such as C. Wright Mills (1956) and Thomas Dye (1995), and "instrumental" Marxists like Ralph Miliband (1969, 1977) and G. William Domhoff (1978, 1998), posit the existence of a strong level of cohesion among private corporations and their elite members. At the same time, these theorists concede that there are forces within the business world that lead to conflict and divergence. For example, there are important divisions between financial and non-financial businesses, retail and manufacturing firms, large international corporations and smaller domestic ones, as well as competition within industries and regional divides. To be sure, differences among those with wealth and power do exist. Members of the economic elite are often divided over a multitude of policies and issues. But unity theorists believe that this does not prevent them from constituting a dominant economic class, possessing a high degree of solidarity and common purpose. Moreover, when disagreement does occur, it takes place within a very narrow conservative spectrum that precludes major conflict. Although there is considerable diversity among them, members of the elite share "a basic political consensus in regard to the crucial issues of economic and political life ... men of property and wealth have always been fundamentally united, not at all surprisingly, in the defence of the social order which afforded them their privileges" (Miliband 1969: 44). Unity theorists also point to the existence of powerful *unifying mechanisms*, which help elites to foster a strong ideological consensus and unified political vision. In contrast to pluralists, who argue that these mechanisms are ineffective or irrelevant, unity theorists maintain that they are highly efficient instruments of elite domination and control.

Many years ago, Karl Marx claimed not only that there was a high degree of class consciousness within the upper classes of society, but that this was where class consciousness could most easily be demonstrated. The term class consciousness refers to the level of understanding one has about one's own class position and the interests one shares with others in the same location. Compared to working classes, elites recognize (perhaps better than anyone else) the need for solidarity in class struggle. Along these lines, the economic elite can be said to form what Marx calls a "class for itself," a social group whose members are conscious of forming a group with shared interests and therefore able to act collectively in pursuit of those interests. Marx contrasted such a purposeful group with the concept of a "class in itself," which refers to members of a group who share a similar position in society's economic structure but are largely unaware of their membership in the group and who consequently do not pursue their interests in a collective manner. (Marx used the latter term to describe the working class.)

I would argue that the economic elite is united on many issues and that this unity assumes a more solid political expression when class conflict is high and the elite face a threat. One reason for this unity is that capital forms something close to an "organized minority," in which there can be and is a high degree of social and political interaction among its members, through interlocking directorates, business associations, family connections, educational similarities and social clubs. Of course, all of this is in addition to the incredible resources the elite controls, both economic and cultural, which can be used for coordination and planning. In the words of Peter Newman (1975: 385), "power tends to connect; absolute power connects absolutely."

Even successful managers and entrepreneurs of working class origins are quite easily assimilated into the elite, both in their style of life and their political outlook. Miliband (1969: 42–43) points out that, "some may retain a lingering sense of their antecedents, but this is unlikely to be of great consequence, socially or ideologically. Wealth, in this restricted sense at least, is the great leveler. But wealth is also a great leveler in ideological and political terms." This is as true today, perhaps, as it was in the past. Speaking of the United States, Noam Chomsky explains that

> only two groups are allowed to be class conscious in the United States. One of them is the business community, which is rabidly class conscious. When you read their literature, it's full of the danger of the masses and their rising power and how we have to defeat them. It's kind of vulgar Marxism, except inverted. The other is the high planning sector of the government. (cited in Chomsky and Barsamian 1997: 60)

As we have seen, structuralists reject the idea of class consciousness and solidarity within the elite. Yet this assumption conflicts with structuralism's relative autonomy framework. The theory of relative autonomy assumes that business leaders will respond effectively to the "abuse" of that autonomy. But for the elite to be capable of taking corrective actions, it must have some degree of internal cohesion and a sophisticated understanding of its interests. Essentially, the theory requires that the economic elite, or a portion of it, be class conscious. Yet most structuralists have rejected the usefulness of consciousness as an explanatory concept. Poulantzas, for example, imputes the needs and goals of elites to the capitalist system and argues that "motivations of conduct" should not be used to explain their actions. But even though socioeconomic systems do pressure individuals into particular roles and patterns and have certain requirements for their maintenance, they themselves do not have needs or goals. Robert Brym (1989: 194–195) reminds us that "a capitalist system's 'need' to perpetuate capitalist class relations is no more than a desire on the part of people who benefit from those relations to see things continue pretty much as they are." The same is true of specific institutions. Corporations, for example, do not have objectives other than those instilled in them by people. They are legal devices created to accomplish certain ends. As Mills (1956: 286) points out, corporate elites "are not merely 'bureaucrats': they command bureaucracies." If motivations are ignored altogether, elites are effectively relieved of any accountability. Those in positions of power and authority must be held accountable for the policies they design and implement, and for the often devastating consequences that result.

Block's (1980) discussion of "exceptional periods"—those periods when capital cannot rely on its structural power to ensure state compliance— also implicitly suggests a high level of class consciousness and agency on the part of the elite. During these periods, business leaders will mobilize and use the more direct channels of political influence at their disposal. In order for them to do so, they must be aware of the threat posed by a more independent state and take collective action to "reign the state back in." Mobilization and purposeful action of this sort also imply a relatively cohesive and politically aware class, one that recognizes its own long-term interests, recognizes when those interests are threatened and is able to implement effective solutions.

In general, disagreement among different segments of the Canadian economic elite occurs within a framework of consensus on underlying values. The range of disagreements is relatively narrow, and it is generally confined to means rather than ends. In *The State in Capitalist Society* (1969: 141) Miliband writes, "business, it could be said, is tactically divided but strategically cohesive; over most of the larger issues of economic policy, and over other large national issues as well, it may be expected to present a reasonably united front." For unity theorists, this is a critical qualification. Battles may be fought within corporate boardrooms or policy organizations over *how* to properly defend elite interests, but this does not necessarily suggest conflict over *what* is to be defended. In other words, disagreement over the tactical elements of elite rule is quite common but of less importance than disagreement over their desired results (though not, perhaps, for the victims). Even pluralists have acknowledged that elites are generally united in their support of "the rules of the game," though within these parameters, they maintain, conflict is the norm.

Indeed, it is arguable that elites agree with each other over "large issues of economic policy." For example, a recent project developed by the Ekos research group interviewed 1000 key decision-makers in Canada (top state officials, politicians and corporate executives), as well as 2,500 members of the general public. This study showed the remarkable degree to which the elites were "homogenous in their values and attitudes" and that "a profound gap exists between the public and decision-makers in the area of preferred government values." More specifically, those policies that would facilitate equality, collective rights, full employment and business regulation were routinely low on the elites' list of priorities but high on the general public's (Ekos Research Associates 1995). These findings suggest that the policy preferences of elites are more strongly aligned than disunity theorists acknowledge. As Miliband proclaimed, it may be a mistake to confuse disagreements over tactics with differences in fundamental values.

Earlier studies from the 1980s drew similar conclusions. Michael Ornstein (1982a, 1982b), for one, has argued that Canadian business elites are nearly unanimous in their opposition to the redistribution of income, as well as to the measures that would increase the rights of workers and the power of trade unions. No systematic differences separated medium and big business or different types of industry. Big and medium business also share similar attitudes with respect to social welfare issues, most notably a concerted opposition to the expansion of the social welfare system and a willingness to use social welfare policy to regulate economic conditions and the size of the surplus labour force (Williams 1982).

The importance of maintaining a relatively stable consensus over key issues of public policy is surely recognized by some elites. For this reason, corporate officials will sometimes support positions that are detrimental to the short-term interests of their companies. That class considerations can outweigh more immediate company concerns is quite remarkable, given the importance attached to profit and market share. As unity theorists argue, this suggests a high degree of political awareness and flexibility on the part of corporate executives, as well as a steadfast dedication to maintaining their position of dominance.

Over-riding Class Interests

Capitalist ideology tells us that the short-term profit motive ultimately determines the rationality and strategies of the economic elite. This is true to a large extent. But sometimes broad class interests appear to overshadow narrow economic concerns. For example, when the Tobin Tax was proposed in 1978 to penalize the movements of financial funds for speculation against currency, most businesses reacted in a united fashion against the initiative. Even the sectors of capital that would benefit from it did not support it. Economist David Felix has argued that this was because they had an over-riding class interest, which overcame their narrow duty to shareholders. According to Felix, the over-riding class interest involved using the government deficit crises to undermine the social contract that had been built up over the years—to roll back the gains in welfare benefits, workers' rights, union rights and other unfavourable developments (cited in Chomsky and Barsamian 1997: 223). This interest was important enough to lessen concern for short-term profits. It is for similar reasons that Chomsky believes American elites prefer military spending to social spending:

> if it turned out, as is likely, that using taxpayers' money for socially useful purposes was even more profitable than sending it through the military system, that still wouldn't change the decision to prefer military spending—because social spending is going to interfere with the basic prerogatives of power, it's going to organize popular constituencies, and have all those other negative side effects that [business wants] to avoid. (Chomsky et al. 2002: 122–123)

Business support for the privatization of healthcare in Canada follows a similar logic. Why have the Canadian economic elite not spoken up to protect Medicare from this encroaching threat, given that Medicare provides such a huge competitive advantage to Canadian business? Indeed, some corporate sectors are eager to open up the healthcare system to private profit. Notably, however, those sectors that significantly benefit from the current system have not been critical of recent privatizing initiatives. Dobbin (2000: 22), for example, suggests the reason is that "there is such a determined dedication to [free market] ideology that even the fiduciary duty to shareholders succumbs to corporate unity on free market doctrine." At times, it would seem, there are some things that are more important than profits, like maintaining the entire system of power and privilege.

There are, of course, some issues over which the elite is divided and where fractional divisions are strong. For example, there has been a fairly consistent division in perspective and orientation between capital-intensive, internationally oriented financial and industrial sectors (big business) on the one hand, and the more labour intensive, domestically oriented sectors on the other (Chomsky and Barsamian 1997: 264). The former group is typically more willing to accept an expanded welfare state, including measures such as social assistance, minimum wage laws and other rights for workers because these politically sophisticated "business liberals" understand more clearly the benefits of an orderly workforce and of keeping class conflict to a minimum. In keeping with this perspective, they often adopt "progressive" attitudes toward labour unions and accept the necessity of state intervention. In Canada, many of these corporations and their members are represented by the CCCE.

The idea that the welfare state is supported by some economic elites to serve their own ends is sometimes referred to as "corporate liberalism" (Olsen 2002: 122). This support is not rooted in a "commitment to reform, nor in an enlightened acceptance of labour and government opponents, but rather in the recognition that the entire business community and the future of the private economy will best prosper if it assumes a position of compromise" (Useem 1984: 114). To the same end, Chomsky argues that many of the policies and legislative initiatives that have improved the lives of people in the United States, like the New Deal programs of the 1930s,[4] were partly spearheaded by big business. Some business leaders are willing to support this kind of legislation because they understand that the system is going to collapse if there aren't policies available to bring things under control (Chomsky et al. 2002: 392). It should be noted that although some business leaders felt the New Deal was necessary to protect American capitalism, others were outraged and formulated a plot to overthrow the government (Bakan 2004: 85–86)!

Such insights into corporate liberalism offer us a useful indication of the extent of class consciousness within the business community. However, the argument that elites are aware of the need for this kind of social policy can be somewhat misleading. It tends to downplay the significance of the labour movement, activist groups and waves of popular ferment that have contributed to social wage government legislation over the years.[5] While there may be some business leaders who recognize the stabilizing benefits of such legislation, the initial political push usually comes from those groups who are directly affected. Elites "get on board" when they recognize that particular reforms will reduce class conflict and stabilize the system. Thus, social policies in the interests of the working and poor classes are not merely concessions designed to control them. Often, they are the outcome of difficult battles that have been fought and won, sometimes under conditions of extraordinary violence and repression.

Unity theorists do recognize that the state is (potentially) responsive to interests other than business. This is also understood, for example, by rural workers in Brazil, who have a slogan called "expanding the floor of the cage" (Chomsky and Naiman 1998: 85). The workers understand that they are trapped inside a cage—the capitalist state. But they also realize that they need to protect some elements of the state that are potentially responsive to their needs, as well as to extend the limits of what the cage will allow. These are essential preliminaries to dismantling it. As the floor of the cage gets larger, the possibilities for further change increase. In other words, the state is inherently class based and will act to defend capitalist interests, but popular organizations can significantly influence its organization, structure and policies.

Though some corporate leaders may be willing to support policies that conflict with their company's interests, certainly many will not. Pluralists view this reluctance to compromise on short-term gain as evidence of weak and incidental class loyalties. However, the existence of pragmatic, company-rational firms does not mean that the pluralist model of business relations is accurate. For the economic elite to develop and maintain solidarity, it is not necessary that every elite member be in agreement on every issue. If a particular group within the elite can think and act in the overall interests of capital and has the ability to persuade other groups to more or less accept its mandate, business unity can be largely and effectively generated.

The Inner Circle and Class-wide Rationality
Michael Useem (1984) suggests that there is a segment of the elite with the capacity to promote the broad, overall needs of big business and to act as political leadership for business as a whole. He calls this group the "inner circle." While Useem's analysis specifically concerns the United States and Britain, his framework can be applied to other industrial democracies, including Canada. Most business leaders are not part of the inner circle; their concerns do not extend much beyond the well being of their own companies. However, there is a leading edge of highly class conscious executives who "constitute a distinct, semi-autonomous network, one that

transcends company, regional, sectoral, and other politically divisive fault lines within the corporate community" (Useem 1984: 3). By virtue of their special positions within corporate networks and extensive business connections, this group is uniquely suited to mobilize corporate resources and act at the forefront of business-government relations. Notably, they have the ability to promote compromise among competing sectors of the business community and reconcile their demands. It is this politically charged group of leaders, with distinct political outlooks, that comprises the inner circle.

The inner circle is informed by a "class-wide rationality" derived through common participation in various policy network associations and multiple board interlocks. Mills (1956: 121) argues that the executives of large corporations often broaden their outlook from their own company's policies and interests to those of the industry. But some go a step further, moving from the industrial point of interest to the interests and outlook of the economic elite as a whole. These executives are keenly aware of the wider social environment in which business operates.

Class-wide rationality helps inner circle executives to successfully advance public policies of significant concern to large numbers of firms. Useem (1984: 16) elaborates, noting that "if they promote these concerns, both individually and through select organizations, government policymakers will hear, though of course not always heed, a point of view far more indicative of the general outlook of business than representatives of individual companies could ever provide." In fact, Useem (1984: 88) says that this class-based commitment among inner circle executives partly accounted for their willingness to receive him for an interview. They generally felt a responsibility for getting the business point of view across to the public, and communication with researchers was one means of doing so.

A number of features of capitalist economic development and business organization may contribute to the development of a class-wide outlook. First, heightened corporate concentration in recent decades has created a situation in which fewer individuals have become responsible for the management of the private economy. Potentially, these arrangements could lead to easier coordination and planning. The spread of intercorporate ownership has meant that the investments of top owners and managers have become dispersed among a larger number of companies, further interlacing the interests of individual elites. As well, the existence of an extensive network of interlocking directorates among major corporations compels managers to assume some responsibility for the prosperity of several different corporations. As Mills (1956: 122) put it, those holding multiple directorship positions constitute "a more sophisticated executive elite which now possesses a certain autonomy from any specific property interest. Its power is the power ... of class-wide property." Whether or not these tendencies lead to a unified and effective elite is an empirical question taken up in Chapters Two and Three.

Major business policy organizations may also aid the inner circle in its political role. These organizations are very different from the everyday trade association, whose primary purpose is to defend the interests of a particular industry. A small number of "intersectoral" organizations have been created to provide a forum for debate around issues affecting big business generally. In addition, they provide a potentially unique and useful setting for selecting those corporate executives who possess the class-wide business focus and who therefore deserve promotion as business representatives and government consultants. In Useem's (1984: 101) view, major policy organizations "both groom and screen the select number of business leaders who are to act on behalf of all." Examples include the Canadian Council of Chief Executives, the Business Roundtable in the United States and the Confederation of British Industry. If a case can be made that these organizations have been developed with the purpose of bringing together various sectors of capital in support of key public policy issues, this would lend considerable support to the elite unity perspective.

Corporate inner circles have assumed a more prominent political role over the past few decades. Since the early 1970s, corporate political activities have expanded in Canada and around the world, in conjunction with what has come to be known as economic globalization.

THE 1970S CORPORATE OFFENSIVE
AND THE RISE OF NEOLIBERALISM

An example of collective political action by big business that appears to lend support to the unity perspective is the well-recognized "corporate offensive" that accelerated throughout the developed capitalist world in the early 1970s (the initial stages of what is today referred to as globalization). Fed up with falling profits, government regulation and stagnating economic growth, corporate leaders attempted to mobilize their collective resources to increase their power and control over the global economic system. A second major factor behind the offensive was that a number of new weapons had come into the hands of capital. Revolutionary changes in telecommunications, financial deregulation and the enhanced capacity for corporate mobility provided business elites with more leverage and power. Finally, the offensive represented a response to the widespread political upheaval that took place in the late 1960s and early 1970s, when normally marginalized groups such as workers, ethnic minorities, women, the elderly and others began to get organized and enter into the political arena. These popular grassroots movements took various forms in different countries, but at the core of the struggle was a desire for a more responsive democratic system and a growing resentment of state and corporate power.

In the United States, for example, public attitudes toward government and business underwent a remarkable shift (Crozier et al. 1975: 78).

At the end of the 1950s, approximately three quarters of the American public believed that their government was run mainly for the benefit of "the people" and only 17 percent thought it primarily responded to "big interests." By 1972, the numbers shifted to 38 percent and 53 percent respectively. Corporations were also experiencing a public relations crisis. As Daniel Bell (1971: 7) pointed out in the early 1970s, the "benign attitude toward the corporation has receded ... the sense of identity between the self-interest of the corporation and the public interest has been replaced by a sense of incongruence." U.S. public opinion polls in the 1960s indicated that large U.S. corporations enjoyed a high degree of public confidence, whereas by 1974 this support had been cut in half (Clarke 1997: 19). At the same time, public confidence in big business was declining rapidly in Canada. One indicator of this transformation came in the 1972 Canadian federal election when the New Democratic Party, led by David Lewis, was able to organize broad public support for its campaign against "corporate welfare bums." Similar developments were occurring around the world, in tandem with social movements of various stripes.

If falling profits and the popular uprisings of the 1960s were the major impetus behind the corporate offensive of the 1970s, the expanding power of capital was a primary means to execute it.

The aggressive corporate offensive was designed to accomplish a number of objectives. Business leaders sought to lower what they saw as unrealistically high or economically counter-productive living standards by reducing wage gains, inducing "normal" levels of unemployment, cutting state provided social services and benefits, weakening or destroying unions, and generally dismantling the (already weak) popular structures that enable ordinary citizens to fight for their rights in opposition to the owners and managers of the economy. The media was attacked because it was viewed as too "liberal" and independent (as were universities for the same reason), while the public education system was targeted, once again, as a potential tool for profits and propaganda.[6]

Clearly, a crucial element in the corporate offensive was an attack on the state itself. Because many elites blamed the state for their economic difficulties, their solutions included large reductions in taxes for the wealthy, cutting state spending for the poor and less business regulation. It is important to keep in mind that it was not *less* government intervention that was called for but a different *kind* of intervention. Only state intervention in the interests of workers or that which constrained capital mobility and profit-making was to be reduced. The reasoning was simple: business wanted the popular aspects of government (those programs that serve the needs and interests of the general population) weakened, but still wanted a powerful state—one that protected it, directed resources its way and was generally removed from public control. Aside from these specific goals, the offensive represented a more broad objective—to attack the very concept of democracy and the way it had developed (Carnoy 1984: 233). Elites sought to roll back the social contract that had been won through decades of bitter struggle. Chomsky summarizes their broad mandate this way,

> if you look back to the 1970s it began to appear ... as if it might be possible for ruling groups to do something that they've always hoped to do but couldn't, namely, to roll back everything connected with the social contract ... go right back to the days of 'satanic mills' where they believe they have enough weapons against the population—and it's not implausible—that they can destroy human rights, eliminate the curse of democracy except in a purely formal way, move power into the hands of absolutist, unaccountable institutions which will run the world in their own interests ... eliminate workers' rights, political rights ... destroy it all. (cited in Chomsky and Barsamian 1997: 154)

In the Canadian context, the goals of business leaders were consistent with the general objectives of the corporate campaign. In short, Canada's largest corporations aimed to solidify a business consensus regarding their long-term strategy, assert themselves more forcefully in the policy-making process and alter the political culture of the country to an environment more suitable for business prosperity.

The program of economic and political restructuring which coincided with the offensive later became known as neoliberalism. Neoliberalism incorporates a range of elite policy imperatives such as trade liberalization, privatization of publicly owned enterprises, deregulation, emphasis on deficit and/or debt reduction and business-friendly tax reform. Crucially, it involves "rethinking" the role of the state by replacing its functioning with market mechanisms. Along the same lines, neoliberalism encourages a sharp reduction of the role of government in economic life, particularly income security programs that may discourage workers from accepting low-wage jobs. To help advance the neoliberal agenda, business leaders set out to create and, in some cases, transform, a number of global economic and political institutions. Some of these institutions include the International Monetary Fund (IMF), the World Bank, the World Trade Organization (WTO), the Organization for Economic Cooperation and Development (OECD), the World Economic Forum (WEF), the Trilateral Commission (TC) and the G-7 Forum.

The fact that corporate leaders recognized and quickly responded to the popular challenges of the 1960s and 1970s suggests that business cohesion was already quite strong prior to these events. But Useem (1984: 171) argues that the rise in corporate activism "would not have been as rapid ... nor its thrust as effective were it not for the presence of the transcorporate networks of the inner circle, the class-wide social organization that had

Table 1.1: Typology of Corporate Political Action: Business Disunity and Unity

Generalized Model of Corporate Political Action	Motivations and Political Expression	Actors
Business Disunity Theoretical Schools: • Pluralism • Structural Marxism	Selective: Economic/ Organizational Interests	Complex Organizations: Corporations/ Trade Associations
	Company Rationality	
Business Unity Theoretical Schools: • Power Elite • Instrumental Marxism	Solidaristic: Collective Interests Class-wide Rationality	Class Segments: Inner Circle

Adapted from Dreiling (2000: 26)

gradually developed over the years." These networks facilitated the mobilization of corporate political power in Canada and elsewhere.

The 1970s offensive is one historical example of the power that can be generated through business solidarity. Though the offensive was international in scope, most of the research in this area has focused on the consequences of the corporate offensive within respective nations. In addition, the majority of empirical work on the general issue of elite unity has been nationally focused, while relatively few studies have examined the unity and political capacity of the global economic elite, or what some refer to as a "transnational capitalist class" (Robinson and Harris 2000; Sklair 2001; Carroll and Carson 2003; Robinson 2004). As a global orientation among business elites takes shape and the power of transnational corporations (TNCs) increases, the working of the economic elite in the global political arena is becoming ever more relevant to the elite unity debate. From the perspective of disunity theorists, globalization has the potential to increase division and fragmentation among national corporate classes. Unity theorists, on the other hand, contend that many of the same mechanisms that integrate elites within nations are now working at the global level, albeit in a much larger and potentially more complex context. While a comprehensive investigation of these matters is well beyond the scope of this book, the process of worldwide elite integration represents an important area for future investigation.

To conclude, it would appear that, at least in some instances, the economic elite is able to develop, articulate and advance a class-wide interest in the policy-making process. But how does this happen? To answer this, a number of empirical questions need to be explored. First, are there concrete structural mechanisms within the economy that serve to unify the elite? If so, how do these mechanisms facilitate elite cohesion? Second, how do organizations outside of the economic realm organize members of the elite around specific public policy issues? Lastly, are there socio-political channels by which the elite can effectively advance a unified agenda in the political arena? These questions form the focus of the discussion to follow.

NOTES

1. The disagreements between "unity" and "disunity" theorists constitute an important part of what has been termed the "Miliband-Poulantzas" debate, which accelerated in the 1970s and represented a more general set of divisions in Marxist theory between instrumentalism and structuralism.

2. Block is introducing an idea developed much further by state-centred theorists. State theorists argue that state officials might pursue their own distinctive goals, rather than those of interests groups or capitalists. As well, state structures, such as bureaucracies, party systems, rules of electoral competition and relations among different levels of government, are viewed as important determinants of social policy (Olsen and O'Connor 1998: 19). See, for example, Evans, Rueschmeyer and Skocpol 1985; Steinmo, Thelen and Longstreth 1992; and Olsen 2002.

3. Theda Skocpol (1985: 27), a state-centred theorist, asserts that capitalists "lack the political capacity to pursue class-wide interests in national politics." Claus Offe, a structuralist/systems theorist, says that "the anarchy of competition-geared capitalist production" makes it "extremely unlikely" that a class interest could emerge from among the competing special interests of different business groupings (cited in Barrow 1993: 47). This "anarchy" is primarily due to the stubborn and short-sighted interests of individual corporations.

4. The New Deal was a series of government-led programs in the 1930s that marked the beginnings of the modern American welfare state. It was primarily designed to stimulate and stabilize the economy after the Great Depression. The New Deal measures included the introduction of unemployment insurance, minimum wage laws, old age security, social assistance, farm subsidies and a public works program.

5. The social wage refers to provisions made by the state to reduce the burden placed on the direct earnings of workers through the funding of public services, such as healthcare, education, housing, social welfare, unemployment insurance and public transportation.

6. A useful book dealing with the corporate takeover of the Canadian education system is *Class Warfare: The Assault on Canada's Schools* (1994), by Maude Barlow and Heather-Jane Robertson.

2. CONCENTRATED ECONOMIC OWNERSHIP

In January of 2001, America Online (AOL) and Time Warner merged in a transaction valued at $164.7 billion (Gaughan 2002: 4). The merger combined Time Warner's extensive holdings in music, movie, television and magazine production with AOL's Internet resources. The combined company is a true multi-media powerhouse, boasting impressive market share and power. But this is only one example of the mega-mergers that characterize the last twenty-five years, and mergers are only the most visible symptom of a much broader phenomenon that joins corporations into integrated networks of economic and political cooperation. Increasing levels of concentration mean fewer conflicting interests in the domestic market, as previously competing financial and industrial interests become economically and socially intertwined. Vast blocks of economic resources are brought under the control of fewer and fewer individuals, potentially expanding economic cooperation and concentrating corporate power. The result is that a relatively few large enterprises have come to control a dominant (and ever-expanding) proportion of all economic activity.

Concentrated ownership has obvious implications for our understanding of corporate networks and elite unity. Because corporate ownership is generally confined to a small and increasingly entangled circle, the dense web of interconnections among dominant firms makes it easier for owners and managers to perceive and articulate their common interests. The leaders at these corporate empires are often mutually acquainted and tend to have outlooks that extend beyond the prosperity of their own companies. Those with the abilities and necessary connections to reconcile competing interests wield an extraordinary level of power and influence within Canada's economic system. As well, because so few individuals control such a large proportion of economic assets, they are in a position to exercise "veto power" over government policy proposals. Of the approximately one million incorporated businesses in 2001, the top twenty-five accounted for 41.2 percent of all business assets in Canada. Across all sectors of the economy, dominant corporations (firms with assets larger than $25 million or annual revenues greater than $100 million) accounted for almost 80 percent of total assets (Carroll 2004: 201).

MERGERS AND ACQUISITIONS

Contrary to one of the key myths about modern capitalism, the huge corporations—those of which most Canadians are aware—did not grow to their huge size by "slugging it out" in a competitive economic arena. These giants grew and expanded their operations by combining with other companies through mergers and acquisitions. When two companies merge, there are two possible end results. In some mergers, one company is absorbed by the other and loses its independence. In 1998, for example, Nortel merged with Bay Networks, creating a much larger "Nortel." In other mergers, an entirely new company is formed by the consolidation of two firms. For example, in 1998, Alberta Telecom and GTE Canada combined to form Telus, a larger telecommunications company. Acquisitions occur when one company buys the majority of the ownership shares or voting stock of another firm and then runs the acquired company as a subsidiary. Put simply, one company acquires and takes over the operations of another company. Throughout the 1990s, the mining giant Noranda gradually acquired shares of Falconbridge, a smaller Canadian mining company. Today, Noranda owns nearly 60 percent of Falconbridge and runs the smaller company as a subsidiary.

Three kinds of corporate integration are based on mergers and acquisitions. The first kind, horizontal integration, is the consolidation of firms that operate in the same industry. This is the most common way to increase concentration, and it often involves a large firm buying out its smaller competitors, as the example of Noranda and Falconbridge demonstrates. If this process occurs regularly it can lead to the formation of a monopoly, meaning the exclusive control of a product or service in a given industry. A second kind of integration is vertical, in which the linking brings together discrete elements of the production and distribution processes within one single operating structure. Thus, a vertically integrated company is one whose activities include some or all of the steps of production, ranging from the attainment of raw materials to the sale and/or servicing of the finished product. For example, a car manufacturer may acquire parts manufacturers that produce the materials necessary for automobile production, as well as the transportation companies and retail outlets at the distribution end. Such control over many stages of production gives the corporation a titanic boost in its power and profitability. Ben Bagdikian (2000: xvii) argues that vertical integration used to be looked upon negatively by governments, as it was widely recognized that "corporations which have control of a total process, from raw materials to fabrication to sales, also have few motives for genuine innovation and the power to seize out anyone else who tries to compete." Today, however, governments have become sympathetic to large vertical corporations that have merged into incessantly larger "total systems."

A third kind of corporate integration is the conglomerate merger, which links companies in different fields of production. In this type of merger, the firms involved have no intrinsic relationship in their activities, either horizontally or vertically. A dramatic example of a conglomerate merger was the 1980s takeover of The Bay by the Thomson Corporation (which already controlled half of Canada's newspaper market and had considerable oil and gas interests) (Veltmeyer 1987: 40). At the time, The Bay was Canada's largest retail merchandising chain, and it had recently purchased 50 percent of Simpsons-Sears, Canada's second largest retailer. Since the incursion of transnational corporations in the 1950s, conglomerate mergers have become an increasingly popular form of augmented concentration, although their popularity has appeared to be waning in recent years. The top ten Canadian conglomerates in 2001, ranked by revenue, are presented in Table 2.1. The top three alone—George Weston Ltd., Onex Corporation and Power Corporation of Canada—received over $66 billion in revenues in 2001 and presided over approximately $105 billion in assets.

It is important to acknowledge that the three kinds of corporate integration discussed above are not discrete categories. Today's complex corporate giants are often mixtures of all three forms of consolidation, and the varieties of combination are endless. Nevertheless, in whatever form it takes, the continual merging of capital serves to potentially "unify an already small and cohesive group, reducing dissension because interests and concerns become more congruent. Political organization and mobilization are made much easier ... capital can more readily speak with 'one voice'" (Olsen 1991: 116).

Corporate concentration through mergers and acquisitions has been increasing in Canada for many decades. Using an approach similar to John Porter's (1965), Wallace Clement (1986: 125–126) found that the 183 dominant corporations identified by Porter in the 1950s had been melded down to a significantly smaller number of dominant companies by the early 1970s. The key reason for this was augmented concentration, as forty-one of the dominant companies were reduced to seventeen through mergers and acquisitions. Concentration continued to increase in the late 1970s and into the 1980s. Newman (1981) shows that the number of what he calls "major and significant" corporate mergers climbed steadily from 1975 to 1981. In 1983, the top 500 Canadian firms (representing only about one-eighth of one percent of all companies) accounted for more than one-half of total sales, over two-thirds of assets and profits, and almost three-quarters of equity (Veltmeyer 1987: 23). Between 1977 and 1986, as measured by the shares of corporate sales, assets and profits, concentration increased for the vast majority of available indicators (Krause and Lothian 1989: 3.27).

Remarkably, the degree of concentration and monopoly permitted under Canadian laws during this period surprised even the editors of the

Table 2.1: Top Ten Canadian Conglomerates, 2001

	FP 500 Rank	2001 Revenues $'000s	2001 Assets $'000s	2001 Profits $'000s
George Weston Ltd.	4	24,661,000	16,227,000	582,000
Onex Corp.	5	23,803,000	20,870,000	798,000
Power Corp. of Canada	14	18,360,000	68,730,000	618,000
The Jim Patterson Group	53	5,200,000	3,100,000	n.a.
ATCO Ltd.	69	3,754,300	n.a.	124,400
Siemens Canada Ltd.	80	3,300,000	n.a.	n.a.
James Richardson and Sons, Ltd	136	1,812,015	1,018,373	58,342
Bayer Inc.	167	1,560,259	1,017,546	n.a.
Brascan Corp.	195	1,229,000	21,467,000	311,000
MDC Corp. Inc.	209	1,113,272	918,315	139,360

Source: National Post Business (2002)

New York Times. In a 1980 article called "Monopoly by Oligarchy?" the *Times* reports the following:

> Canada's corporate concentration grows by the day. Economic power is flowing to fewer and fewer individuals. And because of the weakness of Canada's antimonopoly laws and the lack of strong public sentiment against bigness in business, the Anti-combines branch of the Department of Consumer and Corporate Affairs is virtually powerless to do anything. (*New York Times*, March 1980, cited in Veltmeyer 1987: 42)

These developments accelerated in the years that followed. In 1985, merger and acquisition activity skyrocketed and remained exceptionally high until the end of the decade (Green and McNaughton 2003: 19). This jump was likely related to the relaxed ownership restrictions and deregulation of the Canadian economy in the 1980s, which continued into the 1990s. Since 1984, for example, banks have been permitted to increase their control of investment dealers from zero to 70 percent, and of trust companies from 36 to 69 percent.

The economic depression in the early 1990s saw many companies get "lean and mean," and, consequently, the number of merger and acquisitions declined. But this reduction was short lived, as just a few years later the number of deals was again on the rise. The rate of transactions in Canada increased steadily throughout the decade, but more than doubled in the year 2000. This latest surge, which began in the late 1990s, echoed developments in many other countries, as transactions accelerated around the globe in both volume and value (Gaughan 2002: 53-54). These trends show little sign of slowing down.

DIVERSIFICATION

Accompanying concentration through mergers and acquisitions has been diversification. This is a process whereby many large firms become economically integrated with a wide variety of related and unrelated products and industries. A company diversifies by establishing or acquiring production units engaging in different industrial activities, thereby moving either into areas closely related to the company's main line of business or into new unrelated areas. Thus, diversification involves a decline in the number of companies involved in a single line of business as they become more familiar with a range of different labour forces, market conditions and business climates. A typical diversified firm is usually considered a corporate conglomerate. These types of enterprises have existed in Canada since the late 1800s, when the Canadian Pacific Railway Company began to expand into other industries such as transport, mining and natural resources, communications, hotels and real estate (Minister of Supply and Services Canada 1978: 103).

Because they must be cognizant of developments in various sectors of the economy, the top executives of heavily diversified firms are less prone to narrow, industry-specific viewpoints. A firm that expands the breadth of its industrial activities will be less vulnerable to rapid changes in any single market. Indeed, managing risk is one of the reasons why many companies choose to diversify. Diversification thus links the fate of one company to the fate of many others, cutting across industries and economic sectors.

There are few studies of diversification, largely because of the difficulties inherent in obtaining comprehensive information on the operations of firms across industries. Using 1995 data, Green and McNaughton (2003: 9) discovered that the most heavily diversified companies in Canada were financial intermediaries, insurance companies and business financing firms. They note that the most extreme example of diversification is represented by the Canadian Depository for Securities, which is privately held by many of Canada's major banks, trust companies and brokerage houses. Strikingly, it had established 173 ownership ties in 30 different industry groups by 1995. Again using 1995 data, Green and McNaughton (2003: 9) found corporations in other sectors of the economy that were also heavily diversified. In primary and manufacturing sectors, for example, these include James Richardson and Sons with twenty-seven ties to twelve industry groups, MacMillan Bloedel with twenty-five ties to eleven groups, and Alcan Aluminum with twenty ties to eleven groups.

Diversified corporations are central to the Canadian economy. One

Table 2.2: Top Ten Diversified Financials, 2001

	2001 Revenues $'000s	2001 Assets $'000s	2001 Profits $'000s
Power Financial Corp.	17,889,000	67,069,000	879,000
Fairfax Financial Holdings Ltd.	6,125,700	35,438,700	346,000
RBC Dominion Securities Ltd.	3,854,020	59,018,170	n.a.
Caisse de dépôt et placement du Québec	3,750,000	121,808,000	3,543,000
Canada Trustco Mortgage Co.	3,551,747	40,649,359	439,876
TD Securities	3,100,000	n.a.	n.a.
Scotia Capital Inc.	2,794,000	115,000,000	686,000
Canada Mortgage and Housing Corp.	2,207,000	23,822,000	345,000
Bank of Canada	2,149,200	41,804,500	1,980,400
Ford Credit Canada Ltd.	2,085,670	13,835,104	103,820

Source: *National Post Business* (2002)

type is "multi-unit firms," companies whose multiple operating units span different industrial sectors. Simply possessing two or more units does not ensure that a firm is diversified, as many multi-unit firms consolidate all of their operating units within a single industry (often through vertical integration). Nevertheless, "the proportion of multi-unit firms within an industry will, in part, determine its overall level of diversification. Other things being equal, the more multi-unit firms within an industry, the more diversification occurs" (Baldwin et al. 2000: 17). As presented in Table 2.3, over 13,400 companies have multiple units within their operating structures, accounting for less than one percent of all companies in Canada. Yet, despite comprising only a tiny fraction of Canadian companies, these multi-unit forms employ one-third of the Canadian workforce and account for one-half of total business revenue. Not surprisingly, diversification occurs more frequently in industries with higher levels of corporate concentration, further strengthening the position of Canada's largest firms and integrating their fortunes.

INTERCORPORATE OWNERSHIP AND CONTROL

The networks of relations among companies are also becoming more inclusive through the rise in intercorporate ownership. This refers to a situation where many of the top shareholders in a large company are other corporations. The intercorporate network of ownership is diffuse; that is, most of the ownership links are broadly spread, and they are not usually formed to link specific pairs or cliques of firms (Useem 1982: 207). In other

Table 2.3: Characteristics of Multi-Unit Firms, Third Quarter 1998

	Multi-Unit Firms	All Firms	% Accounted for by Multi-Unit Firms
Number of Businesses	13,421	1,701,821	0.79
Revenue ($ billions)	1,254	2,265	55.4
Employment (millions)	4.96	14.53	34.1

Source: Baldwin at al. (2000: 17)

words, most shareholding of this kind is the result of investment strategies that treat other large companies as relatively equivalent. Similar to the diffuse network of interlocking directorates discussed in the next chapter, the diffuse structure of intercorporate ownership suggests that it too may serve as an effective unifying mechanism.

As in the case of diversification, one obvious and important result of the spread of intercorporate ownership is to connect the fate of many companies. The decisions taken by one large corporation become increasingly meaningful to others. The same is true of political challenges facing particular firms: they become challenges to many. Because profit is the fundamental objective of the capitalist system, "joint ownership among the dominant enterprises [ties] them inexorably together in pursuit of common goals." Intercorporate ownership affords the elite a "structural foundation for the ascendancy of common interests over narrow and parochial ones" (Richardson 1992: 312). Therefore, elites who are entangled in these ownership networks can easily develop a set of attitudes and commitments that are broad in focus and class-based. This outlook emerges quite naturally, spawned and maintained through the merging of corporate interests.

Corporate concentration and intercorporate networks cannot be fully grasped without employing the concept of *control*. Another means of concentrating economic power is for an individual, a family or a corporation to acquire enough equity in a set of companies so as to control them without complete ownership. All that is necessary for full legal control is to own the majority of another company's stock, and a minority will sometimes be sufficient for *effective* control if the stock is widely held. Control can also be exercised through the ownership of the majority of another company's voting shares. As in the case of stock ownership, however, a minority of voting shares will often be adequate, sometimes as low as 5 percent, if the shares are widely held or if some of their owners are known to be inactive (Veltmeyer 1987: 53).

As Veltmeyer (1987: 47) explains, "by tracing links of common ownership and control among [dominant] corporations, it is possible to reduce

the entire economy to a much smaller group of corporate complexes—
groupings of companies that are independently registered but effectively
controlled by one source." These groups of companies are known as
"enterprise groups"—sets of firms unified under a single controlling interest, which are able to function as one integrated unit of capital. Seen in
these terms, we have a much clearer picture of corporate linkages and a
more accurate description of the staggering degree of corporate concentration in Canada. Clear examples are the empires built by Conrad Black
and Paul Desmarais in the mid-1980s. Together, these two groups pulled a
total of 350 corporations under their control and, through their subsidiaries, another 1500 companies with combined assets of $60 billion.[1] Despite
claims of a recent dispersal of shareholding, fewer than one-fifth of the top
250 Canadian corporations in 1996 were without an identifiable controlling interest (Carroll 2004: 44). In this instance, control does not usually
refer to actual influence on the everyday affairs of another company but
rather to the power to determine the broad policies guiding that firm's
behaviour.

Enterprise groups can best be conceptualized as "control pyramids"
consisting of many ownership layers. A pyramid ownership structure allows
a wealthy family or corporation to control assets worth vastly more than
their own wealth by holding controlling interests in particular companies,
which in turn hold controlling interests in other companies, and so on
down the pyramid. A control pyramid ten layers high, with 51 percent
ownership at every level, magnifies a billion dollars of wealth into control
of over $840 billion (Morck et al. 2000: 323). As this suggests, pyramids
allow corporations to compound their control far beyond their immediate
assets and income. Moreover, because they enable the controlling interest
to use the resources of firms low in their pyramids (whose profitability is
relatively unimportant to them), pyramids create incentives for controlling
families or corporations to engage in political lobbying. Over the past few
decades, wealthy families and individuals in Canada have made much
greater use of intercorporate ownership as a means of exerting strategic
control. Using the Statistics Canada Directory of Inter-Corporate
Ownership database, Randall Morck et al. investigated the group of firms
controlled by Canadian billionaires Edward and Peter Bronfman in 1998.
They summarize the pyramid as follows:

> They own Broncorp Inc., which controls HIL Corporation with a
> 19.6 percent equity stake. HIL owns 97 percent of Edper Resources,
> which owns 60 percent of Brascan holdings, which owns 5.1 percent
> of Brascan, which owns 49.9 percent of Braspower holdings, which
> owns 49.3 percent of Great Lakes Power Inc., which owns 100
> percent of First Toronto Investments, which owns 25 percent of
> Trilon Holdings, which owns 64.5 percent of Trilon Financial,

which owns of 41.4 percent of Gentra, which owns 31.9 percent of Imperial Windsor Group. (Morck et al. 2000: 329)

Incredibly, the Bronfman's actual equity stake in the Imperial Windsor Group works out to 0.03 percent, but they have *full control* of it, and of all other firms in the pyramid. Carroll (2004: 56–57) notes that in 1996, the Bronfmans were one controlling interest in a sub-network that pulled thirty-seven dominant Canadian corporations into a single connected component of Canadian capital.[2]

A related form of ownership that clearly emphasizes control is a holding company. Rather than a merger or an acquisition, the acquiring company may choose to purchase only a portion of another company's stock—enough to establish a controlling interest in the other firm—and act as a holding company. This is sometimes accomplished through the purchase of voting shares. In the 1980s, a trend away from mergers and toward holding companies as the preferred form of concentration had already begun (Veltmeyer 1987: 52). This practice allows one company to control another without putting up much money. When minority voting control is combined with pyramiding, a voting control pyramid is created that, for a relatively small investment, can lead to the control of billions of dollars worth of assets. A famous example of this method of control is provided, once again, by Conrad Black and his associates. By 1983, with an investment of only a few million dollars, Black's team had acquired voting control of companies worth between $6 and $7 billion (Veltmeyer 1987: 53). Their success appeared to have caught the eye of other executives shortly thereafter, as there was a 65 percent increase in holding companies between 1986 and 1991 (Green and McNaughton 2003: 14).

The concentration of economic ownership through mergers and acquisitions, diversification and intercorporate ownership networks provides a powerful structural basis for elite cohesion in Canada. The existence of such structures does not guarantee that cooperation and cohesion take place. But it clearly strengthens the potential for elite unity and effective political action.

CANADA'S MASS MEDIA:
A CASE STUDY IN CONCENTRATED OWNERSHIP

It is not surprising that the concentration of media ownership has increased remarkably in recent years. This runs parallel to developments in other sectors of the economy. However, the media warrants special concern, as it represents a vehicle through which the economic elite can set the agenda for public debate and propagate the ideas, values and policy initiatives that represent an elite consensus. Thus, while it is highly significant that a group of integrated and powerful individuals controls the large industrial corporations and the big banks, it is especially noteworthy that they are in charge of the major systems of public information. Indeed, the Canadian mass media represents a striking example of concentrated ownership, one which has particularly devastating effects on democracy. Media institutions function as one of corporate Canada's most effective weapons of class domination.

The major mass media organizations in Canada are in many ways akin to other business organizations. At the most basic level, they are lucrative corporate enterprises owned and directed by members of the economic elite; they are not just business but *big* business. Media corporations are also extensively connected and integrated with other large firms. And, like other businesses, the media has a product which its sells. The buyers are corporate advertisers, and the product is readers and audiences (with a bias towards wealthy audiences, which improves advertising rates). Thus, the elite media is essentially large corporations "selling" privileged audiences to other businesses. Chomsky (1989: 8) points out that, under these institutional arrangements, it should hardly come as a surprise if the picture of the world they present were to reflect the interests and perceptions of the sellers, the buyers and the product. In fact, it would be very surprising if this were not the case.

The basic picture is almost the same today as it was decades ago when Wallace Clement (1986) showed that members of Canada's media elite tended to be part of the broader corporate community. He suggested that the corporate news media shared an "elective affinity" with business values and business interests in general. These commitments emerged through a set of common social interests and interactions, shared social backgrounds,[3] interlocking directorates and, notably, a highly integrated system of concentrated corporate ownership, in other words, through many of the same structures and processes that integrate the economic elite as a whole. Indeed, there is a final similarity between the media and the rest of corporate Canada: economic concentration within the media has increased dramatically over the past few decades.

Media Concentration in Canada—A Brief History
The concentration of media ownership into fewer hands and the business orientation of the commercial media have been sources of widespread concern in Canada for decades. Clement (1983: 101) discussed the *Senate Report on the Mass Media*, a commissioned study that identified the largest media complexes in 1970. The report found an enormous concentration within the media and argued that this was detrimental to everyone's interests except the few corporations and individuals who controlled it. Fallout from the report actually resulted in an antitrust action against the Irving media interests in New Brunswick (the first of its kind in the media industry), although the ruling was eventually overturned. The Senate Report pointed out that although the structure of the media had changed,

the mythology encompassing it had not; "conventional wisdom still cherishes the image of the 'independent' owner-editor, a tough but kindly old curmudgeon who somehow represented the collective conscience of his community. If this image ever had validity, it hasn't now" (cited in Clement 1986: 288).

Trepidation over media ownership intensified through the 1970s as some of the largest media empires identified in the Senate Report continued to consolidate. Telemedia Quebec, for example, one of the largest fifteen, was acquired by Montreal Trust, itself a subsidiary of Power Corporation. This increased Power Corporation's already widespread newspaper holdings in Quebec. As well, Standard Broadcasting, a subsidiary of Argus Corporation, took over Bushnell Communications, which was also one of the largest in the country (Clement 1983: 101–102). In 1981, spurred by the closing of the Winnipeg Tribune (owned by Southam) and the Ottawa Journal (owned by Thomson) on the same day, the federal government launched the Kent Commission. After much discussion, the commission made a number of detailed recommendations to protect journalistic integrity, including limiting the number of newspapers any single person or company could own to five, and barring ownership of more than one newspaper in a 500 kilometre radius. The Commission also admitted that "it was left-wing viewpoints that tended to be underrepresented as commercialism increased its hold" (cited in Hackett and Gruneau 2000: 67).

The Commission's proposals to restrict ownership concentration and protect editorial independence in papers owned by big chains or conglomerates outraged the powerful media owners in Canada. One media baron, Pierre Péladeau, reminded the commission that "profit is the name of the game" (cited in Hackett and Gruneau 2000: 37). Other owners stressed the same point, insisting that it was a newspaper's first duty to thrive economically. The government eventually retreated, and the proposals of the Kent Commission were never implemented. Since the Commission's report, Hackett and Gruneau (2000: 37) argue that the media's "bottom-line orientation to profit" has intensified. Many of Canada's family-owned chains have been swallowed up by huge multi-media conglomerates owned by shareholders. This type of ownership intensified the purely economic objectives of media companies, as managers became more concerned with maximizing short-term profits. Another casualty of media consolidation has been "independent dailies," which are newspapers published by a company owning no other daily papers. By 2001, the number of independently owned daily newspapers had dropped to just five, down from twenty-nine in 1970. The biggest loser was Ontario— it had eighteen independent newspapers in 1970 and none in 2001 (Thunderbird online magazine, December 2001: volume iv, issue ii). The circulation battles between the large media zeniths and the smaller independents were understandably lopsided, with predictable consequences.

In the early 1990s, a number of newspaper chains consolidated and struggled to increase profits during the economic decline. As a result, significant cutbacks were made in newsroom resources, most notably in the area of investigative journalism. Newspapers across the country began to look increasingly similar (Hackett and Gruneau 2000: 11). In 1996, following the dazzling array of takeovers by Conrad Black, the level of corporate concentration in Canadian newspapers was among the highest in the world. After buying a dozen Thomson newspapers and a regional chain in Saskatchewan, Black acquired Canada's largest chain, Southam. At the time, many Canadians were stunned by this latest incident of media consolidation. In contrast, the federal government no longer seemed concerned about growing media concentration; it "reacted to Black's takeover with a yawn. No Royal Commission. No legal challenge from the competition policy bureaucrats. On the contrary, the takeover was pre-approved" (Hackett and Gruneau 2000: 11).

By the end of 1996, Black's company Hollinger comprised the third largest newspaper empire on the planet. It owned 58 of Canada's 104 dailies as well as titles in the United States, Britain, Israel and Australia (Hackett and Zhoa 1998: 62). To put this in perspective, in the years following his takeovers Black presided over 40 percent of daily newspaper circulation in Canada. At the same time, ten companies were in charge of roughly the same share in the United States (Hackett and Gruneau 2000: 55). The newspaper industry definitely stood out in the mid-1990s, but other media sectors had also become highly concentrated. According to James Winter,

> In Canadian television, five corporations reached 62 percent of viewers in 1993. In the cable industry, three companies now have 68 percent of the audience, up from 36 percent in 1983, even though the number of subscribers has increased by more than 40 percent. In radio, with 479 stations, just ten companies control 55 percent of the revenue share, up 50 percent in the last decade. In magazine publishing, the largest eight publishers controlled 52 percent of circulation in 1993–1994. In book publishing and distribution, Statistics Canada reported that for 1991–1992, just 21 out of 370 firms (6 percent) accounted for 51 percent of total sales. (Winter 1997: 3)

In the late 1990s, Conrad Black decided to divest himself of many media holdings. But this did not result in greater distribution of media assets or a less concentrated media landscape. Rather, most of these assets were bought by CanWest Global, which instantly emerged as a newspaper giant in 2000 when it purchased most of Conrad Black's Hollinger holdings, including many from the Southam chain. Overall, the purchases included thirteen metropolitan dailies, 50 percent of the *National Post*, 136 community newspapers and Internet portal Canada.com. The bill was $3.5 billion Hollinger kept half of the *National Post* and, in addition to cash, got 15 percent of CanWest shares, 6 percent of voting shares and two seats on the board of directors (Grace 2001: 10). Also in 2000, CanWest bought the nine television stations of Western International Communications (WIC) for $800 million. This completed a new national Global Television network stretching from coast to coast.

By the middle of 2001, CanWest had amassed an impressive media empire. It owned the *National Post* (after purchasing the other half from Black earlier in the year), fourteen large metropolitan daily newspapers and hundreds of smaller daily and weekly community papers. The twenty-seven papers grouped together in the Southam chain accounted for approximately one-third of the total circulation per week of Canadian daily newspapers in mid-2001, and 41 percent of the circulation of English-language dailies (Knox 2002: 505). Its television holdings included the Global network, made up of eleven stations in eight provinces across Canada (reaching 94 percent of the English speaking public), Prime TV, as well as five independent stations, in Kelowna, Red Deer, Victoria, Montreal and Hamilton. In addition, the company had private TV networks in Australia, New Zealand and Ireland, among other holdings. CanWest Entertainment (its film and TV production division) was now comprised of three separate units: Fireworks Entertainment, based in Toronto; Fireworks Pictures, based in Los Angeles; and Fireworks International, based in London, England. Also in 2001, CanWest's Interactive division operated the Canada.com Internet portal, which included Globaltv.com and sites corresponding to Southam newspapers across the country (CanWest Global 2004; Chen and Graves 2002; and Wilson 2002).

In July 2002, in an attempt to pay down its debt of about $4 billion, CanWest sold a dozen community newspapers and thirty-two other publications in Atlantic Canada and Saskatchewan for $255 million (Knox 2002: 520). These were taken over by Transcontinental, a new player in the newspaper industry. Despite dropping their share in the newspaper market by a few percentage points, CanWest Global Communications is still the most imposing example of concentrated media ownership in Canada.

A final trend in media consolidation deserves mention. In the past decade or so, and especially in the last few years, the accelerating processes of concentration and profit maximization in the media have coincided with an acceleration in cross-media ownership or "convergence." At the industry level, convergence generally refers to the trend of consolidation of media ownership among information, entertainment and retail companies. Wilson (2002: 6) argues that a small number of convergence "champions" have emerged and grown into positions of dominance as a result of horizontal integration within industry sectors, combined with the vertical integration of these consolidated firms within newly constructed media/ communications empires. In 1999, for example, two cable operators, Shaw and Rogers, were the second and third largest radio ownership groups in Canada (Wilson 2002: 11). All but one of the main English-Canada newspapers in 2001 was the property of a TV or telecommunications giant, while in Quebec both private TV networks were in the hands of Quebecor, a newspaper and printing firm.

Appendix A presents the interlocking directorship ties between dominant Canadian corporations and seven of the largest and most dominant media corporations in Canada (Chapter Three explains interlocking directorships in detail).[4] Although relying simply on revenue as an indicator of dominance is problematic, the intercorporate linkages between the media and the "top 500" provide an important indicator of elite integration.[5] Subsidiaries of the media corporations themselves are not included. Other subsidiaries are included only if their parent is listed in the top 500 (and the director does not sit on the parent company's board) and if the subsidiary is listed in the top hundred subsidiaries. As these data indicate, Canada's largest media corporations are heavily interlocked with other dominant Canadian corporations.

Legitimation and Ideology

In other ways, however, the mass media represents a unique area of interest. Media agencies play a crucial role in the legitimation of the capitalist economic system and in the construction, dissemination and reinforcement of ideologies. They work to gather acceptance for those policies and programs advocated by business and, just as significantly, to saturate political discourse with the capitalist "ethos"—the values, commitments and goals of the economic elite. Numerous studies suggest that despite the official context of free expression of ideas and opinions within the media, the reality is that these institutions generally act to limit public understanding and discussion in accordance with the needs of the powerful, which includes the elites who own them. While divisions and disagreements among elites are reflected in media debate, departure from their relatively narrow consensus is rare (see, for example, Herman and Chomsky 1988; Chomsky 1989; Winter 1997; Taras 1999; Hackett and Gruneau 2000; and McChesney 2000).

Even if media owners had no political motives, or if they never influenced editorial policy, concentrated ownership could still highly affect the content and diversity of media output. Most media corporations are controlled by owners and managers who are subject to sharp, market-oriented constraints. Like other corporations, they are primarily accountable to the dominant shareholders and hence the "bottom line." It is therefore not surprising that ownership has a heavy impact on resource allocation, hiring and firing, and the content of media output. The directions in which owners and managers typically steer media content are remarkably consistent and hardly surprising, given that "those who own and control the capitalist mass media are most likely to be [persons] whose ideological dispositions run from soundly conservative to utterly reactionary" (Miliband 1969: 204).

Direct intervention by owners to regulate media content is rare. Most reporters, directors and editors are pre-selected, and their views fall safely within the limits of tolerance and the framework of assumptions of their corporate bosses. Spirited debate, criticism and even dissent occur but mostly remain within the system of presuppositions and assumptions that define this consensus. For those with a more independent outlook, most screening is subtle but remarkably effective. As Chomsky notes, "there's a whole filtering process that enables people to rise through the system into managerial roles only if they've demonstrated that they've successfully internalized the values demanded by private power" (cited in Chomsky and Barsamian 1997: 127). In part, this process is predicated on fear, as the power of owners to hire and fire creates an unspoken but chilling effect in many newsrooms. It should be pointed out, however, that there is no shortage of cases in Canada where the intervention of owners has been direct and heavy-handed (see, for example, Clement 1986; Hackett and Gruneau 2000; Grace 2001; Knox 2002; Macklem 2002; and Winter 2002).

Another crucial source of influence is advertisers. Most media corporations depend on advertising revenue for their financial survival. Therefore, its incentive encourages the media to treat advertisers' products and their broader interests with the utmost of care. There is little doubt that advertisers are interested in the program content and editorial information of any medium, partly for basic ideological reasons but also because the nature of the content determines the segment of the population likely to be reached. When advertisers do find fault with particular stories, they can use their financial muscle to downplay or even eliminate potentially damaging news coverage. This is sometimes known as "flak," which is a negative response to a media statement or program. The ability to produce flak is directly related to power, and advertisers are certainly in a position of power when it comes to the media. Herman and Chomsky (1988: 26) argue that serious flak has increased in close parallel with the corporate offensive of the 1970s, when business was becoming increasingly resentful and intolerant of media criticism.

Despite illusions to the contrary, elites have always recognized the media's value. Today, the importance of media influence is usually taken for granted. In 2002, for example, media relations made up 41 percent of the average public relations budget of Canadian corporations (Watson 2002: 136). The mass media is comprised of effective ideological institutions that have become even more efficient in recent decades through greater corporate concentration, as well as the improved sophistication of public relations and news management. These matters are clearly relevant to the unity debate, as the media is the primary means of expressing the ideas and values that represent an elite consensus. This consensus is forged, in part, by the highly concentrated ownership of the media.

The concentration of capital into a relatively small number of colossal institutions is occurring not only within countries but also at the global level among corporations that are not tied to any one nation. For example, no more than a dozen giant corporations now dominate the global media market, including AOL-Time Warner, Disney, Viacom, General Electric and Sony. The transnational concentration of capital has implications similar to, and perhaps more far-reaching than, capital concentration at the national level.

CORPORATE CONCENTRATION AND INEQUALITY AROUND THE GLOBE

Until the 1980s, most merger and acquisition activity did take place within national boundaries. In the past couple of decades, however, cross-border activity has become one of the primary means for corporations to expand their operations and activities. Cross-border mergers represent the integration of firms from at least two different countries, and cross-border acquisitions involve firms incorporating foreign companies into their own operations. Both cross-border mergers and acquisitions have grown at an astonishing rate since the beginning of the 1990s (Robinson 2004: 58). The actual number of deals jumped from 14 in 1980 to 3,516 in 1990 to 9,655 in 1999. In 1991, the value of these activities was $85 billion, in 1998 it was $558 billion, and in 1999 it surpassed $1 trillion. Between 1980 and 2000, mergers and acquisitions had a total combined value of more than $12 trillion, and about one-quarter of these involved cross-border takeovers (Gabel and Bruner 2003: 8). According to Kang and Johansson (2000: 14), the value of cross border mergers and acquisitions in relation to global foreign direct investment (FDI) climbed from 53.7 percent in 1991 to 85.3 percent in 1997. In other words, less than one-fifth of the money in 1997 went into new investments. From 1998 to 1999, overall merger volume increased 36 percent globally, moving forward at an amazing $1.6 billion per business hour (Grubb and Lamb 2000: 9). These trends have not been confined to the most globalized sectors of the world economy but have also embraced "mega-retailers, companies trading in primary commodities, chemicals, and numerous services, from legal firms to insurance and management" (Robinson and Harris 2000: 34).

For nearly all Canadian industries, a considerable majority of the mergers and acquisitions involve Canadian companies integrating with one another. Recently, however, many of the *largest* transactions have

Table 2.4: Fifteen of the Twenty Largest Mergers and Acquisitions in Canada, 2001

Deal	Value in Billions
Conoco buys Gulf Canada	6.7
Duke Energy buys Westcoast Energy	5.5
Devon Energy buys Anderson Exploration	5.3
Newmont Mining buys Franco-Nevada and Normandy Mining	5.3
Solectron buys C-MAC Inds.	4.1
Nortel Networks buys JDS Uniphase's fibre-optic assets	3.8
Royal Bank buys Centura Bank	3.5
Barrick Gold buys Homestake Mining	3.3
Burlington Resources buys Canadian Hunter Exploration	3.3
Sun Life Financial buys Keyport Life and Independent Financial Marketing	2.6
Domtar buys Georgia-Pacific's paper mill assets	2.3
Celestica buys Omni Industries	1.3
Calpine buys Encal Energy	1.3
Deutsche Lufthansa buys Sky Chiefs	1.3
Canadian National buys Wisconsin Central	1.2

Source: Davies (2002: 54)

included foreign companies. Of the twenty largest mergers and acquisitions completed in Canada in 2001, fifteen were cross-border deals (Davies 2002: 54). These are shown in Table 2.4. Canadian banks have been particularly active in cross-border shopping, led by the Royal Bank of Canada (RBC). In 2001, RBC acquired Dain Rauscher Corporation in a U.S. $1.8 billion deal, as well as the Boston-based Tucker Anthony Sutro Corporation. In one of the largest deals of 2001, the bank picked up Centura Banks for U.S. $2.2 billion. Including the mortgage and insurance companies it purchased in 2000, the Royal Bank gained two million U.S. customers in just eighteen months. The Bank of Montreal has also been quite active, spending more than $2 billion on U.S. operations from 1999 to 2001. Not to be left out, the Toronto-Dominion Bank recently bought two U.S. enterprises, the Stafford and LETCO groups, and has been negotiating to offer banking services in Wal-Mart stores across the United States (Davies 2002: 52). It appears that when Paul Martin closed the door in 1998 on the proposed mergers between the Bank of Montreal and Royal Bank, and the CIBC and TD Bank, the banks collectively decided to look internationally.

Among the thousands of transnational corporations (TNCs) in the world today, the top two hundred are the major players. A large majority are headquartered in the United States, followed by Japan, Germany and France. Between 1983 and 1999, their combined sales grew to the equiva-

Table 2.5: The One Hundred Largest Economies in the World

Company or Country	2002 GDP (countries) or 2002 Revenue (companies) US $millions	Company or Country	2002 GDP (countries) or 2002 Revenue (companies) US $millions
1 United States	10,416,818	52 CHEVRONTEXACO	92,043
2 Japan	3,978,782	53 Egypt	89,845
3 Germany	1,976,240	54 NIPPON TELEPHONE	89,644
4 United Kingdom	1,552,437	55 ING GROEP N.V.	88,102
5 France	1,409,604	56 Singapore	86,969
6 China	1,237,145	57 ITOCHU	85,856
7 Italy	1,180,921	58 IBM	83,132
8 Canada	715,692	59 VOLKSWAGEN	82,204
9 Spain	649,792	60 Colombia	82,194
10 Mexico	637,205	61 SIEMENS AG	77,205
11 India	515,012	62 Philippines	77,076
12 Korea, Rep.	476,690	63 SUMITOMO	75,745
13 Brazil	452,387	64 MARUBENI	72,165
14 Netherlands	413,741	65 Czech Republic	69,590
15 Australia	410,590	66 Puerto Rico	67,897
16 Russian Federation	346,520	67 VERIZON	67,625
17 Switzerland	268,041	68 AMERICAN INTER. GRP.	67,482
18 Belgium	247,634	69 HITACHI LTD.	67,228
19 WAL-MART	246,525	70 US POSTAL SERVICE	66,463
20 Sweden	229,772	71 Hungary	65,843
21 Austria	202,954	72 HONDA MOTOR	65,420
22 Norway	189,436	73 CARREFOUR SA	64,979
23 Poland	187,680	74 Chile	64,154
24 GENERAL MOTORS	186,763	75 ALTRIA GROUP	62,182
25 Saudi Arabia	186,489	76 AXA	62,051
26 Turkey	182,848	77 SONY	61,335
27 EXXONMOBIL	182,466	78 NIPPON LIFE INSUR.	61,175
28 ROYAL DUTCH SHELL	179,431	79 MATSUSHITA ELECTRIC	60,744
29 BP p.l.c.	178,721	80 Pakistan	60,521
30 Denmark	174,798	81 ROYAL AHOLD	59,455
31 Indonesia	172,911	82 CONOCOPHILLIPS	58,384
32 FORD MOTOR CO.	163,871	83 HOME DEPOT	58,247
33 Hong Kong, China	161,532	84 New Zealand	58,178
34 DAIMLER CHRYSLER	141,421	85 NESTLE S.A.	57,279
35 TOYOTA MOTOR	131,754	86 MCKESSON HBOC	57,129
36 GENERAL ELECTRIC	131,698	87 Peru	56,901
37 Finland	130,797	88 HEWLETT-PACKARD	56,588
38 Thailand	126,407	89 NISSAN MOTOR	56,041
39 Portugal	121,291	90 Algeria	55,666
40 Ireland	119,916	91 VIVENDI UNIV.	54,977
41 Israel	110,386	92 BOEING	54,069
42 MITSUBISHI	109,386	93 ASSICURAZIONI GENERALI	53,599
43 MITSUI & CO. LTD.	108,631	94 FANNIE MAE	52,901
44 Iran	107,552	95 FIAT S.P.A.	52,613
45 South Africa	104,235	96 DEUTSCHE BANK	52,133
46 Argentina	102,191	97 CREDIT SUISSE	52,122
47 ALLIANZ AG.	101,930	98 MUNICH GROUP	51,980
48 CITIGROUP	100,789	99 MERCK & CO. INC.	51,790
49 TOTAL FINA ELF	96,945	100 KROGER	51,760
50 Malaysia	95,157		
51 Venezuela	94,340		

Source: Erosion, Technology and Concentration (ETC) Group (2003)

lent of 27.5 percent of world GDP, yet they employed less than one percent of the world's workforce. Through the same period, their profits grew 362 percent while the number of people they employed grew by just 14 percent (Anderson and Cavanagh 2000). The combined sales of the top two hundred are also greater than the combined economies of 180 countries in the world, and eighteen times the combined income of the world's 1.2 billion poorest people (Derber 2002: 71). Even some individual TNCs—like Wal Mart, General Motors and ExxonMobil—are so large that their GDP/sales dwarf that of several nations combined. In fact, over half of the hundred largest "economies" in the world are now represented by corporations (see Table 2.5). By 2002, Wal-Mart had become the nineteenth largest world economy. It was larger than Sweden, Austria, Norway and Poland. In economic terms, General Motors was the same size as Saudi Arabia, ExxonMobil the size of Turkey, General Electric as big as Finland, Mitsubishi nearly equal to Israel, and IBM larger than Columbia. Entire national economies can now be significantly affected by the actions of a single company. For example, between 1992 and 1996, General Motors laid off approximately 100,000 U.S. workers. At the same time, it became the biggest private employer in Mexico by moving many of its operations south of the border (Draffan, 2000). Commenting on the impact of these corporations on people's lives, Charles Derber writes:

> The top 200 hold 90 percent of the world's patents; grow, refine, and sell much of the world's food; supply the oil that runs our cars and heats our homes; operate the global media and entertainment companies that reach billions of people; and create most of the world's software and manufacture the computers it runs on. They build the airplanes and cars we travel in, make most of our clothes, provide most of the world's banking and financial services, and increasingly dominate services from health care to retailing. Finally the top 200 produce nearly all the weapons that cram the arsenals of nations everywhere. (Derber 2002: 71)

A look at the concentration levels in a few global industries also illustrates the magnitude of the inequities between corporations and the majority of the population. In the mid-1990s, no more than five transnational corporations in each industry controlled over 50 percent of the global marketplace in the automotive, aerospace, airline, electrical and electronics, consumer durables and steel sectors. In oil, personal computers and media, the top five companies in each industry controlled more than 40 percent of sales (Korten 2001: 207). Today, the top ten pharmaceutical companies currently control an estimated 48 percent of the $317 billion world market. The top ten leading grocery retailers account for over one-sixth of the global food retail market, estimated to have a value of $2.8

trillion (Erosion, Technology and Concentration Group, 2001). Three agro-food giants (Cargill, Phillip Morris and Nestle) had revenues that totaled $260 billion in 1998, while the total Canadian gross farm revenue was estimated to be $29 billion in the same year (Canadian Centre for Policy Alternatives 2000: 21). Around the same time, just six food companies controlled roughly 95 percent of all American corn and wheat exports, 90 percent of corn and wheat trade in the European Union, and 90 percent of Canada's barley exports (Gabel and Bruner 2003: 98). In the agricultural chemicals industry, sixty-five companies were competing in the world market just a few decades ago; today, just nine of them account for 90 percent of pesticide sales (McNally 2002: 35).

The sheer size of these companies is something to behold. Enormous planetary empires have been crafted, largely through cross-border mergers and acquisitions, as well as the intercorporate ownership networks of transnational corporations. Global monopolies and oligopolies have become increasingly commonplace. Capital has also become more integrated through a mass of strategic alliances among TNCs. Strategic alliances incorporate a wide range of links among firms, including "joint ventures, minority equity investments, equity swaps, joint research and development, production and marketing, technology sharing, long-term sourcing agreements, and shared distribution and services" (Robinson 2004: 64). These cooperative relationships increased more than six-fold from 1989 to 1999, with two-thirds of all new alliances emerging across countries (Robinson 2004: 65). Global alliances now link a very large proportion of the world's corporations, including almost all of the giant oligopolistic "competitors." Corporations also reduce competition by conspiring to fix prices and divide up markets, otherwise know as collusion. This all suggests that contrary to mainstream economic theory, the global economy is not a free market economy, in which production, investment and distribution are determined by market forces.

Despite what the public is encouraged to believe, corporations disburse great effort to eliminate competition and to avoid risk and uncertainty. The relationships among global corporations make it clear that the last thing capital wants for itself is competition or a "free" market. On the contrary, corporations attempt to overcome competition in whatever way possible and to maximize control over markets. They specifically set themselves up to violate market discipline. Of course, any "barrier" to market discipline imposed by governments—whether designed to protect the public's health, labour, the environment or local industry—is likely to be attacked by the corporate sector as a violation of market principles. In fact, under today's global trade treaties, corporations can now sue governments for these practices. The real reason why elites so loudly proclaim the virtues of the free market is that

it is the philosophical rationale for the advancement of the interests of private property and for undoing much of the postwar
[welfare state].... It is the rationale for privatizing public corporations and for deregulating the operation of the economy, for
relieving the state of any functions that restrict private accumulation. It is also the rationale for countering the principles of trade
unionism. (Teeple 2000: 86)

Along the same lines, free trade agreements have little to do with
freeing trade. Rather, the primary purpose (and corresponding effect) of
these agreements is to free *capital* to pursue investments and profit-
making without interference. Indeed, trade may be more restrictive today
than it was twenty years ago (McNally 2002: 32). Approximately half of
world trade consists of the transfer of goods and services within
transnational corporations. While these activities are technically referred
to as "trade" (imports and exports), they typically amount to little more
than the internal transfer of parts, components and services from one
corporate unit to a corporate unit in a different country. In Chomsky's
words, "it's as if someone who has a small vegetable store moved a can of
beans from one shelf to another. It's just that this takes place across
international borders, but it doesn't have anything to do with trade; it's an
organized act by a centralized management" (cited in Chomsky and
Dieterich 1999: 82).

Furthermore, although more conventional trade restrictions (such as
tariffs) have declined, non-tariff trade restrictions, such as strategic alliances, quotas, production and export subsidies and import-limiting agreements, have been on the rise. These non-tariff trade restrictions have
become so common that, according to one estimate, only about 15 percent
of world trade is actually "free" in the conventional sense (McNally 2002:
33). Despite repeated claims by elites that central economic planning is
inefficient and unresponsive to consumer demands, the reality is that large
corporations maintain a very high degree of control over the economies
defined by their product networks. Most economic activity is controlled
by the visible hand of corporate managers and not, as we are led to believe,
by the market's "invisible hand." As Dobbin (2003c: 11) correctly points
out, "surveying this incredible concentration of economic power, and
control over markets nationally and globally, exposes the sheer nonsense
of any talk about competitive markets, the free market, the free enterprise
system, and the critical economic role of the entrepreneurial spirit."

Typically, TNCs are only seen as contributing to the processes of
economic globalization, which downplays the determined *political* motives
of these huge institutions. In the words of Dreiling (2000: 22), "the liberal
assumption that the diverse economic interests of business generate political division leaves us with a paradox regarding the political sources of

globalization." This assumption—taken up by more than "liberals"—detracts from the importance of global corporate unity in shaping politics at the international level. The global elite have the power to create and/or modify international organizations and forums, such as the WTO, the World Bank, and the IMF. They also play a key role in the policy-formation process, as evidenced by international agreements such as the North American Free Trade Agreement (NAFTA), the General Agreement on Tariffs and Trade (GATT), the Free Trade Agreement of the Americas (FTAA) and the General Agreement on Trade in Services (GATS). According to Noam Chomsky, these organizations and agreements are representative of a new "de facto world government," one designed to serve the needs of the "new international corporate ruling class" and to ensure that the general population is shut out of the political process (cited in Chomsky et al. 2002: 381). As concentration has continued to increase in tandem with declining capital regulation and a proliferation of strategic relationships, the elites who run these global empires can easily become more cohesive and far more powerful. The transnational integration and political unity of global elite networks have become much more robust since the corporate offensive of the 1970s.

Of course, such a dramatic concentration of wealth and power has serious consequences for the enormous multitude of people who are left behind in the global economic system. It has contributed to a sharp and mounting disparity between the rich and poor, and to astonishing levels of inequality and poverty. When examined on a global scale, the inequalities involved are obscene. The richest two hundred people in the world more than doubled their net worth between 1994 and 1997 to over $1 trillion, and this has since increased. Just three billionaires collectively have assets greater than the combined gross national product of the world's poorest nations and their six hundred million inhabitants. Overall, the assets of the world's wealthiest two hundred people are greater than the combined income of 41 percent of humanity. Contrast this with the situation in the developing world, where 1.2 billion people live in absolute poverty, surviving on one dollar a day or less. Another billion are illiterate and have no access to safe water, while 2.4 billion lack basic sanitation (McNally 2002: 46–47, 91). Two hundred million of the world's children under the age of five are malnourished, one hundred million children are living or working on the streets, and fourteen million children die every year from hunger related diseases. Even in an extremely wealthy country like the United States, over thirty million people do not have enough food to meet their basic needs. This represents roughly 10 percent of U.S. households (Cavanagh et al. 2002: 7). It should be obvious, even to the most cynical observer, that there are horrific inequities in the allocation of the world's resources. Equally disturbing is that they continue to increase, under the guise of "free enterprise."

Clearly, the dramatic rise in corporate concentration and strategic alliances among companies, both nationally and globally, creates a corporate structure that is conducive to elite cohesion. These increases also point to some of the shortcomings of assumptions underlying "free market" economic theories and pluralist interest group competition. Capitalist economies are not built on competition and pluralities. To the contrary, capitalist economies tend to the destruction of competition and the creation of economic monopolies.

In the next chapter, we will see how interlocking directorates provide another example of how the structure of corporate capital acts as a mechanism for elite cohesion.

NOTES

1. Black and Desmarais were not the only ones to employ this strategy. Carroll and Lewis (1991: 493) noted a significant rise in the prominence of family-based enterprise groups within the Canadian economic system from 1976–1986. Today, these empires account for much of the economic activity in Canada.

2. The Bronfmans are one of Canada's wealthiest families. A controversial tax ruling in 1991 by Revenue Canada allowed the family to move more than $2 billion worth of Seagram company stock to the United States tax-free. It is estimated that this decision permitted the family to avoid paying as much as $750 million in taxes, money which otherwise could have been used for healthcare, education and numerous other social services. In response to the ruling, a social activist from Winnipeg filed a class action suit against the federal government. For more information on the tax ruling, see Smith (2002).

3. For example, Clement (1986) discovered that over 70 percent of his sample of "media elites" were of upper class origin and 46 percent attended private school. In a more recent study, Fleming (1991) found that the majority of his sample of elite publishers and editors of major daily newspapers had attended private school and over 85 percent had attended university. Many had also obtained post-graduate and professional degrees and enjoyed elite business backgrounds.

4. For an in-depth ownership breakdown of Canadian newspapers and television stations, see Thunderbird Online Magazine (2001).

5. The 2001 company revenues and assets were taken from the 2002 *Financial Post 500* (published annually by *National Post Business*). The sample of dominant Canadian corporations is taken from a list of the top 500 Canadian corporations found in the 2002 *Financial Post 500*. Information on the directors was taken from the 2003 Financial Post Directory of Directors (published annually by *National Post Business*).

3. INTERLOCKING DIRECTORATES

One of the most obvious indicators for identifying linkages between individual corporations and the elites who run them is interlocking directorates. Corporations are governed by boards of directors elected by shareholders. These boards are responsible for evaluating major policy proposals and for hiring and firing top management. In addition, directors have the legal authority to make decisions concerning wages, working conditions, capital investment policies and many other matters related to the disposition of corporate assets. At times, shareholders choose to elect themselves as directors, allowing them more direct control over the company's operations. Interlocking directors are individuals who simultaneously sit on two or more corporate boards of directors, whereas interlocking directorates are stable networks of interlocking directors among particular groups of companies.

There are important structural differences between *public* and *private* corporations that have an impact on the interlocking directorate network. When a corporation is said to be publicly traded, its ownership shares are exchanged in the stock market by members of the public who have little involvement with the company's operations (other than hoping for a financial return on their investment). In contrast, the shares of a private corporation are not publicly traded. Typically, private corporations are owned and operated by a small collection of individuals or family members. The number of large private corporations is relatively small compared to the public variety and, as we will see, are far less integrated into the network of interlocking directorates in Canada.

The typical board of a large corporation consists of a range of inside and outside directors. Inside directors are those whose primary affiliation is with the firm, usually the company's top executives. Outside directors are individuals whose primary affiliations are with other organizations. These organizations are usually other large corporations but may include, for example, law firms and policy organizations. Retired politicians also sometimes occupy outside directorship positions. Those companies at the top of the corporate world—the dominant firms—are the ones with the strongest intercorporate ties. They make up the core of the network, in and around which the majority of all other interlocks are focused (Carroll

1986: 106). The core of the directorate labyrinth solidifies a much broader network of intercorporate alliances and is not isolated from middle range or small companies. Many executives from dominant corporations are recruited to sit on the boards of smaller companies, and the opposite also occurs frequently. Most of the research on interlocking directorates, however, concerns the interlocks between large, economically dominant firms.

Networks of interlocking directorates can be analyzed on two levels: that of the corporation (the institutionalized relations between firms), and that of the individual interlocker. Both levels are important because "adequate analysis requires examination of the structure both as a network of capitalists (and their functionaries) and as a network of the organizational units within which capital accumulates" (Carroll and Lewis 1991: 495). Corporate board interlocks draw individual directors into a socially integrated corporate elite, just as they draw directorates into a network of intercorporate relationships. This dual focus allows for a more complete picture of class organization.

THE DETERMINANTS AND CONSEQUENCES
OF INTERLOCKING DIRECTORATES

The Disunity Position

An inter-organizational perspective informs much of the research on interlocking directorates.[1] Here, board interlocks are viewed as a device that corporations use to monitor and control other companies: "to co-opt threats in their environments from competitors, suppliers, customers, and regulatory agencies; and, generally, to coordinate their business activities with other corporations" (Ornstein 1984: 210). Some interlocks involve reciprocity and an exchange of resources between firms, while others are asymmetrical, extending to the outright control of a subsidiary through interlocking with a parent company. From the inter-organizational perspective, interlocks are used by corporations in a straightforward and practical manner to coordinate and pursue their interests. Interlocking directorships act as instruments for reinforcing intercorporate resource exchanges, or, more specifically, as a means of securing the buying and selling of products, the formation of joint ventures, the borrowing of money and other forms of economic exchange. For example, large manufacturing firms often maintain many ties to major commercial banks. Inter-organizational theorists infer that the manufacturers maintain these ties to protect their lines of credit, while the banks do so to protect their investments in and loans to specific firms. In either case, pairs of corporations are interlocked by their directors to "pacify" the resource provider's management and to serve the specific economic relations between them.[2] The role of the director in this formulation is largely parochial, that is, to promote the joint interests of pairs or cliques of firms, or to advance the interests of one firm at the expense of the other.

It is true that some interlocks are created by virtue of these instrumental considerations. Many of the interlocks that are formed between large industrial corporations and the big banks are cases in point. But there are also other factors "underlying the creation of many, perhaps even most, interlocking directorships," as Useem (1984: 43) points out.

The Unity Position

The class dominance perspective represents the alternative to the inter-organizational approach. This perspective explains the role of interlocks as expressing and maintaining class solidarity. Interlocks serve as a means of political and ideological coordination and act as a network of shared social ties among members of the elite. "'Interlocking directorate' is no mere phrase: it points to a solid feature of the facts of business life, and to a sociological anchor of the community of interest, the unification of outlooks and policy, that prevails among the propertied class" (Mills 1956: 123). Three qualities of interlocking directorates make them an effective organizational tool for the elite (Useem 1984: 38). First, the bulk of their members are fulltime senior managers of large corporations. Second, the network of directorates includes almost all of the large, dominant companies. And third, the ties are dispersed in a fashion that favours class-wide integration.

This third quality—how the ties are dispersed—is particularly important. When a high level executive of one corporation sits on the board of another, he or she establishes a *primary interlock* or *strong tie*. Put simply, the executive represents their own company on the board of the other. Inter-organizational theorists pay special attention to this type of interlock and to the role of the inside directors. But there are other types of interlocks embedded within the corporate network. *Secondary interlocks* are created in two ways. One is by outside directors who sit on multiple boards; for example, a retired politician who sits on the boards of two companies but does not "belong" to either company—meaning he or she has no representational function—establishes a secondary interlock or *weak tie* (Carroll and Alexander 1999: 340–341). The other type of secondary interlock is "induced," that is, created as a byproduct of primary interlocks. So, if an inside director of company X sits on the boards of companies Y and Z, he or she creates two primary interlocks. However, these two primary relations also induce a secondary interlock between Y and Z. A director of four corporations, involving three primary interlocks, establishes three additional induced interlocks, and so on.

Class dominance theorists view board interlocks as a means of generating elite cohesion. Hence, they tend to give more weight to the secondary interlocks or weak ties, which weave together entire networks of companies in a more general way. Carroll and Alexander (1999: 341) comment that "although secondary ties may be less important in the accumulation process, such connections do figure in the other face of corporate power: they serve to integrate the corporate elite along sociocultural lines." Ornstein (1989: 162) argues that the secondary ties which are not induced are of particular importance. They are the ones most likely to serve the general interests of business, partly because outside directors are often well suited to represent the economic elite in the political arena. Their suitability is the result of their many resources, including "their own wealth, their directorships at other corporations and non-profit organizations, their general understanding of business and investment, and their many relationships with other wealthy people, fund-raisers, and politicians" (Domhoff 1998: 36).

The way these ties are dispersed determines network "diffuseness." Diffuseness is the degree to which network ties are spread widely rather than concentrated within small groups or cliques. Networks are considered less diffuse when the directorships shared by corporations are the product of specific ties among cliques of firms, whereas networks are more diffuse when connections originate from processes unrelated to these specific relations. Whether a network is diffuse influences its ability to serve as a vehicle for political coordination among the elite. A highly diffuse network facilitates such coordination; a network characterized by low diffuseness usually does not.

Only a small portion of interlocks are the result of specific resource relations. Networks of interlocking directorates tend to be highly diffuse, with most ties emerging out of a desire to do more than just exchange resources between firms. For example, Koenig et al. (1979), Ornstein (1980) and Palmer (1983) all studied the frequency with which "accidentally broken" interlocks between firms were reconstituted. In Palmer's study, for example, interlocking directorates are classified as accidentally broken if they are severed by changes in the director's personal circumstances rather than changes in the economic relations between the companies. These researchers found that most broken ties were not reconstituted with the same firm, suggesting that most interlocks reflect social ties and diffuse class interests rather than organizational requirements. If interlocks were created for resource exchange or other firm-specific relations, then we would expect to see these broken ties quickly re-established.

In his study of high level executives in the United States and Britain, Useem (1984) found that resource exchange considerations were of minor importance in crafting the makeup of corporate boardrooms. Although senior managers were usually expected to join the boards of other large firms, from the company's standpoint it did not matter which ones, so long as the firms fell within broadly required categories. The same was true of the perspective of the inviting firms. Moreover, these invitations were usually unexpected by directors who received them. When asked why certain directorships were initiated, a strong majority of executives identified factors unrelated to trade or any other business relation between the companies. What motivated many board invitations and acceptances was the desire to improve the company's "business scan" (Useem 1984: 45). In other words, executives wanted to learn about the general economic and political environments in which business operates—an objective consistent with the broad ideological and political goals emphasized in the class dominance (unity) perspective.

According to both American and British executives, few experiences were more useful for obtaining information on the business environment than was service on the board of another major corporation. As one American executive explains, "it extends the range of your network and acquaintances.... You get a more cosmopolitan view—on economic matters, regional differences, and international questions.... It just broadens your experience, the memory bank that you have to test things against." Another executive offers this synopsis, "if you want to just bottomline it, it's a hell of a tool for top management education" (Useem 1984: 47–48). The predominance of these motivations is not the pattern that would prevail if intercorporate resource considerations were a major factor in the makeup of the network. Multiple board membership increases the knowledge and experience of corporate managers, and it creates a pool of highly skilled, class conscious executives.

MULTIPLE DIRECTORS: BACKBONE OF A CLASS CONSCIOUS BUSINESS ELITE

Multiple directors are in a unique and powerful position within the world of business. Through multiple board memberships, these directors are well situated to recognize and help reconcile the problems of many companies, which often operate in very different corporate environments. Mizruchi (1996: 288) argues that heavily interlocked directors constitute a vanguard of the economic elite, as they are well integrated into the corporate community and at the cutting edge of innovations. In contrast with members of the elite who are responsible for the operation of only a single firm, multiple directors tend to have higher levels of political consciousness and broader outlooks. This is one reason why the corporations with the greatest number of director interlocks are also the ones most heavily involved in political lobbying (Burris 1991: 547).

In his famous study of Canada's "vertical mosaic," John Porter (1965: 255) concluded that Canada's interlocking directors "are the ultimate decision makers and coordinators within the private sector of the economy. It is they who at the frontiers of the economic and political systems represent the interest of corporate power. They are the real planners of the economy." They are also an appealing source of government council because they come equipped with an integrated corporate vision and they possess a "special aura of stature, legitimacy, and influence that is but faintly shared by directors of single companies, however eminent they may be in their own company or sector" (Useem 1984: 62). Interlocking directors have been shown to sit on more nonprofit boards and to be appointed more frequently to government advisory positions than single directors. The number of directorship positions is also strongly associated with participation in business policy organizations (Useem 1979; Domhoff 1998). Thus, directors sitting on numerous boards are in a very strong position to coordinate corporate activity and represent the overall interests of the economic elite. Even pluralists have acknowledged the impact of multiple directors. Arnold Rose (1967: 133), for example, has stated that interlocking directorates give large corporations "a high degree of cohesiveness." Where the pluralists disagree with class dominance theorists is in the assumption that such interlocks are widespread; pluralists see these interlocks as the exception rather than the rule and therefore as an ineffective mechanism of elite unity.

MAPPING THE NETWORK: INTERLOCKING DIRECTORATES IN CANADA

There are few up-to-date Canadian studies of interlocking directorates. In part, this may be explained by a general decline in empirical research on social structure and social inequality in Canada (Ornstein 1998: 173). A small number of contemporary studies do exist, however, three of which (Ornstein 1989; Carroll and Alexander 1999; and Carroll 2001) help to answer this question of the extent to which board interlocks effectively integrate Canada's business community.

Like such networks in other advanced industrialized countries, the Canadian directorate network is centred around "finance capital." Socio- logically, finance capital involves the integration of finance and industry. It represents an alliance of banking and industrial corporations, under the control of a relatively small group of powerful investors: "the largest and most profitable financial and non-financial corporations that dominate the economy are interconnected ... into a cohesive network that provides the social cement for this dominant group" (Richardson 1992: 309). Thus, there is a symbiotic relationship between large industry and high finance, allowing industrial firms access to borrowing and solidifying the ability of financial institutions to secure their loans and investments. Theories of finance capital suggest that corporate interlocking will be structured "around a densely connected, domestically owned financial-industrial axis with banks and financial institutions at its centre" (Carroll and Alexander 1999: 348).

The central position of financial institutions, and banks in particular, creates an effective communication system among financials through their direct links to the same major industrial corporations and between different non-financial industries and sectors. As a result of their special position within the network, Mintz and Schwartz (1985) argue, banks are more concerned with the overall functioning of business than are other corporations and, as such, are well suited to mediate conflicts within the business world.

The Canadian Network in Comparative Perspective: The 1980s

Michael Ornstein's (1989) comparative analysis of interlocking directorate networks built upon a previous study by Stokman, Ziegler and Scott (1985), which looked at the networks in Austria, Belgium, Britain, Finland, France, Germany, Italy, the Netherlands, Switzerland and the United States. Data from these ten countries provided the context for Ornstein's analysis of the Canadian scene. Following the model advanced by Stokman et al., his study included the top 250 Canadian corporations: the fifty largest financial corporations (ranked by assets) and the two hundred largest non-financials (ranked by sales).

Ornstein found broad networks of both primary and secondary interlocks in Canada. Specifically, 30 percent of the interlocks between Canadian corporations involved primary ties, 27 percent were induced by those primary ties, and 43 percent did not involve a primary tie and were carried by outside directors. The high percentage of interlocks in the last category is particularly meaningful, since these are the ties that are most likely to serve the general interests of the elite.

Ornstein also looked at the density of ties among different sectors of the economy. Table 3.1 presents the mean number of ties with all other corporations for different ownership categories. As we can see, with means of 29.1 and 30.3 ties, the widely held Canadian non-financial corporations and the Canadian financial corporations, respectively, had more ties with other corporations than any other group. Least integrated into the network were provincial crown corporations and different categories of foreign capital. The five most heavily interlocked non-financial corporations averaged 54.6 interlocks. The five big banks carried the financial network, with an average of 85 ties, while the other financial corporations averaged 21.4. Overall, when interlocking directorates were analyzed at the level of the corporation and their institutionalized relationships were mapped, the Canadian network fell somewhere in the middle of the range of variation among the other nations in terms of network integration.

When analyzing the distribution of individual positions, it appears that the Canadian network stands out more prominently. Ornstein looked at differences in what he calls the *autonomy* of the corporate network; that is, the extent to which the network can be said to represent more than the interests of individual corporations. First, the ratio of positions to directors

Table 3.1: Mean Number of Ties with Other Corporations by Ownership Categories

Ownership Categories	Mean Number of Ties with Other Corporations
Non-Financial Canadian Corporations	
Widely held	29.1
Family Control	13.8
Federal Crown	12.5
Provincial Crown	6.5
Non-Financial Foreign	
American	6.4
British	5.9
Foreign	12.1
Financial Sector	
Canadian	30.3
Foreign	4.3

Adapted from Ornstein (1989: 164)

was 1.39, higher than the ratio found in all of the other nations surveyed. This ratio is calculated by dividing the total number of directorship positions by the total number of directors. The larger the ratio, the more autonomous the network is said to be. Put another way, if the number of positions were held constant for every country, a more autonomous network would have fewer directors occupying all of the available positions. Such a network is more likely to have a greater number of individuals who hold many board positions simultaneously, increasing its capacity for elite integration. In Ornstein's research, Canada ranked highest in terms of the proportion of multiple directors relative to single directors and was third in the total number of multiple directors, with 464.

Two other related measures of network autonomy are included in Ornstein's analysis. "Big linkers" are directors that occupy four or more board positions, whereas "network specialists" are big linkers that are *not* executives in any of the corporations. Because network specialists have no primary affiliation with any corporation in the network, they play a special role in unifying the system. Canada's 118 big linkers were found to be the most of any country in the sample (accounting for 69 percent of all Canadian interlocks), and its forty network specialists also ranked among the highest. As this illustrates, the composition of the Canadian network in the 1980s is among the most autonomous of the sample. It is also among the most centralized and dense of the European and North American economies. Ornstein (1989: 169–170) concludes the following:

In Canada, there is a very cohesive network, which is tied together

by a relatively small number of individuals with many board positions.... In terms of the more general questions about the organization of the Canadian network, the analysis lends support to the
models of capitalist class relations which emphasize unity.

The Canadian Network and Elite Integration in the 1990s

Carroll and Alexander (1999) compared the social organization of corporate elite networks in Canada and Australia for 1992. They examined the
top 250 corporations (200 non-financials ranked by sales, and 50 financials
ranked by assets) in each country. One of the issues of concern to the
authors, which has relevance here, is the extent to which interlocks integrate
the directors of leading corporations into a dominant stratum or inner
circle, thereby providing an organizational basis for elite unity and class
consciousness.

Table 3.2 compares board sizes and the mean degree of interlocked
boards for different subgroups of Canadian corporations. The first row
compares industries. It shows that the boards of financial companies are
significantly larger than those of other sectors, a feature consistent with
their status as important meeting places for members of the elite. They
also experience a greater degree of interlocking; the large boards of financial
institutions interlock directly with an average of 15.5 other firms. The
second row compares domestic and foreign corporations. As is evident
here, the boards of domestic firms tend to be larger than their foreign
counterparts and, on average, they interlock with a far greater number of
other companies. The third row compares types of strategic control. In
contrast to public firms, wholly owned or private companies typically have
small boards comprised of insiders (those who already "belong" to the
company). The evidence in Table 3.2 thus suggests that companies with a
greater dispersal of shares and/or a more widely held controlling interest
tend to have larger boards and interlock with a greater number of companies.
Their boards often include a fair number of outside directors, who may
also be involved in other elite forums.

Carroll and Alexander (1999) also analyze the different kinds of ties
present within each country's network, and it is here where a comparison
is useful. Table 3.3 presents the density of interlocking for the two countries,
defined as the proportion of all pairs of firms that are actually interlocked
though a particular type of tie. Corporations in Canada are three times
more likely to be interlocked than corporations in Australia. This difference
becomes even larger when secondary ties are considered in isolation, as
they are far more common in Canada. As Carroll and Alexander (1999: 341)
highlight, "in Canada, much of the network is carried by outside directors;
by the same token, the Australian network is less integrated in part
because of a lack of outside directors who sit on multiple boards." The

Table 3.2: Canadian Top 250:
Composition, Mean Board Size and Mean Degree of Interlocked Boards

	% of Top 250	Mean Board Size	Mean Degree Degree of Interlocked Boards*
Industry			
Resources	11	11.7	13.4
Manufacturing	31	11.3	11.0
Other Industrial	16	12.3	11.3
Financial	20	20.1	15.5
Investment	3	14.0	11.1
Trade	16	10.1	5.0
Location of Control			
Domestically controlled	70	15.0	13.4
Foreign control in N. America	19	8.8	6.7
Foreign control in Europe	6	10.3	7.6
Foreign control in Asia-Pacific	4	7.6	1.8
Strategic Control			
Wholly owned	36	9.2	4.7
Majority-controlled	29	14.4	12.7
Minority-controlled	16	16.4	15.2
No identified controlling interest	19	16.4	18.3
Total Sample	100	13.2	11.3

* Degree of interlocked boards refers to the number of other corporate boards with which a firm is interlocked

Adapted from Carroll and Alexander (1999: 339)

large number of secondary ties and the abundance of outside directors in Canada suggest that its interlocking network is better able to act as a mechanism of elite unity than its Australian counterpart.

Another way to analyze elite integration is to look at the core of the interlocking network. Carroll and Alexander (1999: 343) define the "4-core" as the largest set of companies, each of which has strong ties with four or more members of the same set. In Canada, the 4-core includes seventy-five firms, very few of which are foreign controlled. More specifically, foreign companies make up only 12 percent of the 4-core, and such limited penetration does not significantly fragment the national network.[3] Canadian controlled, publicly traded industrial and financial institutions are heavily interlocked within the group of seventy-five. Together, these two types of corporations make up fifty of the seventy-

Table 3.3: Density of Interlocking for Four Types of Ties

Type of Interlock	Australia	Canada
All Ties	0.015	0.045
Primary Ties	0.008	0.014
Induced Ties	0.003	0.012
Secondary Ties	0.006	0.026

Source: Carroll and Alexander (1999: 341)

five corporations in the 4-core, a proportion consistent with theories of finance capital.

Not only is the network centred around finance capital, it is also highly concentrated around a relatively small number of individuals. The authors found 122 big linkers (directors who occupy four or more board positions) in the Canadian Top 250. As a group, the 122 made up 22 percent of all interlockers in Canada and carried 68 percent of all interlocks. The density of corporate networks is heavily influenced by the number of big linkers, and Canada's 122 stands in stark contrast to the 34 identified in Australia. According to Carroll and Alexander (199: 348), "big linkers play a pivotal social role in class integration, cutting across particular capitalist interests and weaving the leading corporations into a socially integrated block." The abundance of secondary interlocks, often provided by outside directors serving on multiple boards, provides a further basis for class coordination.

The "Geography" of Corporate Power: Spatialized Interlocking

The integration of Canada's economic elite is further illuminated by charting the "geography of corporate power." In his recent study, Carroll (2001) maps the changing network of large Canadian corporations following the Second World War, using the location of corporate head offices—the decision centre of a company—as an indicator of the corporate power structure. In this analysis, Canada's spatialized corporate network is compared at three points in time (1946, 1976 and 1996) and is defined as including the top 103 corporations in each year. More specifically, the top 103 is composed of the largest 23 financial and 74 non-financial corporations (ranked by assets) and six large investment companies (each owning key blocs of shares in other dominant firms).

In 1946, the central position of Montreal was dramatic: 35 percent of all corporate interlocks in Canada connected Montreal-based firms to each other, making it the dense core of the network. Toronto had secondary status; 12.7 percent of all interlocks linked Toronto-based companies to each other, and approximately the same proportion connected Toronto firms with Montreal firms. Very few interlocks connected corporations based outside these two cities. Most of the interlocking extending beyond Montreal and Toronto drew outlying firms *into* the Montreal-Toronto bloc (Carroll 2001: 129). By 1976, the total volume of interlocking had grown, and Toronto had replaced Montreal as the core city. The majority of interlocks now linked Toronto-based companies to each other as well as to Montreal-based firms. The volume of interlocking within the Toronto-Montreal bloc represented 64 percent of the total network, up slightly from 60 percent three decades earlier. A few dozen ties now linked this eastern core of companies to those based in Winnipeg, Calgary and Vancouver, and a small number of ties had been created among companies in the West.

In the period from 1976 to 1996, the spatial network of Canadian directorates underwent significant change. Most dramatically, there was a major redistribution of head offices westward, especially to Calgary and Vancouver. In 1946, the ratio of corporations based in western cities to corporations based in the Toronto-Montreal core was 0.078; it increased to 0.181 in 1976; and to 0.475 in 1996. This rise of the West as a centre for top corporate management was mainly an industrial phenomenon. In other words, there was a shift in the geography of corporate power in the industrial sectors (oil, gas, forestry and mining), but not in finance.

By 1996, a major proliferation of ties had emerged among western firms, and interlocking within the Toronto-Montreal bloc had decreased. The bloc now represented slightly less than half of all interlocks in the national network, representing a major decline from 1976. Although a small regional network did emerge in the West, the dominant tendency was for western companies to interlock with firms in the East. In Carroll's words (2001: 130), the core of the network in 1996 "remained centred around the Toronto-Montreal axis, but major spokes had been extended westward to new sites of corporate command."

The Contemporary East-West Network

Of the top 103 corporations in 1996, 181 interlocking directorships linked Montreal- or Toronto-based corporations with those based in the far West. This involved 42 eastern and 27 western firms, comprising over two-thirds of the Top 103. Twelve of the eastern firms were financial companies, and they participated in 45 percent of the east-west interlocks. All but one of the 27 western firms were industrial corporations. A select few of these industrials—specifically energy corporations based in Calgary—accounted for one-third of the entire east-west volume of interlocking. More specifically, each of the five Calgary-based industrial corporations were interlocked directly with three of the five large Canadian banks and with at least one other financial institution in the network. The Bank of Nova Scotia, for example, was interlocked with Nova, TransAlberta, TransCanada PipeLines and PetroCanada. In contrast, there was no evidence of an autonomous western network detached from the East; the rise of the West should be considered as an expansion of the national network, furthering the spatial integration of the Canadian economic elite.

Table 3.4 presents the network of individual corporate directors that comprise the current east-west network. The second largest regionally defined category—the seventy-three directors of corporations based in both eastern and western cities—deserves attention. They are the most well-connected directors in the network, carrying an average of 5.42 corporate ties. Sixty members of this group are east-west directors who sit on the boards of both major industry and high finance. These "finance capitalists" are the most important players. They carry nearly half of the entire 1996 network, even though they make up only a quarter of inner circle members. This is in stark contrast to the ninety-six directors whose companies are based in the Toronto/Montreal zone, who carry only 1.88 interlocks on average. This spatial network has implications for elite integration:

> Across half a century, even as its contours were reshaped by the westward shift of command centres... the Canadian corporate elite had largely maintained its cohesiveness... [it is] well-integrated across the main urban centres of economic power, across the financial and industrial forms of capital, and across the anglo-French ethnic difference. Viewed in light of related research on the elite's reach into civil society, this pattern of spatial, sectoral, and ethnic integration presented a structural basis for strong business leadership in both economic and extra-economic fields. (Carroll 2001: 137)

The Impact of Globalization on the Canadian Directorate Network

Each of the three studies presented above points to the existence of a well-integrated and dense network of *nationally based* interlocking directorates in Canada. Foreign controlled corporations have only marginal interlocking status and are much more likely than domestic firms to be isolated from the network. In Carroll's (2001) spatial analysis, for example, only one of the network's twenty-six most central corporations—General Motors Canada—was foreign controlled in 1996. These studies all suggest that while the penetration of foreign capital has the potential to fragment national corporate networks it has yet to do so in Canada. On the surface, these findings appear to strengthen the position of unity theorists. But it could also be argued that the weak integration of foreign capital in Canada adds some credibility to the disunity claim. Some large, foreign U.S. corporations in Canada do wield significant power in many sectors of the national economy. The isolation of these corporations from the Canadian

Table 3.4: Inner-Circle Members Cross-Classified by Region and Economic Sector, 1996

Region(s) in which Directors Participate		Sector(s) in which Directors Participate			Total
		Industrial Firms Only	Financial Institutions Only	Non-Financial Firms & Financial Institutions	
Toronto-Montreal	N	35	1	60	96
only	Mean	1.83	1.00	1.92	1.88
East-West (Tor/Mont	N	13	0	60	73
to Cal/Ed/Van)	Mean	3.77		5.78	5.42
West Only	N	16	0	0	16
	Mean	1.31			1.31
Other	N	6	8	38	52
	Mean	1.83	1.00	2.71	2.35
Total	N	70	9	158	237
	Mean	2.07	1.00	3.58	3.03

N refers to the number of directors with directorships in the sectors and regions indicated; mean refers to the average number of corporate interlocks carried by directors of a given type.

Source: Carroll (2001: 132)

network supports the disunity contention that significant divisions exist within Canada's economic elite. Further, as Mel Hurtig (2002) has shown, there is a recent trend toward the reduction of corporate head offices located in Canada. As a result, corporate decisions once made by Canadian directors in Canada are now being made by "absentee managers" from the United States and elsewhere. This trend also raises questions about the structure and unity of the Canadian economic elite.

Despite the limited penetration of foreign capital noted in the three studies, changes in the international economy have had an impact on the directorate network. How has economic globalization impacted the organization of Canada's economic elite, specifically? One possible source of disintegration is the transnationalization of investment. While the multifaceted nature of this process and the resulting structural changes to the Canadian corporate network are too complex to be detailed here, a few general observations can be made. William Carroll's (2004) analysis of transnationalization corroborates the three studies mentioned above; the penetration of foreign capital has not led to network disintegration. But what about the other side of transnational investment—transnational capital emanating from Canada? Over the course of the past few decades, the number of transnational corporations (TNCs) operating within the country has proliferated. As a result, the network's "core" has shifted from nationally based finance capital to a transnational sector of companies. It is important to note, however, that these TNCs are overwhelmingly Canadian controlled. Specifically, only one of the forty-four TNCs forming the dominant component of the transnational sector was foreign controlled in 1996. Moreover, these firms were also well integrated with non-TNCs. Given this, Carroll (2004: 85) concludes that "transnational finance capital has radiated from Canada in a way that has not disorganized the national network, but has *embedded* it more extensively in a circuitry of global accumulation." For the most part, the Canadian network has remained domestic in terms of its locus of control and retained a predominantly national base.

In addition to transnational investment, a second possible source of network disintegration is corporate governance reform. Following a series of financial scandals in 1993 and the eventual collapse of Confederation Life, the Toronto Stock Exchange (TSE) struck a task force to look specifically at the issue of corporate governance. The task force made fourteen recommendations (adopted by the TSE in 1995), which have since significantly impacted the structure of the Canadian interlocking network. For our purposes, two of the recommendations are particularly relevant: (1) boards should be constituted by a majority of outside, unrelated directors, meaning directors should be selected independent of management so that they can pursue the best interests of the corporation; and (2) every board should examine its size and, where necessary, reduce the number of directors to facilitate more effective decision-making. These reforms were aimed at making corporate boards "more active and effective centres of governance—independent of management, beholden only to shareholders, small enough to function efficiently, and composed of well-oriented, high-performance directors" (Carroll 2004: 34). In part, they can be understood as a reaction by Canadian elites to the competitive pressures of globalization. While the reforms were primarily motivated by the need for efficiency and profit, they may also be seen as a project of "moral reform" within the corporate community. Sound corporate governance was seen as a way to give business a higher degree of legitimacy and allow it to respond more actively to public demands and pressures.

Without a doubt, corporate governance reforms have created a sparser directorate network. Specifically, smaller board sizes have had the effect of reducing the number of interpersonal elite contacts. Between 1976 and 1996, the mean number of interpersonal contacts among the elite declined from 34.0 to 20.8. Smaller boards have also decreased the number of multiple directorships. For example, the number of big linkers fell from 128 in 1976 to 82 in 1996 (Carroll 2004: 24). The move away from inside directors—those who create primary interlocks (and induce secondary interlocks) through multiple directorships—also resulted in network decline. An average of five inside directors sat on the boards of major firms in 1976. Twenty years later, the average was reduced to just three. Moreover, in 1976 a total of sixty-eight inside directors were big linkers, compared with only twenty-eight in 1996. By weakening all segments of the primary interlock network, corporate reforms have significantly reduced the overall number of network ties. Hence, corporate governance reforms have resulted in smaller boards populated by fewer officers, and they have produced a network linked together mostly by outside directors.

Most changes in board size (and the density of the network) can be attributed to changes at the major Canadian banks. As mentioned earlier in the chapter, banks exist at the heart of the network and serve as a central meeting place for elites. In 1976, a total of 172 members of the elite sat on the boards of Canada's five largest banks. This number was reduced considerably to just 97 in 1996 (Carroll 2004: 26). At the same time, inside bank directors nearly disappeared from the boards of other dominant corporations. Despite the declining prominence of banks, they continue to represent "central nodes"—through secondary ties—in the directorate network.

At first glance, it would appear as if changes in corporate governance present a threat to elite unity in Canada. Fewer multiple directors and an overall decline in interpersonal contacts among the elite suggest that the directorate network may no longer be as useful in its unifying role. However, the decline in the number of interpersonal contacts is offset to some degree by the *kind* of directors around which the network is now primarily structured—outside directors. As noted earlier in the chapter, outside directors play a key role in unifying the system, as they do not represent a particular corporation and can more "objectively" promote the economic and political interests of the elite as a whole.

The third international change involves the globalization of elite networks and the formation of a transnational capitalist class. A more connected network of global elites has taken shape over the past few decades, centred around transnational corporations. A recent study by the U.S. Conference Board of TNCs from sixteen different countries illustrates the nature of the changes. The study found that the percentage of companies with "non-national" directors (a director from one country that sits on the board of a TNC based in another country) increased from 39 percent in 1995 to 60 percent in 1998; companies with three or more non-national directors increased from 11 percent to 23 percent over the same period. Based on their data, the authors conclude that "non-national directors are gaining an influential role in boardrooms around the world" (cited in Robinson 2004: 63). A globalized network of interlocked directorates and a greater proportion of directors could come to pose a threat to the non-national composition of nationally based networks.

However, compared to interlocking among Canadian corporations, transnational interlocking involving Canadian elites is quite rare (Carroll 2004: 151) With the exception of the complex of companies under the control of Paul Desmarais, the elite is not well integrated into the global system. Further evidence of this is provided by William Carroll and Meindert Fennema (2002), whose research investigated whether or not the global network was composed of one interconnected component or whether it was primarily a collection of separate national components. The authors note a modest increase in transnational interlocking between 1976 and 1996. They also found, however, that the emerging global network of the world's largest firms did not appreciably fragment the complex of ties within nations. The organization of business communities, at least via board interlocks, appears to still be a predominantly national affair. Their conclusions are worth quoting at length:

> the process of transnational class formation did not fragment national corporate networks but occurred in tandem with their reproduction.... There has been no massive shift in corporate interlocking from a predominantly national to a predominantly transnational pattern. By 1996, three-quarters of all the lines linked companies domiciled in the same country, down only slightly from 1976. Even when we examine the 20-odd companies that have the most extensive transnational ties—forming the center of the transnational network—we find nationally based clusters. All of this suggests that the transnational network is a kind of superstructure that rests on rather resilient national bases. (Carroll and Fennema 2002: 414)

Also worth noting is a shift away from the participation of inside directors in the global network from 1976 to 1996. In 1976, only about one-quarter of transnational linkers were outside directors; most were officers in one of the top global firms. By 1996, well over half of transnational linkers were outside directors, anchoring a network composed mainly of secondary ties. The tendency by 1996 for transnational directors to be uninvolved in managing specific corporations means that the potential for unity within the global economic elite has markedly increased.

Have these changes associated with globalization weakened the national network of interlocking directorates in Canada? While the evidence is mixed, the answer appears to be no. The resilience of "the national factor" in the directorate network suggests that, at least for the time being, globalization has not disrupted elite integration in Canada. Despite corporate governance reforms and other changes, the Canadian directorate network remains cohesive.

Clearly, the potential for unity and control is not equivalent to actual control. While corporate concentration and corporate board interlocks show us that the economic structures for cohesion are in place, there are other mechanisms for translating these into political action. In Part Three, the discussion shifts to those mechanisms of elite unity that comprise the "policy formation network" intersectoral policy organizations, advocacy think tanks and free-enterprise foundations. These organizations figure prominently in producing policy consensus among members of the elite. Agreement on policy issues requires extensive deliberation and consultation in order to transform political problems into manageable objects of policy. This largely occurs within the context of the policy formation network.

NOTES

1. For an overview see Ornstein (1984) and Mizruchi (1992, 1996).
2. Mizruchi (1996: 276) suggests that resource exchange could even take the form of "legitimacy." Firms may not be seeking specific alliances but rather the prestige associated with being linked to other high profile companies. This type of association signals that the firm is worthy of support and may help to secure important resources such as capital, raw materials and markets.
3. Carroll and Alexander (1999) make clear that most firms that are isolated or excluded from the Canadian network as a whole are not controlled by domestic capitalists. The largest category of these is American-controlled industrial corporations.

4. INTERSECTORAL POLICY ORGANIZATIONS

Literally hundreds of trade associations in Canada have been organized to defend the interests of specific industries. These customary associations are seen in the context of larger investigations of pressure groups. Yet a few organizations have been established with a much different mandate. These organizations, which can be described as "intersectoral," exist to provide a forum for discussing and articulating policies that affect most large companies, regardless of sector or region. In Canada today, there are four influential policy organizations of this type: the Canadian Council of Chief Executives (CCCE), the Canadian Chamber of Commerce (CCC), Canadian Manufacturers and Exporters (CME), and the Canadian Federation of Independent Business (CFIB).

Pluralists view business policy organizations as one of many voices in the policy-making process. Put another way, they contend that a diversity of interest groups compete to have their wishes met and that there are no consistent "winners and losers." This process of competition is said to be magnified by the sheer number of competing interest groups and organizations, and by their diverse strategies and resources. Some pluralists, however, do concede that business is in a favoured or privileged position when it comes to policy formation. In making this concession, these pluralists seem to acknowledge that there is a connection between economic and political power (Smith 1990). Nevertheless, they also maintain that constraints exist to ensure that corporate power does not overwhelm the state or government. For one, countervailing power groups (such as organized labour) have the capacity to challenge more influential groups (like the economic elite). If countervailing groups fail to be effective, powerful interests are still held in check by the existence of "potential groups" (Smith 1990: 305). Potential groups are unorganized clusters of individuals with shared interests who could become organized if business tried to push its agenda too far. If, for example, the government does not take these interests into account when developing or advocating policy, then a potential group could organize itself and pose a threat at the polls. Because (re)-election depends on majority support, pluralists argue that governments have no choice but to consider a wide range of interests and concerns. Thus, they see countervailing and potential groups as ultimately preventing big business from taking advantage of its vast resources and privileged position.

For more critical theorists, broadly focused, intersectoral policy organizations comprise some of the key coordinating points in the capitalist power structure. Carroll (2004: 172) goes so far as to say that "the mobilization of business activism within neoliberal policy-planning groups has been the most important means by which the Canadian corporate elite has formed and exercised its collective will in recent decades." Unity theorists point to several ways that policy organizations can help to advance elite interests. First, they provide a setting where business leaders can meet with each other and with government representatives to familiarize themselves with policy issues and discuss general concerns. Second, policy organizations help to infuse the information and concepts provided by other "experts" into the perspectives of corporate leaders and government officials, who are then better able to use the information for political ends. Third, they supply a possible forum from which the elite can informally select business leaders capable of serving in government. This informal recruiting ground may extend as well to other experts, such as elite academics. Policy organizations—in concert with the economic elite—evaluate whether academics are capable and committed enough to represent their interests within the state and political arena. In turn, academics help business leaders to hone and clarify their political thinking and strategizing (see Domhoff 1987: 193–194).

There is one other crucial function of policy organizations: the mediation of conflicts within the economic elite and the generation of class-wide rationality. This function is regularly overlooked, not surprisingly, since many prominent business representatives are already highly class conscious before becoming members. Indeed, an awareness of class and politics among incoming policy-group members is necessary, as these organizations constitute an important interface between the highest levels of government and dominant corporations in all sectors of the economy. But a broad, class-based outlook is also fostered within policy organizations, and a greater degree of unity is cultivated among their various participants.

Interesting testimony on this is offered by prominent executives in the United States in talking about the kinds of people they would suggest for government positions. The most valued traits were "character and integrity," which were exemplified by "an executive's capacity to transcend the immediate imperatives of his or her own company to express a broader vision" (Useem 1984: 96-97). The persons who fit this criterion were selected specifically for their experience in policy organizations. One executive who sat on four company boards and served in the Department of Defense for several years remarked that the executives who best represented business "are down in Washington undertaking responsibilities beyond the requirements of their own operation ... [H]eading the

Roundtable and the Business Council, [they are] willing to step out and accept public responsibility even while they carry out their private responsibility" (97).

Thus, individuals who direct the activities of intersectoral policy organizations typically have a significant influence on the policies collectively endorsed or opposed by business. These participants must have demonstrated an ability to bring forward information about the common concerns of a broad range of companies and to translate these concerns into realistic policy alternatives. Their abilities become more sophisticated through continuous rounds of meetings, negotiations, conferences and planning seminars. As well, these activities allow corporate executives to judge each other's capacities at close range and weed out those whose outlooks are not sufficiently broad or class-based. In short, policy organizations both attract inner circle business leaders and refine their political perspectives and skills.

TRANSFORMING CANADIAN PUBLIC POLICY: THE CANADIAN COUNCIL OF CHIEF EXECUTIVES

The Canadian Council of Chief Executives (CCCE) is Canada's most powerful and effective policy organization. It is composed of the chief executive officers (CEOs) of the country's 150 leading corporations. Together, they represent every major sector of the economy. These companies administer assets worth upwards of $2.3 trillion and employ approximately 1.5 million Canadians. Presided over by CEO Thomas d'Aquino, the CCCE consists of an eight-person executive committee and a twenty-four member board of directors (who together provide governance and overall direction for the Council), as well as the general membership. Known until December 2001, as the Business Council on National Issues (BCNI), the name change coincided with the organization's expanding global outlook and the "need for a clearer identity worldwide" (CCCE website). In conjunction with its increasingly global mandate, the Council now consists of three separate policy committees which cover Canadian, North American and global policy issues.

According to David Langille (1987: 51), "if there is an 'inner circle' amongst Canadian [business leaders], it would certainly be dominated by the members of the Business Council." Nearly all of the organization's members are professional managers, but some "owner-managers" (such as the Thomsons) are represented within the Council by companies under their control. Senior officers in Canada's other major policy organizations, such as the Canadian Chamber of Commerce and Canadian Manufacturers and Exporters, also participate as associate members in the affairs of the Council. Most members engage directly in policy work through committees, roundtables, task forces and other initiatives. Over the years, committees and task forces led by council members have dealt with a wide range of domestic and international issues.[1] The overarching mandate of the CCCE and the structure of its many task forces have made it a virtual "shadow cabinet," overseeing developments in every cabinet portfolio (Dobbin 1998: 167).

The Business Council was created as part of the corporate offensive of the 1970s. The Council united the "greatest collection of heavyweight executive talent in Canada's history" to deal with "organized labour and governments that have grown in size as well as propensity to regulate and intervene in the economy" (Davies 1977: 30). In addition to other powerful affiliates, its initial membership list included the presidents or CEOs of Canada's eight chartered banks, the top ten insurance companies and eighteen oil and pipeline corporations (Clarke 1997: 20). Canadian capitalists were concerned that the welfare state had grown too large; the state, they believed, was dangerously out of control and no longer capable of adequately representing business interests or organizing the compromises that would sustain corporate dominance. Furthermore, the political parties had become unreliably "pragmatic" and too willing to sacrifice business priorities. The period was also marked by a growing tide of labour unrest and increasing public criticism of corporate power. In response to these pressing concerns, business leaders Alfred Powis and W.O. Twaits formed the BCNI in 1976 to enhance the influence of the private sector in Canada.

The BCNI was also formed to meticulously transform Canadian public policy. As part of its mandate, the Council outlined broad areas of policy that required attention and aimed to exert its influence in a timely fashion. Prior to its development, business leaders had appeared capable of reacting only negatively and after the fact to government policies and programs (Langille 1987: 48). According to former Council president William Archibald, the BCNI would reverse this pattern of business-government relations and anticipate public policy, developing approaches and solutions that could be put forward in the early stages of the policy-making process (cited in Dobbin 1998: 167). The overall objectives of council members were very ambitious:

> to challenge the whole notion of the social state, the sharing for survival, the whole notion of paying taxes because you believe there is something greater than your own set of rights. They knew that if they were going to ... replace democracy with economic freedom as the most fundamental right, then they had to change the political culture.... It wasn't going to happen overnight. I believe they knew it was going to take 20 years. (Barlow 1999: 20)

However, in order to bring the state back in line and successfully contour Canada's public policy terrain, business leaders needed an organization that would speak for the business community as a whole. The various trade associations had considerable expertise about the specific industries they represented but were not capable of establishing long-term policy initiatives or coherent political strategies. Furthermore, policy organizations like the Canadian Chamber of Commerce and the Canadian Manufacturers' Association were not sufficiently broad in focus and the CEOs of Canada's largest corporations no longer played an active role in them. According to Michael Pitfield, then Secretary to Cabinet in the Trudeau administration, the existing organizations had atrophied so badly that they had become part of the problem (Langille 1987: 47). Government officials shared the desire of Canada's business elite for an organization that could reflect the wide range of views within the business community and offer an integrated approach. It is likely that "some credit goes to Trudeau himself for encouraging the BCNI. He kept complaining about the mixed messages being received from business" (Cameron 1988: 19).

In the words of Tom d'Aquino, the Council's creation and structure reflected the fact that "major business leaders wanted to be able to move quickly on issues and address them at the highest level ... at a level most large organizations are unable to do and with a degree of speed and consensus most large organizations find difficult" (cited in Langille 1987: 53–54). Thus, a primary motive for the creation of the BCNI in 1976 was to facilitate cohesion and consensus among Canada's elite and to ensure the maximum degree of coordination and planning in matters of overall concern to Canadian business.

Given that the BCNI was forged as a new organizational model for Canadian business, it is useful to ask how business leaders chose its particular structure and membership guidelines. By many accounts, the Council was modeled after the Business Roundtable in the United States, an organization whose members include the CEOs of the largest U.S. corporations (Langille 1987; Dobbin 1998; and Barlow 1999). Barlow (1999: 20) argues that there were "enormously close ties" between the BCNI and U.S. business leaders "right from the beginning." Since its creation in 1974, the Roundtable has developed into an extraordinarily effective policy organization. Like the BCNI, it materialized out of the corporate offensive of the 1970s, as business leaders in the U.S. sought to reduce state autonomy and unite the array of industry-specific business groupings. Canadian business leaders were impressed by the Roundtable's success and particularly by its ability to integrate the U.S. business community. Tony Clarke comments on how the structure of the Roundtable facilitates corporate unity:

> In this forum, the head of General Motors works side by side with his counterparts in Ford and Chrysler; the CEO at Exxon sits down with his rivals at Mobil, Texaco, and Chevron; the head of Citicorp

works with his counterparts at Chemical Banking, Chase Manhattan, and First Chicago; the president of DuPont collaborates with his competition at Dow, Occidental Petroleum, and Monsanto. (Clarke 1997: 47)

Useem (1984) contends that the Business Roundtable enhances the political awareness of its members and sensitizes them to the political consequences of actions taken by their own firms. Following this, the Roundtable attempts to bring companies together to support policies they may not otherwise support, at least not with the same degree of enthusiasm or certainty.

Enter Thomas d'Aquino

Until 1980, the profile of the BCNI was fairly low. This changed, however, in 1981 when Tom d'Aquino was chosen to lead it. The Council first targeted the Trudeau Liberals, who now faced a more united and far more aggressive business class. One indication of the shift came when business requested that the government re-examine the tax system. Contrary to the BCNI's goal of promoting business-friendly tax reform, finance minister Allan MacEachen and his advisors focused on how billions of dollars were being lost to corporate tax breaks and how to close the loopholes. The resulting legislation outraged corporate Canada, prompting immediate action. According to Neil Brooks (who worked for the finance department on the tax reform package), Canadian corporations launched "a classic example of what's called a capital strike. I mean, business simply said to the government that if you go ahead with these measures we will stop investing in Canada.... Literally the next day they were closing down jobs" (cited in Dobbin 1998: 168–169).[2]

The above incident was but the beginning of the BCNI's efforts to alter the relationship between big business and the state. Bradford (2000: 67) argues that by 1983, "business had responded in a coherent and strategic fashion to changed economic and political conditions ... demonstrating little uncertainly or confusion about its interests and exhibiting unprecedented capacity for political articulation." For the remainder of the decade, the BCNI pushed its neoliberal agenda. It focused much of its attention on the new Conservative government led by Brain Mulroney and the elimination of Canada's National Energy Program (NEP). Energy policy had been one of the most difficult areas for members of the Council to reach a consensus on, as they faced divisions between the conflicting interests of the oil companies, manufacturers and utilities, as well as between domestic and foreign-owned firms. Nevertheless, through "a series of secret meetings involving oil executives and the Alberta government, industrialists and the Ontario government, and bankers and the Federal Government," the BCNI helped engineer a new energy accord, "one that would virtually scrap the NEP, adopt world market prices, and involve substantial changes in taxation policies" (Langille 1987: 62–63).

Not long after the energy victory, d'Aquino set out to officially revise Ottawa's competition bill, something that he had laid the groundwork for years earlier (Newman 1998: 155–156). In the early 1980s, the BCNI spent a million dollars on the competition project alone and by 1985 (with the help of twenty-five lawyers) it had produced a comprehensive 236-page report, which was given to the government and eventually became Canada's new competition law. Not surprisingly, the new legislation contained no provision for class-action suits, and prosecutions were moved from criminal to civil courts. Newman (1998: 156) laments the fact that this may be "the only time in the history of capitalism that any country allowed its anti-monopoly legislation to be written by the very people it was meant to police." By all accounts, the first half of the 1980s was a period of considerable accomplishment for the BCNI, and the Council was aware of the reasons for its success. In 1986, they wrote the following:

> One of the Business Council's most remarkable attributes is its ability to forge common positions on major issues.... Consensus has been achieved in virtually every task force initiative since 1981. There are several reasons for this. First, the Council asks members to consider issues from a national perspective. Advocacy of individual company concerns is discouraged. Second, great emphasis is placed on balancing interests when specific issues are under consideration. This requires compromise and long-term thinking. (Business Council on National Issues 1986: 7)

In the late 1980s and early 1990s, new matters of policy and politics surfaced. Inspired by previous successes, the BCNI continued to convey its unified vision to government and, in effect, to write policy. In 1987, for example, both the government and the BCNI hired the same person to construct a paper on Canadian defence policy. Predictably, the Council's paper closely mimicked that of the government's own White Paper, likely because the retired general who wrote the policy simply gave the same paper he wrote for BCNI directly to the government (Barlow 1999: 20). They were so similar that d'Aquino agreed to delay the release of the BCNI paper for several months so as not to embarrass the Tories. A few years later, the Council staunchly supported the introduction of the Goods and Services Tax (GST). "So powerful was the corporate consensus on this issue that the Conservative government of Brian Mulroney virtually committed political suicide to get it through" (Dobbin 1998: 172).

The BCNI's influence over deficit reduction was also considerable, first with the Conservatives and later with the Liberals. In this crusade, they were aided by the Canadian Manufacturers' Association, the Canadian Chamber of Commerce, the C.D. Howe and Fraser institutes, the National Citizens

Coalition and the Canadian Taxpayers Federation. The media also played a key role, producing hundreds of articles and reports which focused on the deficit "crisis." According to d'Aquino, when Chrétien was elected "we took [the deficit reduction] campaign in hand, and we scared the hell out of people. We said it over and over again for so long that people began to believe the deficit was really wicked" (cited in Newman 1998: 159). Canadians were repeatedly told that if the deficit was not reduced, economic disaster would soon follow. The impact of this campaign was vividly reflected in public opinion polls. According to a survey by Gallup Canada (1995), in 1992 only 3 percent of respondents identified "government debt/deficit" as the country's most important problem. Just one year later in 1993, this number jumped to 20 percent, peaking in 1995 at 27 percent.

A core part of the campaign was the message that "excessive" government spending, especially on social programs, was the primary cause of the spiraling deficit. However, as Linda McQuaig has argued, the deficit campaign was largely a fraud, a way to reduce government spending and shrink Canada's social safety net. She writes:

> A frontal assault against social programs was out. What was needed was something that attacked from an unprotected flank, something that would lead to cuts in social spending without coming right out and saying so.... [T]he deficit became a crucial weapon in the business arsenal, a powerful concept that could be trotted out to back up the business claim that government spending was out of control. (McQuaig 1991: 102–103)

Another indicator that the deficit scare was initiated as a means to reduce public spending was that the primary reasons for the deficit were largely ignored. A solid body of evidence suggests that deficits have little to do with social program expenditure. Many authors note that the major causes of Canada's rising deficit were high interest rates and revenue shortfalls resulting from tax breaks to wealthy individuals and corporations (See Clarke 1997; McBride 2001; McBride and Shields 1993; McQuaig 1995; Dobbin 2003c). Nevertheless, according to James Winter (1997: 128), a 1995 Statistics Canada report which argued that social spending was not the cause of the deficit/debt was "furiously attacked" in the news media.

Both the Mulroney and Chrétien governments, acting in the interests of big business, seemingly ignored the primary causes of the debt. Instead, they chose to focus squarely on government spending, implicating the welfare state as the cause of the problem. What followed were tens of billions of dollars in cuts to social programs—unnecessary cuts, since many other countries had managed to eliminate their deficits by the late 1990s without radical spending cuts. In fact, if program spending had simply been frozen from 1994 to 1999, the deficit would have shrunk from 4.8

percent of GDP in 1994 to zero in 1999 (Stanford 2001). The deficit scare was an impressive and highly successful campaign organized by Canada's elite. Yet even it pales in comparison to corporate Canada's actions in support of the Free Trade Agreement (FTA) with the United States. Spearheaded by the BCNI and its allies, the FTA represented one of the most important victories for Canadian business.

Strength through Solidarity

The notable success of the Council is largely due to its unparalleled ability to forge a business consensus over policy recommendations and to negotiate the compromises which ensure that those recommendations become policy. The Council does not simply respond to government initiatives but anticipates issues, making detailed recommendations to policy-makers while the initiatives are still under consideration. Indeed, it has "conducted its affairs with a strategic intelligence that has, with few exceptions, allowed the state to implement a comprehensive corporate agenda while appearing to act in the public interest" (Dobbin 1998: 178). Part of this strategy has involved careful public posturing. The Council has always maintained a cautious, arm's length relationship with the extremist agendas advanced by the National Citizens' Coalition (NCC) and other visible right-wing groups (Clarke 1997: 36). In this way, the NCC creates a political space for the Council's pro-business but less radical ideas.

Another cause of its success (and one that is often overlooked) is its workers' high level of class consciousness. A decade ago, in an interview with Murray Dobbin, d'Aquino ironically remarked, "whenever I look around and see enormous power blocs exercising influence vastly greater than they should and seek to do it consciously, I get very upset" (Dobbin 1992: 7). To be sure, the Council, closely attuned to political sensibilities, is careful not to be perceived as simply a creature of the economic elite. Its business leaders recognize that they are fighting what amounts to class warfare and know that this takes persistent effort and a keen awareness of public relations. For example, in their tax reform proposals, the Council aimed both to reward the rich and to "protect" the poor, by lowering taxes at both ends of the spectrum and using tax credits to protect low-income earners. Thus, "by championing the cause of the poor, they appear magnanimous at very little cost to themselves, since most of the reforms they propose would be borne by the middle class" (Langille 1987: 60). Similarly, when the Mulroney government's attempt to de-index pensions provoked widespread public opposition in the late 1980s, the Conservatives were forced to abandon the initiative, not only because of the public's distaste for the plan but also because the BCNI, normally a supporter of Tory policies, opposed it. It later turned out that BCNI members did not want to see the broad campaign against social programs threatened by any single issue (Archer 1997). A final example of the BCNI's strategic approach is its dealings with labour. Compared to the Business Roundtable in the U.S., the BCNI has taken a less confrontational stance towards organized labour. Rather than directly attack the power of trade unions, council members established a dialogue with labour leaders in order that these leaders might become more receptive to concessions and gain a better "appreciation" of market forces (Langille 1987: 50).

As the above arguments illustrate, the Canadian Council of Chief Executives is an incredibly organized and persuasive policy group. Arguably, it has been even more pivotal in Canada than the Roundtable has in the United States. It may, in fact, be unique in the developed world in terms of its ability to dominate political life. As d'Aquino boasts, "no business community in the world at the CEO level has taken such an active interest in politics" (cited in Newman 1998: 159–160). The Council's non-confrontational approach, combining "the skills of the senior policy analyst with the sensitivity of a politician," has helped it to succeed where other organizations fail (Dobbin 1998: 167). Potent and unrelenting business activism, coupled with a unique ability to forge a sturdy elite consensus, has enabled it to become an instrument of unprecedented political power in Canada.

OTHER PLAYERS IN THE NETWORK: THE ALLIES OF THE CCCE

Canada's other policy organizations play an important role in generating corporate unity as well, partly because the Council's policy vision has permeated these institutions. Three of the CCCE's key allies are the Canadian Chamber of Commerce, Canadian Manufacturers and Exporters and the Canadian Federation of Independent Business.

An influential advocate for business in Canada since 1925, the Canadian Chamber of Commerce (CCC) confidently describes itself as "the national leader in public policy advocacy on business issues" and "the leading organization that brings all types of Canadian business together to act as a powerful single voice." Interestingly, it also depicts itself as "non-political" (CCC 2003). A second ally of the CCCE is the powerful Canadian Manufacturers and Exporters (CME), known as the Alliance of Manufacturers and Exporters Canada until October 2000. It was formed through the merger in 1996 of the Canadian Manufacturers' Association (CMA) and the Canadian Exporters' Association (CEA). The members of the CME represent 75 percent of the country's manufacturing output and 90 percent of exports. Historically, both the CCC and the CMA have had extensive ties to the most successful Canadian corporations (largely through board interlocks) and to the state (Fox and Ornstein, 1986). Finally, the Canadian Federation of Independent Business (CFIB) began in 1971 as a political action organization for small and medium-sized businesses. The organization describes itself as "a unifying force for small business" which is committed to "being the most courageous, persistent, creative and constructive voice of independent enterprise in Canada" (CFIB 2003).

Part of the mandate of each of these organizations is to advocate for small and medium-sized companies in Canada, companies whose interests often conflict with those of the large corporations. What is worth noting, however, is that the positions advanced by these organizations often coincide with those of the CCCE, even when such positions may not be in the interests of the majority of their members. This cooperation, some evidence suggests, has been going on since the inception of the BCNI. In 1976, one of its founders, William Twaits, remarked that the Canadian Chamber of Commerce and Canadian Manufacturers Association (together with the media) would help to disseminate the Council's research information to the general public (Davies 1977: 31). In the 1980s, thanks to the BCNI, these organizations began to express an increasing degree of unity on many issues despite their somewhat different priorities and power bases (Langille 1987: 51). One of these issues was free trade.

THE FIGHT FOR FREE TRADE IN CANADA

Did corporate political action influence the passage of the North American free trade agreements? If so, how? Specifically, was business leadership organized in defence of the agreement "formed as a result of converging company rationalities, specified by various organizational interests, or as a result of a much broader, class-wide rationality forged in cohesive associations across the policy formation process" (Dreiling 2000: 23)? Dreiling's analysis of the situation in the United States strongly suggests that the mechanisms and motivations leading to collective action "were formed within a social milieu best characterized by Useem's 'inner circle' and Domhoff's 'policy-formation network'" (43). Here, the question will be addressed within the Canadian context, focusing primarily on the original free trade agreement with the United States (FTA). The events that solidified the passage of the FTA in 1988 (and subsequently NAFTA in 1993) offer a compelling example of corporate political unity in action.

The BCNI, headed by Tom d'Aquino, began promoting free trade as early as 1981. At the time there was little interest in the idea within the Liberal and Conservative parties, and considerable uncertainty existed even among the CEOs on the Council. Rather than lobby the Liberals directly, d'Aquino began a campaign to influence the outcome of the Macdonald Royal Commission into Canada's economic future. Through meetings, presentations, press conferences and "serious looking documents," the BCNI convinced the Commission that free trade was the most adept way to deal with American protectionism and the best future economic strategy (Cameron 1988: 20–21). A few years later, before its own research was even completed, the Commission publicly announced that it was in favour of the deal and called on Canadians to take a "leap of faith" (Doern and Tomlin 1991: 24).[3]

Beginning in 1983, d'Aquino publicly promoted free trade and lobbied aggressively for its support. The Council took a lead role in convincing the Canadian business community to move away from its traditional protectionism. According to Duncan Cameron (1988: 29), those business leaders who were not members of the BCNI were courted with the help of the Canadian Chamber of Commerce. That same year, d'Aquino went to the United States to advance the idea with the Reagan administration and the U.S. Business Roundtable. In 1984, a business task force was formed whose forty-five members included many powerful business titans. Their goal was to garner support from other business leaders on freer trade with the United States. Largely as a result of their efforts, most Canadian business leaders were onside by the mid-1980s.

Having achieved a strong working consensus among the business elite in Canada, the BCNI next sought to secure the support of the Conservatives under Brian Mulroney (who had opposed free trade during the 1984 election campaign) and the U.S. business community and political leadership. In an effort to convince Mulroney, the BCNI utilized the task force it had created in 1984. Mulroney proved an easy sell. Within a few short months, he had bought the argument for free trade advanced by the BCNI. Following Mulroney's lead, many other high government officials reversed their positions. In a remarkable turnaround, "all the key Tory ministers had suddenly become free traders" (Cameron 1988: 20). In March 1985, with the support of the Canadian government now all but assured, a group of seventeen members of the BCNI travelled to Washington for three days of discussions with American business leaders and government representatives. In the months and years that followed, BCNI members would deliver numerous speeches in the U.S. and meet with many key members of the American political elite. The Council would also secure the endorsement of the Business Roundtable, the two organizations agreeing to work together in order to expedite the process (Langille 1987: 68–69). In April, following the Shamrock Summit between Prime Minister Mulroney and President Reagan, d'Aquino pressed Mulroney to push for a comprehensive deal on trade liberalization.

Although the Canadian government now tacitly supported free trade, members of the government did not want the public to know it. In fact, they thought it best that the public not be informed about the proposed agreement at all. A government document leaked from the Prime Minister's Office, in September 1985, revealed the Tories' media communications strategy regarding the free trade issue. There is no escaping the anti-democratic thrust of the document:

> Our communication strategy should rely less on educating the general public than on getting across the message that the trade initiative is a good idea. In other words, a selling job ... a substantial majority of the public may be willing to leave the issue in the hands

of the government and *other interested groups*, if the government maintains communications control of the situation. Benign neglect from a majority of Canadians may be the realistic outcome of a well-executed communications program. (cited in Winter 1990: 46–47, emphasis added)

Although the other "interested groups" were not identified, it is not difficult to surmise whom the document was referring to. Clearly, the public was not one of these groups. The government recognized that the initiative was politically weak and that, if the issue was debated openly, any public support generated for the agreement was likely to evaporate quickly. They were fearful that most Canadians—when they became aware of the deal—would view free trade as serving the narrow interests of corporate Canada. Accordingly, the document also called on the government to discredit opposition members who raised concerns about the deal and to "divide and neutralize" dissenting organizations (Barlow 1990: 25). When it looked as if the Mulroney government was mishandling the negotiations or the public relations campaign, "business rescue missions" were launched to ensure that things proceeded as planned. Partly as a result of these strategies, many Canadians felt confused and uninformed about the deal in the time leading up to its passage (Rick Salutin cited in Winter 1990: 47).

With the seeds of the agreement firmly in place, the BCNI and its allies stepped up their campaign. From 1985 to 1988, the BCNI spent upwards of $20 million in one of the largest lobbying efforts in Canadian history (Newman 1998: 156). Canada's business community rallied around the Tories, showering them with massive campaign contributions and an unprecedented degree of support. In the two years leading up to the "free trade election," in 1988, the Conservative government spent an estimated $32 million promoting the deal, mostly through the International Trade Communications Group in the Department of External Affairs (Dobbin 1998: 46). In 1987, in the face of growing public opposition to the deal, the BCNI decided that a public advocacy campaign was needed. Once again, the goal of the campaign would not be to educate Canadians but to implant the idea that free trade would ultimately be beneficial to all. Much of the campaign was conducted through the Alliance for Trade and Job Opportunities, which consisted of many corporations and banks who were BCNI members, as well as dozens of business organizations. Alcan, Noranda and the Royal Bank each contributed $400,000 to the Alliance, while other corporations donated another $3 million. The major donors were mainly members of the BCNI and included some US-based transnationals (Barlow 1990: 8). In the months leading up to the 1988 election, the Alliance spent over $5 million on an advertising campaign, which included a four-page tabloid called *Straight Talk* inserted into every major newspaper across the country just two weeks before the election. The advertising blitz sold the idea that free trade would lead to rising living standards, would increase employment and would not adversely affect social programs.

Some Canadian corporations even lobbied their own employees by putting pro-FTA materials in pay packages and by sending pamphlets to their workers and clients. Crown Life Insurance, for example, went so far as to intimidate their employees with the possibility of plant closures and layoffs if they did not vote for the deal (Dobbin 1998: 47). Just two weeks before the election, both the Canadian Chamber of Commerce and the Canadian Manufacturers' Association urged their members to hold workplace meetings with employees to pressure them to support free trade (Richardson 1992: 322). As well, journalist Doug Smith argues that Canadian business leaders threatened to strike by withholding capital and investments if the Conservatives were defeated. "Day after day, business leaders were paraded before us, explaining how they would be forced to rethink their investment plans unless the FTA was approved." Smith added that "they appeared to have almost unlimited access to the media" (cited in Winter 1990: 67).

There was also, of course, a dedicated coalition of anti-free trade groups as well. While the pro-free trade forces united around the Alliance, the opposition gathered around two umbrella groups, the Council of Canadians (COC) and the Pro Canada Network (PCN). The PCN brought together thirty national organizations and ten provincial coalitions, including church groups, women's groups, environmental lobbies, aboriginal organizations, senior citizens' groups and representatives from the labour movement. The activists in the COC and PCN battled hard right up to the final days before the election—although they could not match the tens of millions of dollars put forward by Canadian business.

The degree of elite consensus in the free trade battle was quite remarkable, thanks mainly to the BCNI and its allies. In fact, the consensus was so powerful that some of the corporations whose interests were harmed by free trade were said to have "fallen on their swords," sacrificing themselves for the overriding principles of corporate domination (Dobbin 1998: 178). Yet securing a united business front on the free trade issue was not as easy as the BCNI would have liked. For one thing, the leaders of the Canadian Manufacturers' Association (CMA) were initially hesitant about the idea, believing that the majority of their members would oppose it. Although some elements of the Canadian Federation of Independent Business were also skeptical at first, the BCNI played an instrumental role in bringing them on board. In fact, the CFIB supported free trade virtually from the beginning, even though only one-third of its members said they would benefit from the deal (Dobbin 1998: 179).

Behind the scenes, there was considerable discord between, and even within, business sectors. When the beer industry threatened to mount a public campaign against the deal, the BCNI calmed their fears and eventually got them special protection under the agreement (Doern and Tomlin 1991: 107-108). Other industries—such as food manufacturers—also made threats to oppose free trade publicly. Barlow (1990: 15–16) notes that over 80 percent of the members of the Grocery Products Manufacturers of Canada expressed "grave concerns" about the impact of the deal on their businesses, yet the transnational corporations that dominated the association made sure that their fears were never made public. There were also outright defections from the business alliance. For example, an umbrella group called the Business Council for Fair Trade aligned itself with the Pro Canada Network. Crucially, though, these backroom struggles never cracked the united business front. In the end, the only major companies to oppose the FTA were the Bank of Nova Scotia and McCain Foods (McBride 2001: 76).

Although free trade proponents said time and time again that the deal would not damage Canada's social safely net, when Mulroney won the election in 1988 and the FTA was passed Canada's policy organizations immediately turned the agreement into a weapon to be used against social programs. According to the Canadian Centre for Policy Alternatives (CCPA), just a few weeks after the election the BCNI, CCC and CMA all began to lobby for harsh spending cuts. The chair of the CMA, for one, insisted that every federal and provincial program be re-examined and recommended the elimination of those programs that might impede competitiveness (CCPA 1996: 17). The Chamber of Commerce called for cuts to old-age security and unemployment insurance. Their recommendations did not go unnoticed. Mulroney's first free trade budget included a series of severe cuts to old age security, unemployment insurance, health and education. In 1990, the same organizations called for a freeze on increases in federal program spending, the main component of which is social program expenditure. Once again, the government did what they asked.

Linda McQuaig reveals that some BCNI members may have been uncertain about supporting the free trade deal because the final package fell far short of their expectations:

> In part, the reason for the BCNI's willingness to go along with the final package, despite misgivings, was that the business agenda had changed somewhat in the years since the trade initiative was launched. While winning secure access to the American market had been the prime concern in the early eighties, a whole new motive had emerged in the mid eighties. Free trade had become a potential tool for a dramatic overhaul of a country that business had come increasingly to dislike. (1991: 166)

The overhaul was designed to make Canada more competitive in the global marketplace—to get the country ready for tougher competition. This entailed disciplining Canadians into lowering their expectations for their own well-being and that of their families. Once Canadians realized that they were now competing with U.S. workers, who were paid much less, they would respond by accepting lower wages, fewer benefits and less job security. Canadians would come to realize that, in a competitive global economy, generous social programs were no longer possible. Those on social assistance would learn to free themselves from their "addiction" to government handouts. The values of community and entitlement would be replaced by those of individualism and competitiveness. Thus, free trade was a way to "whip them into shape, strip them of their old expectations—expectations of a higher standard of living.... Canadians would have to learn to expect less" (McQuaig 1991: 160).

For the elite, another advantage of free trade was that it tied the hands of government, both present and future, limiting its capacity to actively determine the course of economic development. Future generations would be locked in to the policies of a deregulated, privately controlled market, beyond the reach of democratic challenge. According to Barlow and Campbell (1995: 74), while the FTA (and later NAFTA) formally retained the right of government to expand public sector activity, in practice it dissuades public enterprise and "systematically compresses the boundaries of the public sector. Business has a virtual veto over any decision to provide new public goods or services." Opportunities to reverse the trends of deregulation, privatization or welfare state retrenchment are obstructed by the market principles that have become codified in free trade agreements. Canadian business wanted to ensure that nationalist policies, like the National Energy Program, would never resurface.

Since the passage of the FTA, a torrent of negative developments has impacted the lives of Canadian citizens. These developments include a sharp decline in average income and purchasing power, the deterioration of social programs, a considerable rise in poverty and inequality, and dramatic job losses. Indeed, a growing number of Canadians have become contingency workers—lacking full time employment, job security, pensions and benefits (Barlow 2004: 8). From 1992 to 1999, program spending at all levels of government fell from 45 percent to less than 35 percent of GDP (Economic Policy Institute 2001: 27). Between 1988 and 2002, thirty-nine BCNI/CCCE member corporations increased their combined revenues by 105 percent ($144 billion), while decreasing their workforces by nearly 15 percent, or 100,000 jobs (Campbell and Macdonald 2003: 2). Hundreds of thousands of high-paying manufacturing jobs have been lost, permanently, to the United States.

In the years that followed the passage of the FTA, most likely aware that the Conservatives would probably lose the next election, d'Aquino began briefing the opposition Liberals on the NAFTA issue. Roy MacLaren,

Chrétien's trade critic in opposition (eventually minister of international trade), worked especially closely with d'Aquino to develop a position on NAFTA that would appease "social Liberals" while maintaining the agenda of the economic elite. Many Canadian corporations were active in the fight, as were, once again, the BCNI and its policy allies.[4]

The Multilateral Agreement on Investment

In the mid-to-late 1990s, the BCNI—in concert with transnational corporations and other organizations—began quietly to advance the Multilateral Agreement on Investment (MAI). The MAI was a proposed international agreement that sought to extend the principles of "free trade" and corporate-led globalization around the world. In effect, the agreement would have granted to corporations the power of nation states without any accountability, compromising the ability of any government to impose labour laws, environmental standards or other regulatory policies that might benefit its people. Like earlier free trade agreements, the MAI was designed to protect the rights and privileges of international investors, constituting "a one-way street in which capital-holders are given the power to challenge the laws of democratically elected governments [while] governments have no reciprocal power over them" (McQuaig 1998: 23).

Exhibiting the same anti-democratic mentality that motivated the Mulroney government to keep the public uninformed about the FTA, the planners of the MAI attempted to keep it secret. Of course, while the Canadian public was being kept in the dark, the Liberals were busy consulting Canadian policy organizations (and the corporations they represent) about the MAI. Another clear sign of the government's commitments came in the late 1990s, when the Liberals refused to make public the names of the corporations who had been advising the government on the issue. The Canadian Department of Foreign Affairs and International Trade (DFAIT) worked closely with the U.S. State Department and the European Commission to try to get the agreement off the ground (Barlow and Clarke 2001: 94). According to Alan Rugman, a University of Toronto business professor who prepared a background study on the MAI for the OECD, "there are Canadian fingerprints all over the MAI. The untold story is that we are the real heroes getting it going" (cited in Dobbin 1998: 114).

The same kind of anti-democratic sentiment was evident in the United States. In reaction to inquiries from Congress and to public protests, the U.S. government eventually issued a statement on the MAI that claimed that all of the "domestic constituencies" who have a stake in the MAI had already been consulted. Chomsky comments on the implications:

> So, the public isn't a constituency. Congress isn't a constituency. But the U.S. Council for International Business is. They were informed all the way and were intimately involved. The corporate

sector was involved. The White House is telling us plainly and clearly who their domestic constituencies are. It's very rare that political leaders are so frank in such a clear and vulgar fashion about exactly the way they perceive the world. (cited in Chomsky and Barsamian 2001: 9–10)

Obviously, both the Canadian and American governments understood the profound importance of keeping the public uninformed. They operated under the assumption that policy could be designed and executed by those in positions of elite power, without public scrutiny. (See Chapter Eight for information on the defeat of the MAI.

The opening paragraph of this section asked whether the alliance of Canadian business leadership in support of free trade results from converging company rationalities or from a much broader, class-wide rationality forged in business organizations. The evidence seems clear. The motivations that precipitated collective action and political unity around the FTA resided only partly in the organizational interests of corporations. For the most part, these motives were formed through the activities of Canada's policy organizations and inner circle of business leaders. That some corporations sacrificed their interests and supported the deal supports that conclusion, as does the fact that all four major policy organizations were united despite the particular interests of many of their members. The achievements of the BCNI and its allies in forging a robust elite consensus around such an important piece of legislation confirms the importance of elite cohesion and class-wide rationality in the process of policy formation. Their influence will be felt for many years to come, pushing us to "commit ourselves to a national effort that will require changes in attitude, policies, and behaviour on a scale even greater than those involved in embracing free trade" (d'Aquino 2000: 5).

GLOBAL POLICY ORGANIZATIONS

National policy organizations are important for integrating members of the elite, forging consensus and cohesion, and developing new policies and political strategies. In the era of globalization, similar organizations have taken shape at the international level. Global policy groups can act as vehicles for elite integration as well, connecting powerful business leaders from around the world and embedding them within the structure of global corporate power. As Carroll and Carson (2003: 31) point out, the articulation of elite interests at the global level requires sites beyond the boardrooms— places where business leaders can come together to discuss issues and plan strategy. Such meetings also facilitate class consciousness and a unified vision among transnational executives, helping them to articulate and pursue their interests in a world of liberalized trade. Among the most prominent global policy groups today are the Trilateral Commission, the

World Economic Forum, the International Chamber of Commerce, the Bilderberg Conference and the World Business Council for Sustainable Development. Each serves as an important meeting place for global elites and helps to foster agreement around the priorities of transnational capital. By no means an exhaustive list of global policy groups, these five organizations nevertheless represent a few of the most important international forums for consensus formation and strategizing among global elites.

The Trilateral Commission (TC) was formed in 1973 to promote international leadership and cooperation among the three core regions of global capitalism: the United States, Europe and Japan. Its membership includes over 300 representatives of the world's elite, many of whom are CEOs of large corporations—among them several directors of Canada's largest corporations—along with academics, media executives, politicians and others. The TC has played an important role in reorganizing the global economy around the principles of neoliberalism and corporate-led globalization. In the words of Tony Clarke (1997: 46–47), "the Trilateralists saw themselves as self-proclaimed leaders with a mission to create an ideological consensus around a new economic and political agenda. They knew they could not advance this agenda without changing the direction of public policy-making and general public opinion within nation-states."

The Crisis of Democracy, published by the Trilateral Commission in 1975, offers a compelling account of how elites understand the world, with a particular focus on how they view democracy and the way it ought to function. The "crisis," as they explained it, had to do with the fact that previously passive and marginalized sectors of the population were becoming organized enough to enter the political system and to press for their interests. Of particular concern to elites was that people were starting to challenge established authority. Harvard professor Samuel Huntington, one of the book's authors, lamented the fact that the public was now questioning "the legitimacy of hierarchy, coercion, discipline, secrecy and deception—all of which are in some measure inescapable attributes of the process of government" (cited in Crozier et al. 1975: 93). He was also concerned that people "no longer felt the same compulsion to obey those whom they had previously considered superior to themselves in age, rank, status, expertise, characters or talents" (75). Not only did this create problems for government at home, it also threatened foreign policy goals and the prosperity of transnational capital. For trilateralists, these developments required a "greater degree of moderation in democracy" and a return to "apathy and noninvolvement" on the part of normally marginalized groups (113–114). For most people, the promotion and extension of democracy and democratic rights represents a positive development, but for the elites in the TC these movements were considered to be a major crisis. The timing of the book was no accident. It followed the widespread social upheavals of the late 1960s and early 70s and coincided with the global corporate offensive launched by business leaders shortly thereafter.

Another of these global policy groups, the World Economic Forum (WEF) meets every year in Davos, Switzerland, and in other select venues to discuss global economic strategy. Its core membership consists of CEOs of the world's thousand leading corporations. Also invited to WEF proceedings are influential media groups, senior politicians and policy-makers, academics, NGO representatives and cultural icons. Under the leadership of transnational capital, these participants attempt to construct a unifying political vision (Robinson 2004: 128). Today, when participants disband from the meetings in Davos, they can keep in touch through the WEF's computer-networking service. This new initiative is intended to help global elites stay in contact, share new insights and help each other deal with any crisis situations they might encounter (Dobbin 2003c: 156). In the future, it may not be necessary for global leaders to meet face to face. The touch of a button or a few taps on a computer screen may be all that is required for elites to maintain their cohesion. So powerful is the WEF even now that, in recent years, social activists from around the world have launched the World Social Forum (WSF), designed as a "symbolic and political counterweight" to the WEF (Barlow and Clarke 2001: 203).

One of the oldest and largest global policy groups is the International Chamber of Commerce (ICC), founded in 1919. Its membership includes approximately seven thousand corporations and business associations, representing most countries of the world. The ICC is very politically active; it has lobbied against environmental treaties (including the Kyoto Protocol), the regulation of international trade and investment and even the worldwide anti-globalization movement (Robinson 2004: 126–127). The ICC has been among the most vocal advocates of trade liberalization, deregulation and privatization. One of its specific goals is to strengthen corporate power and influence by providing a venue where business elites can meet and attempt to construct a common international policy framework (Carroll and Carson 2003: 33).

Founded in 1952, the Bilderberg Conference has no formal membership. Instead, its annual assemblies bring together a wide variety of participants, including many powerful figures from the ranks of the economic and political elite. The structure of this group is less formal and business-oriented than that of the others, allowing for a more flexible agenda. While the Bilderberg has no formal purpose, it does secure a location for discussion and consensus-building among corporate and government leaders. Its mandate is echoed by Joseph Retinger, its founder and permanent secretary until his death in 1960: "Bilderberg does not make policy. Its aim is to reduce differences of opinion and resolve conflicting trends and to further understanding, if not agreement, by hearing and considering various points of view and trying to find a common approach to major problems (cited in Korten 2001: 139).

One of the most recent additions to the assortment of global policy groups is the World Business Council for Sustainable Development (WBCSD). It was created in 1995, through a merger of the Business Council for Sustainable Development in Switzerland and the World Industry Council for the Environment in France. The WBCSD consists of 120 international corporations from thirty countries. One of its purposes is to facilitate closer cooperation between business, governments, NGOs and other groups concerned with issues of sustainable development (Draffan 2000). Its formation, then, is indicative of a growing awareness among elites that in order to remain legitimate, business must address the widespread public demands for environmental regulation. From this perspective, the organization is part of the movement towards greater corporate social responsibility, which involves efforts to whitewash an increasingly tarnished corporate image.

Global policy organizations make an important contribution to elite integration worldwide. But can today's international business community be described as unified? Robinson and Harris (2000) acknowledge the existence of global unifying mechanisms, but they also maintain that the global elite is a fundamentally divided group. They write:

> Despite its organization and coherence, the transnational [elite] is not a unified group.... [F]ierce competition among oligopolist clusters, conflicting pressures, and differences over the tactics and strategy of maintaining class domination and addressing the crisis and contradictions of global capitalism make any real internal unity in the global ruling class impossible. (2000: 31)

In a later work, Robinson (2004: 76) claims that a unified vision has been difficult to secure because various segments of the class seek different solutions to global economic challenges. "There has been considerable strategic debate, as well as tactical differences, within the ranks of the [transnational capitalist class]." While tactical divisions are a regular feature of business life, it is not clear that global elites are divided over larger issues such as investors' rights, liberalized trade or long-term foreign investment. Miliband's (1969: 141) assertion that business is "tactically divided but strategically cohesive" and will present a reasonably united front over most large issues of economic policy may apply not just to national classes but to the global elite as well. Again, battles may be fought over how to best defend elite interests but this does not necessarily suggest conflict over what is to be defended.

Recently, William Carroll and Colin Carson (2003) looked at the participation of global elites in these five international policy organizations.

Situating these five groups within the larger structure of corporate power constituted through interlocking directorates, they evaluate their contribution to global elite integration. Those elites who are well connected to the world of corporate business through board interlocks, they suggest, also tend to be well connected to the network of policy organizations. A very small number of elites (105) provide most of the network ties; they weave the corporate-policy network together through their participation in transnational interlocking and/or in multiple policy groups, comprising the network's inner circle. Five of the 105 inner circle members were based in Canada (including Paul Desmarais Sr., a member of the Trilateral Commission, and Conrad Black, a member of the Trilateral Commission and a regular participant at the Bilderberg Conference). Moving closer to the inner circle's core, just seventeen corporate directors, some of whom sat on as many as four policy group boards and all of whom sit on at least two, assume an overabundance of relations within the network. The authors note that while the International Chamber of Commerce is not very well connected, each of other four groups provides a meeting place for between eight and eleven of the seventeen transnational corporate directors, with the Trilateral Commission being the most central. Carroll and Carson (2003) emphasize that additional network ties created by the policy groups make an extraordinary contribution to global elite integration, by knitting together elites and the corporations they represent.[5]

NOTES

1. These issues have included monetary policy, fiscal reform, education reform, employment, pensions, taxation, competition policy, energy policy, foreign policy, international security and international trade.
2. This clearly had an impact on the Liberals, as they removed MacEachen as finance minister and replaced him with lawyer Marc Lalonde. Shortly thereafter, Lalonde reportedly visited d'Aquino's home, where "he is alleged to have signed a peace pact with the business leaders and to have promised them the government's support" (Langille 1987: 59).
3. In concert with the push for free trade, Haddow (1994: 355–356) points out that the Commission also received a detailed report from the Canadian Manufacturers' Association promoting the replacement of existing social security programs with a neoliberal Guaranteed Annual Income (GAI) plan. This was in addition to testimonies at Commission hearings by the BCNI and the Canadian Chamber of Commerce advocating substantial reductions in social expenditure.
4. Meanwhile, in the United States the Business Roundtable was lobbying vigorously for NAFTA in concert with hundreds of large corporations (Dreiling 2000). They were joined in the battle by the U.S. Chamber of Commerce, the National Association of Manufacturers, the National Foreign Trade Council, and the U.S. Council for International Business, among other groups (Sklair 2001: 101).

5.   The authors also point out that corporations and elites from less developed
     countries (the periphery and semi-periphery) are largely absent from the
     corporate-policy network. "In this sense the network seems to present one
     facet of collective imperialism, organized to help manage global capitalism
     from the centre" (53).

5. ADVOCACY THINK TANKS

The BCNI and its policy allies were not the only participants in the business-led coalition to promote free trade. They were supported within the policy-formation network by another set of players—a group of high profile think tanks directed and funded by the economic elite. For decades these think tanks have worked with the Business Council to advance the neoliberal agenda in Canada. Tom d'Aquino writes: "While the BCNI chose to lead with flags flying high, we were not alone in advancing our concerns. Other business organizations were on side. Think tanks such as the C.D. Howe and Fraser institutes and the Conference Board of Canada generated convincing analysis" (Business Council on National Issues 2000). Corporate think tanks are tightly linked to Canada's policy organizations and a few of the largest—most notably the C.D. Howe Institute—aid the Business Council in its consensus formation project.

However, large corporate-oriented organizations are by no means the only kind of think tanks in Canada. As a whole, think tanks are a highly diversified group of institutions, varying considerably in size, resources, research focus, ideological orientation and quantity of output. Their memberships, for instance, range from a handful of people engaged in one specific policy area to dozens of economists, statisticians and researchers providing commentary and analysis on a broad range of issues. Despite this diversity, think tanks share a few defining features. First, they are generally non-profit, non-partisan organizations whose primary interest is public policy research and who seek more or less actively to influence the policy-making process. Second, they attempt to influence public opinion and the intellectual climate in which decision-makers operate. Many are supported in this work by foundation grants, corporate donations and government contracts.

Think tanks qualify for non-profit status by defining themselves as educational organizations, committed to increasing public awareness about policy issues. To obtain tax-exempt status, they must also remain non-partisan (Abelson 2002: 9). In other words, while they are not prohibited from taking ideological positions on matters of policy, think tanks cannot publicly support or oppose any political party. They can provide expertise or advice to politicians and government officials but must refrain from engaging in overtly political activities. Needless to say, the line between what constitutes outright political activities and what does not is murky at best. Although they must remain at arm's length from the party system, this has not stopped some of the largest organizations—like the Fraser Institute, C.D. Howe Institute and Conference Board—from forming a dense collection of ties to the Canadian state (Fox and Ornstein 1986: 491).

THE RISE OF ADVOCACY THINK TANKS IN CANADA

There have been three "waves" of think tank growth in Canada. The first wave occurred in the early 1900s with the establishment of a small number of groups concerned with domestic and foreign policy, such as the National Council on Child and Family Welfare (1920) and the Canadian Institute of International Affairs (1928). The second wave, following the Second World War, saw the formation of the Canadian Tax Foundation in 1946 and the establishment, in 1954, of a branch office of the U.S.-based Conference Board. In the 1960s, the Canadian government created several government contractors, including the Economic Council of Canada (1963), the Science Council of Canada (1966), the National Council of Welfare (1968) and the Law Reform Commission of Canada (1970), to advise it on key policy issues (Abelson and Lindquist 2000).[1]

The third wave of think tank development occurred in conjunction with the international corporate offensive of the early 1970s. There was a growing view—particularly amongst business leaders—that alternatives to government-sponsored policy work were needed and that Canada should follow the United States' lead in this respect. Furthermore, as discussed, the business community actively sought organizations to facilitate corporate unity on important issues of public policy. To accomplish these goals, several "advocacy think tanks" were established, so-named because of their "ideologically derived policy agendas" (Abelson and Lindquist 2000: 42). Due to their firm ideological commitments and blurry distinctions between policy research and political sponsorship, advocacy think tanks more closely resemble lobby groups than traditional think tanks. According to Abelson and Carberry,

> Unlike traditional policy research institutions, advocacy think tanks are not driven by an intense desire to advance scholarly research. On the contrary, their primary motivation is to engage in political advocacy. In short, they do not covet attention in the scholarly community, but are deeply committed to imposing their ideological agenda on the electorate. (1998: 538)

Since the early 1970s, several such institutes have surfaced in Canada, including the Canada West Foundation (1971), the Institute for Research on Public Policy (1972), the Fraser Institute (1974), the Canadian Institute for Strategic Studies (1976), and the Canadian Institute for Economic Policy (1979). Around the same time, other organizations underwent significant transformations. For example, a merger of the Private Planning Association with the C.D. Howe Memorial Foundation led to the creation in 1973 of the C.D. Howe Institute, today one of Canada's most effective advocacy groups. As well, the Montreal office of the New York-based Conference Board was moved to Ottawa in 1971, leading to the rapid growth of business-oriented research (Abelson and Lindquist 2000: 43). While not an advocacy think tank per se, the Conference Board does occupy an important niche within the neoliberal policy spectrum through its provision of market-oriented research and other services (Carroll and Shaw 2001: 198–199). More recently, in 1994, the Atlantic Institute for Market Studies (AIMS) was formed. Although much smaller, the AIMS is an advocacy group with a mandate similar to that of the Fraser Institute.[2]

Of course, not all think tanks to emerge in the "third wave" sought to advance a corporate agenda. The Canadian Centre for Policy Alternatives (CCPA), for example, was established in 1980 by academic, labour and civil society researchers to counter the growing influence of the Fraser Institute. Since its inception, the CCPA has provided policy research and commentary on a wide range of social and economic issues. Today one of Canada's leading progressive research organizations, it is supported by over ten thousand individual and organizational members who share a commitment to oppose the corporate-driven policy agenda in Canada and abroad.

The new breed of advocacy think tanks developed innovative political strategies meant to influence policy-makers and the public. One of their most common strategies has been to increase the exposure of policy issues through well-publicized seminars or conferences. At these forums, academics, journalists, corporate representatives, government officials and the public come together to discuss timely issues. Abelson (2002: 75) notes the success of this strategy, as employed by the Fraser and C.D. Howe Institutes, in harvesting support for free trade. Some think tanks encourage their members to give lectures at universities and other venues (a strategy often used by Fraser Institute head Michael Walker), while others rely on scholarly journals, books, opinion magazines, newsletters and websites to reach their target audiences (Abelson 2002: 76). Sometimes, using a more formal avenue of influence, they offer testimony before parliamentary committees. Providing testimony, especially to a high-profile committee, can generate considerable influence among policy-makers.[3] Yet, of all the political strategies mentioned above, none is more visible or more effective than securing consistent access to the corporate media. The media's relationship with Canadian think tanks is discussed below. Three of today's most prominent corporate-driven, free market-oriented institutes are the Fraser Institute, the C.D. Howe Institute and the Conference Board of Canada.

The Fraser Institute

When the province's first NDP government was elected in 1972, business leaders in British Columbia were unhappy. One of them, T. Patrick Boyle, a senior executive and then vice-president of planning at MacMillan Bloedel, immediately sought counsel on how to bring about the new government's demise. To this end, he met with several other business executives and economists, including Michael Walker, who worked for the federal finance department at the time and now heads the Institute. Walker managed to convince Boyle and fifteen mining executives to invest $200,000 in the establishment of an economic and social research institution that would "educate" Canadians about the crucial role of markets in economic prosperity. According to Dobbin (1998: 188), "while a think tank was not an ideal way to deal with the immediate problem of getting rid of the NDP government, Boyle and his mining-executive friends were apparently willing to take the long view."

Like many think tanks in Canada, the Fraser Institute was initially preoccupied with staying afloat, but as its directors became more adept at fundraising and recruiting new members it grew quickly in size and visibility. By the mid-1980s, the Institute had an annual budget of over $1 million and a staff of eighteen, thanks to the support of over four hundred corporations and prominent right-wing business leaders such as Conrad Black (Hackett and Zhao 1998: 101). Carroll (1989: 102) reports that between 1976 and 1986 the number of dominant corporations interlocked with the Fraser Institute's board of directors more than tripled. Its overall membership (corporations, foundations and individuals) increased from 521 in 1983 to more than 1200 in 1997 (Carroll and Shaw 2001: 201). Its revenues too have continued to grow steadily. By the latter part of the 1990s, its annual income totalled well over $3 million, a figure that has shot up rapidly since 1997, reaching over $5 million in 2002 (Fraser Institute website, 2002 Financial Statements).

The Fraser Institute is unquestionably the most advocacy-oriented think tank in Canada. Dalton Camp describes it as "a heavily bankrolled right-wing propaganda agency serving the interests of corporate Canada" (cited in Hurtig 2002: 131). Much like its sister organizations in the United States, such as the American Enterprise Institute and the Heritage Foundation, the Institute places great emphasis on shaping public opinion and public policy. Since its inception, it has worked tirelessly to secure a dominant position for free market principles in virtually every domain of Canadian society. A primary cause of its success in this regard has been its ability to saturate political debate. While the Institute has had less immediate input into federal policy than other institutes, it has found alternative channels of influence. Cameron (1997: 13) tells us that what the Fraser Institute has lacked in direct influence it has made up for by "pushing the limits of acceptable discourse well to the right, and in creating more space and legitimacy for neoliberalism." Not surprisingly, the change in Canada's political climate spearheaded by the Fraser Institute is reflected in the media's portrayal of the Institute itself. Its ideas and policy initiatives have apparently moved from the extreme-right fringe to the centre, as market solutions become increasingly viewed as conventional wisdom or "common sense." According to Marjorie Cohen,

> the Fraser Institute's image shifted from a comic example of ultra-right hyperbole to the representation of reason, responsibility and authority on economic and social issues. No longer is its almost daily reference in the media prefaced with "right-wing think tank." The right has become the norm and the [Fraser Institute] is now as respectable as the Conference Board and the C.D. Howe Institute. (1995: 30)

The Fraser Institute has propagated the neoliberal agenda in a number of innovative ways. To start, its active research program has resulted in the publication of dozens of books and studies, as well as a monthly opinion journal, the *Fraser Forum*. Over the years, its motivated staff have produced hundreds of op-ed articles and delivered countless speeches, many of which have been used by government officials, particularly members of the now defunct Reform Party, as resources for their policy positions and government critiques. For example, Dobbin (1998: 194) points out that during the 1993–1997 Parliament, twenty-two of the fifty-one Reform MPs used Institute materials for their speeches.[4] In fact, the Institute has even provided special seminars for MPs as well as a "hot line" they can phone to get personal assistance. The Institute also sponsors a host of student programs—such as Student Seminars on Public Policy Issues, Student Leaders' Colloquia, an internship program and student bursaries—and distributes to universities across the country thousands of free annual copies of its newsletter, *Canadian Student Review*.

To reach the largest audience possible, the Fraser Institute regularly holds conferences that are accessible to policy-makers and the public at large. Sometimes these conferences play host to a global audience. One of them, in San Francisco in 1996, followed the Institute's development of the "Economic Freedom Index." The Index is an international measurement system designed to assess the implications of government policies on freedom of investment. For the staff at the Fraser Institute, an economy is "free" only to the extent that investors and corporations are free from government regulations that interfere with profit-making. Those countries which act to reduce social inequality (or even provide for the basic needs of their citizens) are given demerits because these policies supposedly infringe upon the economic freedom. For example, government spending on income security programs lowers economic freedom because it interferes with "non-coercive" agreements between potential employers and employees. Another variable measures the extent to which government policy affects workers' freedom *not* to join unions. The San Francisco Conference provided training in the use of the freedom index for participants of thirty-seven countries.

The profound impact of the Fraser Institute in shaping Canada's political and economic landscape is well recognized within Canada and in other countries. World renowned economist Milton Friedman states that "the Fraser Institute has become a remarkably influential think tank: one of the most influential in the world." Similar sentiments are echoed by former British Prime Minister Margaret Thatcher, who believes that the Institute's "great work ... has had a tremendous influence" (cited in Abelson 2002: 86). Indeed, the importance of the Institute can hardly be overstated, and it is likely to push its extreme variety of corporate libertarianism well into the future.

The C.D. Howe Institute

Probably no other think tank in Canada has attracted more attention in policy-making circles than the C.D. Howe Institute (CDHI). Its predecessor, the Private Planning Association of Canada (PPAC), was founded in 1958 by business and labour leaders to undertake research on economic issues and Canada-US relations. In the early 1970s, PPAC President Robert Fowler sought to expand the Association's advocacy role and "permanently transform the organization into a short-term policy analyst of Canadian economic policy" (Ernst 1992: 121). The expanded mandate required additional resources; in 1973 the PPAC merged with the C.D. Howe Memorial Foundation (which supplied a $2 million endowment) to become the C.D. Howe Research Institute.

The injection of new money allowed the CDHI to hire permanent research staff and finance ongoing policy initiatives. Carl Beigie was hired as Executive Director along with a number of young economists, such as Judith Maxwell, who later became Chair of the Economic Council of Canada. Under Beigie's leadership, the Institute soon became "an active and media-conscious policy advocate" (Ernst 1992: 121) and the "staging ground for the resurgence of free market theories in official circles within Canada" (Clarke 1997: 15). In addition, its policy approach changed; where it once valued Keynesian economic policies and promoted goals such as full employment and social program enhancement, its policy approach now reflected the business agenda (Carroll and Shaw 2001: 199).

By the mid-1980s, the CDHI had fully embraced the neoliberal economic agenda, and its advocacy efforts became predictably aligned with the interests of Canada's economic elite. Overseeing the continuing shift to the right was new Executive Director Wendy Dobson, who replaced Beigie in 1981. The Institute began urging the government to attack the deficit through cuts to social spending. Its most active political role, however, was during the free trade debate, when it emerged as a vocal ally of the BCNI and other business coalition members. A major study prepared by the Institute called *Taking the Initiative*, and lobbying efforts by its staff (particularly Dobson and policy analyst Richard Lipsey) were critical in convincing many senior ministers and bureaucrats to support the free trade deal (Ernst 1992: 132; Doern and Tomlin 1991: 26–27). The CDHI continued to be active and highly visible throughout the 1990s, endorsing measures such as privatization, the reduction of social programs and NAFTA.[5] It also continued to take on the deficit. In 1994, the Institute produced a report called *The Courage to Act*, which urged the government to accelerate its deficit reduction timetable and to reduce transfer payments to the provinces for health, education and social assistance by $17 billion (Clarke 1997: 84).[6] The CDHI—like the BCNI, Fraser Institute and the rest of corporate Canada—put the blame for rising deficits squarely on government spending, especially on social programs such as unemployment insurance, old age security, family allowance and social assistance.

While the CDHI has not matched the tenacious advocacy of the Fraser Institute, it has been extremely prolific and very influential in business and government circles. It has published studies on virtually every major government policy initiative of the past few decades. According to Abelson (2002: 185–186), the CDHI devotes 90 percent of its multi-million budget to research, whose impact is evaluated by its contribution to public policy debate. To help publicize its views, the Institute and its committees organize speaking engagements, meetings and conferences involving business leaders and academics from Canada and around the world. Clearly, the CDHI is not simply a diligent research organization; it actively pressures decision-makers and unifies their perspectives by providing a forum for discussion and strategizing.

Much like the CCCE and unlike the Fraser Institute, the C.D. Howe Institute can be described as a "moderate" organization; that is, it tends to offer policy proposals that are politically sensitive and couched in the language of mainstream economics (Ernst 1992: 134). In this way, it provides some intellectual legitimacy to free market ideologies and legislation. Also like the CCCE, the Institute takes on the dual responsibility of building an elite consensus and changing the political culture to reflect that consensus. According to Dobbin (1998: 179), "it has played a major role in bringing key elements of the elite onside, including senior public policy makers at all levels." Interestingly, the Institute is touted as an independent think tank—yet it is almost entirely funded by corporate Canada and its membership is dominated by many of the same corporate giants who make up the CCCE. (A detailed breakdown of the Institute's extensive ties to the economic elite via board interlocks can be found in Appendix B.) Accordingly, while the proposals and strategies of the Fraser and C.D

Howe Institutes are somewhat different, they both work to advance the same market-driven corporate agenda.

The Conference Board of Canada

The Conference Board is the largest think tank in Canada. Indeed, its staff and revenues rival those of many large American organizations. Its origins date back to 1954, when the New York-based Conference Board opened an office in Montreal to serve its Canadian clients. In 1971, the office was moved to Ottawa, where the branch grew rapidly in size and output (Lindquist 1998: 128). Unlike the other organizations profiled in this chapter, the Conference Board is not an advocacy think tank. Nevertheless, it does play a useful political role. Carroll and Shaw (2001) argue that it occupies a position within the neoliberal policy spectrum in two ways. First, it provides the "ideological toolkit of neoliberalism"; that is, the large body of research it produces offers a seemingly objective perspective on policy issues "organized predominantly around discourses of public choice political analysis and neoclassical economics" (198). Second, in harmony with its global corporate vision, the Conference Board calls for restructuring social and economic policy in Canada to enhance the competitiveness and profitability of capital. Part of this restructuring involves the creation of a flexible, less secure workforce. In the 1990s, international competitiveness became a central theme in Conference Board research and analysis.

Thus, while the Conference Board avoids political advocacy, it supplies the elite with a large body of information on policy issues. Among other features, its diverse research agenda includes economic forecasting and analysis, social trends analysis, corporate social responsibility, innovation and technology, and human resource management. One of its goals is to help business leaders become better prepared to adapt to changes in the global marketplace. Aside from access to publications from its wide variety of research centres, the Conference Board sponsors a large number of conferences, seminars, courses and other events on a regular basis. Many of these events bring elites together to discuss strategies and tactics. The sheer size and quantity of the Board's output has made it an invaluable resource for the economic elite, the state and the mass media. Its commitment to producing reliable and "unbiased" research has enhanced its credibility and reputation.

The Fraser Institute, C.D. Howe Institute and Conference Board have been characterized as "sites of business activism" and credited with consolidating neoliberal supremacy in Canadian public policy (Carroll and Shaw 2001: 195). Through the high volume of research they produce, they offer an aura of intellectual legitimacy to capitalist policy goals. An important part of their mandate has been to entrench free market economic theories within official government circles and the mainstream press. These theories gave corporate Canada some of the intellectual credibility it needed to build support for an attack on government intervention and the welfare state.[7] In concert with policy organizations like the CCCE, they have also served to advance a firm policy consensus within the business community and fundamentally alter Canada's political landscape.

MEDIA COVERAGE AND EXPOSURE

The extent to which think tanks have influenced public policy is not easy to measure. Some indicators, however, do permit us to assess their involvement and degree of visibility in the political arena. One such indicator is media coverage. Equating media exposure with policy influence, think tank directors will try to ensure that they are regularly cited in the print and broadcast media. Abelson (2002: 82) contends that, "at the very least, media exposure allows think tanks to plant seeds in the mind of the electorate that may develop into a full-scale public policy debate." The media not only disseminates the ideas of institute scholars, it also gives the organizations a higher public profile and helps to advance their broader political goals.

The Fraser Institute is one think tank whose trustees are particularly conscious of how much coverage it generates. The Institute regularly holds news conferences, issues news releases and willingly provides interviews:

> Its fax news-broadcasting operation sends a two-page news sheet to 450 radio stations every week. It provides packaged editorials for newspapers and radio designed to explain the merits of the free-market system, issue by issue. As well, its seminars are extensively covered by cable stations, which gave it 105 hours of coverage in 1996. (Dobbin 1998: 192)

One of the Fraser Institute's most popular and widely covered media events is its annual announcement of "Tax Freedom Day," defined as the day in the year when the average family has earned enough money to pay its total tax bill to all levels of government. Staff at the Fraser Institute are also interested in the amount of media exposure that other organizations are able to generate and in the kinds of issues that tend to attract media attention. To this end, the Institute's National Media Archive (NMA) was founded in 1987 and given an annual budget of $200,000. The NMA maintains a live database of news and public affairs programming on CTV and the CBC. Through its monthly newsletter *On Balance*, the NMA claims to examine objectively the extent to which media coverage of public issues is "balanced" and free from bias (Hackett and Zhao 1998: 101–102).

Not all think tanks receive the same access to the media. Large organizations with diverse research programs and dozens of staff members are obviously in a much better position to attract the media's gaze than are

Table 5.1: Media Citations for Selected Canadian Think Tanks 1985–1999

	News-Paper Total[1]	Globe and Mail[1]	CBC Radio[2]	CBC TV News[3]	CTV News[3]	Total
Conference Board of Canada	6,289	2,204	18	57	59	8,627
Fraser Institute	3,790	761	58	47	27	4,683
C.D. Howe Institute	3,053	1,290	110	55	45	4,553
Economic Council of Canada	2,033	1,318	43	40	17	3,451
Canadian Tax Foundation	999	473	8	22	4	1,506
Science Council of Canada	714	618	14	12	4	1,362
National Council on Welfare	952	286	13	13	9	1,273
Canadian Council on Social Development	885	354	10	19	4	1,272
Institute for Research on Public Policy	747	347	10	3	2	1,109
Canada West Foundation	824	210	14	16	5	1,069
Canadian Institute of Strategic Studies	770	162	27	33	15	1,007
North South Institute	497	279	12	3	0	791
Canadian Centre for Policy Alternatives	629	118	21	13	4	785
Canadian Institute for International Peace & Security	558	119	7	10	3	697
Public Policy Forum	490	91	2	1	0	584
Caledon Institute of Social Policy	381	124	21	5	0	531
Canadian Institute of International Affairs	360	159	2	5	3	529
Mackenzie Institute	291	42	18	7	8	366
Canadian Policy Research Networks	136	60	0	2	1	199
Pearson-Shoyama Institute	154	21	10	0	0	185
Parliamentary Centre	60	30	2	0	0	92

1 Includes citations from 1985 to 1999.
2 Includes citations from 1988 to 1996.
3 Includes citations from 1988 to 1999.

Adapted from: Abelson (2002: 98–99)

smaller groups. With few exceptions, the print and broadcast media in Canada rely disproportionately on the same group of institutes. Table 5.1 displays the number of media citations in newspaper, radio and television for selected Canadian think tanks. Four institutes—the Conference Board, the Fraser Institute, the C.D. Howe Institute, and the now defunct Economic Council of Canada—generated the majority (60 percent) of all media citations between 1985 and 1999. The Conference Board alone received close to 25 percent of all coverage, not surprising given the size and range of its research program. In addition to the impact of size, the disparity may also result in part from the fact that these groups are very predictable in their values and orientations, making them reliable sources of information. Unquestionably, too, much of the disparity emerges from the parallel orientations of corporate think tanks and the corporate media. Indeed, the mainstream media in Canada appears to be right at home with the neoliberal policy agendas of these institutes.

Other research has yielded similar conclusions. For example, News Watch Canada analyzed coverage in fourteen daily newspapers, as well as CBC television and CTV news broadcasts. It found that right-wing think tanks, like the Fraser and C.D Howe Institutes, received more than three times as much news coverage as left-wing institutes, such as the Canadian Centre for Policy Alternatives (CCPA) (Taras 1999: 211). Another study by the Canadian Press wire service reports an even more extreme imbalance: during a one-year period, the Fraser Institute was quoted in 140 economic-related stories, while the CCPA was quoted in just 16 (Hackett and Zhao 1998: 158). In 2000, the CCPA's *NewsWatch Monitor* examined right- and left-wing think tanks as sources in seven Canadian dailies during February and March of 1998. They discovered that right-wing institutes were cited 304 times, while those on the left received only 78 mentions (for a ratio of nearly four to one). The *Monitor* also contends that the *National Post* "rolled out the red carpet" for the Fraser Institute, mentioning it in 60 articles, perhaps because at the time Fraser Institute trustee David Radler was president of the *National Post* (Gutstein 2000: i).

The special receptivity of the media to the Fraser Institute is not surprising. Over the years, it has been funded by such large Canadian media institutions as Sterling Newspapers, Southam, Thomson Newspapers and Standard Broadcasting. Their support brings indirect financial benefits as well. Penney Kome (2002: 2) reports that in 2001, there were more than 4000 media stories on the Fraser Institute overall, coverage which the Institute's staff calculated as an estimated $10 million worth of "ad equivalency." The media's willingness to utilize the Fraser Institute as an information source comes in spite of the Institute's tendency to make claims that are unsubstantiated or even completely contradicted by available data. The methods used in their research studies "often would not pass muster in an undergraduate social science class" (Dobbin 2003c: 195).

DIRECT TIES TO THE ECONOMIC ELITE

Instrumentalists and elite theorists see think tank leaders and senior analysts as important elements of elite networks—they regularly interact with business elites and help comprise a nation's power structure. From this perspective, the close ties between think tanks and wealthy corporate and foundation donors play a valuable role for the elite. It is argued here that this role is twofold. First, think tanks help business leaders to establish class cohesion and a common policy perspective, mainly by setting up regular meetings or roundtables between different sectors of the business community. Second, think tanks provide the elite with direct and indirect channels of policy influence within the state, political system and civil society.

Major Canadian think tanks derive a substantial proportion of their operating budgets from corporate and foundation grants. For example, according to the Fraser Institute, in 2001 it received 63 percent of its donations from foundations, 29 percent from organizations (i.e., corporations) and only 8 percent from individuals (2002 Annual Report). Another example is provided by Abelson and Lindquist (2000: 52), who note that in 1997, the C.D Howe Institute received 82 percent of its funding directly from corporations. While these institutes do not release the details of their incoming donations, many of their largest backers are represented on their boards or membership lists.[8] In fact, the C.D Howe Institute has a separate corporate membership list, which displays literally hundreds of powerful corporate supporters, some of whom represent the CCCE. Details of foundation support are easier to access than is direct corporate patronage. A breakdown of foundation grants to the Fraser Institute, C.D. Howe Institute and the AIMS will be outlined in the next chapter.

It is likely that the values and policy preferences of wealthy sponsors set limits on the range of policy ideas that can be advocated by the recipient think tank. In exchange for large donations, think tanks are generally willing to advance the political agendas of their benefactors. Commenting on the CDHI's efforts to promote privatization, Cameron (1997: 13) points out that it "produced reports and commissioned academic studies that provided background for the perspective advanced by the CEOs who funded the Institute and served on its policy committees." Although donors do not usually dictate specific research or advocacy preferences, their capacity to withdraw monetary support (and their ability to influence others to do the same) acts as a constraint. Of course, the relationship between funders and think tanks is not purely beholden. Corporate-driven think tanks receive generous donations because of the business-friendly policies they advocate. In other words, they get money from particular organizations as a result of what they say and publish, as much as they publish particular lines of analysis because of who sponsors them. Indeed, the ideological differences between funders and the large

Table 5.2: Directors in the Corporate Policy Network, 1976 and 1996

No. of Policy-Group Directorships Held	No. of Corporate Directorships Held			
	0	1	2 or more	Total
	1976			
1	92	54	73	219
2	1	1	16	18
3	0	1	3	4
Total	93	56	92	241
	1996			
1	122	67	51	240
2	3	3	10	16
3	0	2	4	6
Total	125	72	65	262

Source: Carroll and Shaw (2001: 204).

institutes are minimal at best.

In addition to funding, think tanks and the economic elite are also connected by overlapping board memberships. In a study of elites in the postwar period, Fox and Ornstein (1986: 501) found that many of Canada's most prominent think tanks were dominated by the top levels of the corporate establishment. As evidence, they cited the substantial degree of overlap between the institutes' boards and those of Canada's largest corporations. This practice is still commonplace. Carroll and Shaw (2001) looked at the overlapping boards of the top 250 Canadian corporations (specifically, the 50 largest financial institutions ranked by assets and the 200 largest non-financials ranked by revenue) and major Canadian policy groups in both 1976 and 1996. In 1976, the sample of policy groups included the BCNI, the Fraser Institute, the C.D. Howe Institute and the Conference Board. The sample was the same in 1996 with one exception; the Atlantic Institute for Market Studies (AIMS) was added.

As Table 5.2 shows, in 1976 a total of 241 people sat on one or more of the four policy boards; while in 1996, 262 individuals sat on one or more of five boards. In both years sampled, most policy group directors also directed one or more dominant corporations, and twenty-two of them sat on multiple policy boards. According to Carroll and Shaw:

> The vast majority of these 22 were also corporate directors, and in 1996, six of them directed three policy groups each, forming a closely knit network core. The many corporate affiliations of these individuals confirm that the governance of neoliberal policy groups

is largely the work of the corporate elite. (Carroll and Shaw 2001: 205)

The table also reveals a clear shift away from interlocking over the twenty-year span. In 1976, 92 policy group directors sat on multiple corporate boards. By 1996, this number was reduced to 65. This is due to the changes in corporate governance discussed in Chapter Three: in the mid-1990s, corporate governance reduced the size of corporate boards, especially those of the banks, resulting in a loosening of the interlocking directorate network which, in turn, affected the corporate-policy network. Despite the decrease in interlocking evidenced here, however, a well-integrated corporate-policy network still exists in Canada. The authors note that "the decline in the integrative role of banks and other corporations renders the policy groups particularly central within the 1996 configuration" (208). Thus, the boards of prominent Canadian think tanks (as well as the CCCE) have become more important as sites where the economic elite forge a policy consensus.

The Fraser Institute is not tied by director–board interlocks to nearly as many large corporations as the CDHI and Conference Board (see Appendix B for the names and corporate affiliations of a selection of directors who sit on the boards of the Fraser Institute, CDHI, AIMS and Conference Board).[9] Most of its ties to the economic elite come through corporate and foundation funding grants. The board of the C.D. Howe Institute includes five individuals (Jack Cockwell, Murray Edwards, Kerry Hawkins, Frank McKenna Jr. and David O'Brien) who also sit on the boards of five or more corporations in the top 500. An additional four board members direct four dominant corporations. One of them is David Kerr, who also sits on the boards of the Canadian Institute for Advanced Research and the World Business Council for Sustainable Development. Another is Roger Phillips, who is also affiliated with the Canadian Steel Producer's Association, the Saskatchewan Chamber of Commerce and the Fraser Institute. The board of the AIMS contains ten corporate directors (four of whom are CEOs), including its past chair and current chair emeritus Purdy Crawford. Crawford also sits on the boards of AT&T Canada, the Canadian National Railway Company, Emera, Maple Leaf Foods and Petro-Canada. What is particularly striking about the Conference Board is the number of CEOs who are directly represented on its board of directors; a total of fifteen CEOs in the top 500 are affiliated with the organization. These examples illustrate the extensive connections between Canada's influential think tanks and the economic elite.

Finally, what about ties *among* the policy groups? As noted in Table 5.2, a small number of corporate-policy interlockers sit on more than one policy board. These individuals exist at the heart of the network, forming an integrated inner circle. Table 5.3 lists the ties among policy groups for

Table 5.3: Ties Among Policy Groups 2003

CCCE ties to Think Tanks

Fraser Institute	Paul J. Hill[1]
	Hassan Khosrowshahi
	Gwyn Morgan
C.D. Howe Institute	Jack L. Cockwell
	F. Anthony Comper
	Paul J. Hill[1]
	N. Murray Edwards
	David W. Kerr
	David P. O'Brien
AIMS	Peter C. Godsoe
	David McD. Mann[2]
	John C. Risley[2]
	Harry R. Steele
Conference Board	John M. Van Brunt
	Patrick D. Daniel
	David L. Emerson
	Paul J. Hill[1]
	John S. Hunkin
	Ed Kilroy
	Jacques Lamarre
	David McD. Mann[1]
	Eric P. Newell
	Gilles P. Ouimet
	Douglas Whitehead

Ties between Think Tanks

Fraser Institute	Paul J. Hill
	Roger Phillips
	Herbert C. Pinder Jr.
C.D. Howe Institute	Paul J. Hill
	John T. McLennan
	Peter J. Nicholson
	Roger Phillips
	Herbert C. Pinder Jr.
AIMS	John T. McLennan
	David McD. Mann
	Peter J. Nicholson
Conference Board	Paul J. Hill
	David McD. Mann

1 Individual is connected to more than one think tank.
2 Individual sits on the AIMS advisory council.

Source: board membership information was gathered from the organizations' websites.

2003. The top of the table presents the overlapping board memberships of the four think tanks with the CCCE. It shows that the Fraser Institute has three such linkages, the AIMS four, the CDHI six, and the Conference Board eleven. At the bottom of the table, the ties between the think tanks themselves are presented. Two individuals, Paul Hill and David Mann, sit on the board of the CCCE and more than one think tank. Paul Hill— affiliated with the CCCE, Fraser Institute, C.D. Howe Institute and Conference Board—is particularly central in the policy-formation network. Although not a director of any of the top 500 companies listed in the *Financial Post 500*, he sits on the boards of many smaller firms (including his role as CEO of Harvard Developments). Clearly, there is a substantial sharing of directors among the groups, mainly through the large board of the CCCE.

DO THINK TANKS MATTER?

Although the Japanese government believed U.S. think tanks to be influential enough to appoint a diplomatic official to monitor their activities (Stone 1996: 218), most observers are more skeptical about their policy impact. Pluralists, for example, characterize think tanks as one of many voices in the policy community. They see think tanks not as elite organizations, but as one of a number of groups that occupy a small niche in the increasingly crowded marketplace of ideas. Like other social interest groups, they must compete for the attention of policy-makers. Moreover, pluralists contend that think tanks' "intellectually independent" research agendas are determined within the institutions themselves and rarely influenced by outside bodies. From this perspective, think tanks do not represent any particular vested interest in society but conduct research for the sake of building a body of knowledge and raising public awareness. While many institutes do seek to inform the policy process, their influence is limited. Like trade unions, policy organizations, lobby groups, environmental organizations and NGOs, think tanks have only sporadic and modest power. Their existence is simply one indicator that power is distributed among a number of interest groups, allowing for the free expression of ideas and opinion. That being said, a few proponents of the pluralist approach acknowledge that some think tanks are in a better position to affect policy-making than are others.

Pluralists are not alone in their claim that think tanks have relatively little influence in the policy-making process. Lindquist (1993: 575), for instance, asserts that "despite their prominence, I do not see [think tanks] as potent forces within policy networks. My research indicates that institute studies are often of limited use to policy-makers and are more geared to educating the attentive public." Policy specialist Hugh Heclo argues that Marxist scholars are overly constrained by their preconceptions of capitalist influence. For Heclo, these presumptions are amplified by being "on the outside looking in at the names on the boards of trustees, the printed recommendations, the assumption of policy influence." He also sees Marxists as enamoured with "the self important and vacuous big names that sit on their boards with little effect" (cited in Stone 1996: 34). The former president of the Montreal-based Institute for Research on Public Policy, Monique Jérôme-Forget, is also unconvinced. She maintains that quantitative measures (such as the number of media citations) only show that particular issues are being discussed, as opposed to revealing the potential of institutes to affect people's attitudes (cited in Abelson 2002: 6).

All of these positions have some merit. However, I believe they miss the central means by which think tanks actually influence politics and policy-making. The argument advanced here is that it is through facilitating and maintaining elite unity that think tanks exercise a decisive influence. Some, like the Fraser and CDHI, have also played a crucial role in shaping Canada's political culture. This is not to say that think tanks play an especially important role in forming and implementing specific policy initiatives (although one can certainly find exceptions, such as free trade and deficit reduction). The important point is to distinguish between think tanks' influence on particular policies and their ability to affect the policy-making environment. As has been argued throughout this book, a cohesive and integrated business class wields far greater power in the political arena and over the state than does a fragmented one. The significance of think tanks, then, is that they show us one way in which the elite achieves consensus. They may also be useful for documenting changes in the political strategy of the elite. As Ernst (1992: 109) explains, by tracing the history and policy discourse of think tanks that are closely tied to the leading fractions of capital, one can gauge changes in the strategic orientation of the economic elite. This is only possible because corporate-funded institutes have been so central in providing the ideological framework for corporate political action.

NOTES

1. As part of the first round of serious budget cutting in 1992, the Mulroney government eliminated the Economic Council of Canada, the Science Council of Canada and the Law Reform Commission of Canada. In 1997, a new Federal Law Commission of Canada was established.

2. The Atlantic Institute for Market Studies (AIMS) was founded in 1994 with a three-year start-up grant from the Donner Canadian Foundation. Based in Halifax, the advocacy-style group seeks to generate market-oriented solutions to social problems, with a specific focus on the Atlantic provinces. Carroll and Shaw (2001: 202) note that in "its ideological discourse, mandate, structure, and modus operandi, AIMS is a much smaller, east-coast version of the Fraser Institute." Like other think tanks, the AIMS organizes and sponsors confer-

ences, meetings, seminars, roundtables, lectures and training programs.

3. See Abelson (2002: 113) for a breakdown of appearances by select Canadian think tanks before parliamentary committees from 1980 to 1999.

4. As mentioned above, think tanks are prohibited from supporting or endorsing a political party. While there may have been no formal links to the Reform Party, there were obvious parallels between the Institute's views and the party's political platforms. In addition, a number of years ago Institute economist Herbert Grubel won a Reform Party seat in Vancouver.

5. The Institute's sweeping mandate is vividly summarized in a 1994 report called *The Case for Change: Reinventing the Welfare State*. As policy analyst David Brown notes in the report, "the structural changes Canada is undergoing are so fundamental as to require that the social contract be rewritten.... [T]he old social contract has been rendered obsolete by global events" (Watson, Richards and Brown 1994: 116, 122).

6. According to Dobbin (2003a: 54), reports such as *The Courage to Act* confirmed how overtly political Canada's advocacy think tanks had become. In contrast to previous studies, which simply offered economic recommendations, these new reports advised governments to act quickly in order to undercut the possibilities for effective organization by opposition groups.

7. In *The Cult of Impotence* (1998), Linda McQuaig provides an interesting discussion on the rise to prominence of neoclassical "laissez-faire" economics, led by University of Chicago economist Milton Friedman.

8. During the course of this research, a representative of the Fraser Institute remarked that due to "certain unpleasant instances" that have occurred to their supporters in the past, the institute no longer discloses the identities of corporate sponsors. According to Dobbin (1998: 186), more than half of the top hundred most profitable corporations in Canada have contributed to the Fraser Institute. He obtained this information through a list of corporate donors published by the Institute in 1989, a practice that has not been repeated since. In the correspondence, the representative also lamented the fact that this policy has not stopped some of their supporters from being "harassed."

9. The sample of dominant corporations is the same as that used in Chapter Three (media-corporate interlocks)—a list of the top 500 Canadian corporations found in the 2002 *Financial Post 500*. Information on the directors was taken from the 2003 Financial Post Directory of Directors. Subsidiaries are included only if its parent is listed in the top 500 (and the director does not sit on the parent board) and if the subsidiary is listed in the top hundred subsidiaries.

6. FREE-ENTERPRISE FOUNDATIONS

Philanthropic foundations are institutions that provide grants to individuals and non-profit organizations to fund a wide range of activities. Although foundations have both a direct and indirect influence within many areas of public policy, their importance is often neglected. Hence, most of us remain unaware that some foundations play a conscious and deliberate political role and that they are integrated into the policy-formation network. Foundations' influence within the network is exercised primarily through their funding activities and, to a lesser extent, through initiating programs.

NOT JUST CHARITABLE BUT POLITICAL

Of the thousands of foundations that exist in Canada, only a select number have the money and desire to involve themselves in public policy. Those that do generally fall into two categories: corporate and family foundations. Corporate foundations derive their funds from corporate profits, and although legally independent of the corporation, the foundation is closely tied to the firm's board and funding (Canadian Centre for Philanthropy 2003: 10). In other words, these types of foundations are very much the offspring of their corporate parents and likely to reflect the same social and political interests. In contrast, a family foundation is established by a wealthy family or individual. These are the most well-known and abundant type of foundation in Canada. Through family foundations, fortunes may remain intact over many generations. In addition, family foundations allow wealthy elites to decide where and when to channel vast sums of money. Table 6.1 displays the top ten corporate and family foundations (ranked by grants) in Canada. Together, they distribute hundreds of millions of dollars to recipients of their own choosing.

Private foundations are often regarded as little more than funders of charity and producers of value-free academic research. However, the web of relationships between foundations and the economic elite—as well as the admitted desire of some of them to influence public policy—brings this conception into serious question. Clearly, foundations do more than "just" donate money. For one, their activities are a significant part of large

Table 6.1: Top Foundations by Grants

Rank	Foundation Name	Assets	Grants	# of Grants
	Family Foundations			
1	David and Dorothy Lam Foundation (2001)	$192,459	$20,734,343	36
2	The J.W McConnell Family Foundation (2000)	$543,044,403	$20,259,327	132
3	Chastell Foundation (2001)	$163,299,567	$18,299,145	82
4	The John McKellar Charitable Foundation (2001)	$131,908	$18,193,024	16
5	H.W. Siebens Charitable Foundation (2001)	$7,248,780	$11,523,842	122
6	Claridge Foundation (2001)	$110,264,796	$11,296,554	131
7	Donner Canadian Foundation (2001)	$159,282,380	$9,847,761	201
8	The W. Garfield Weston Foundation (2000)	$23,109,288	$9,582,299	67
9	Kahanoff Foundation (2001)	$107,132,696	$8,475,356	52
10	La Foundation Marcelle et Jean Coutu (2001)	$143,248,591	$7,456,072	177
	Corporate Foundations			
1	TD Friends of the Environment Foundation (2000)	$2,865,872	$24,000,000	11,000
2	RBC Foundation (2000)	$33,596,086	$23,863,907	3,200
3	Irving Oil Foundation (2001)	$83,018	$12,500,000	1
4	J. Armand Bomardier Foundation (2002)	$155,214,379	$10,828,413	341
5	Imperial Oil Foundation (2002)	$7,477	$6,650,000	402
6	Suncor Energy Foundation (2002)	$600,000	$4,600,000	400
7	The Apotex Foundation (2000)	$83,018,856	$3,255,359	82
8	DeFehr Foundation Inc. (2001)	$1,677,028	$2,908,344	n/a
9	The CIBC World Markets Children's Miracle Foundation (2000)	$809,691	$2,126,444	458
10	Hudson's Bay History Foundation (2001)	$28,574,965	$1,670,950	16

Note: All amounts are from the most current fiscal information. The fiscal year is indicated in parentheses.

Source: Adapted from Canadian Centre for Philanthropy (2003: XIX–XX)

companies' public relations efforts. In the words of Steven Neiheisel (1994: 179) "no major corporation dare go without this form of political risk insurance.... Without a track record of public service that can be paraded ... a corporation is without a major weapon in its defensive strategy should public controversy over its operations arise." Thus, foundations play a leading role in creating the public perception that a corporation cares about more than profits.

In addition, companies and individuals use foundation money to influence the policy-making process. How do foundations accomplish this? Most often, they allocate funds to organizations doing policy work. Trustees may donate money to an organization without attaching specific conditions to its use or request that the money be devoted to a particular topic or research effort. Sometimes, however, the money is meant for a pre-defined project. Foundations may also establish in-house projects in the absence of approved recipient organizations. Directors and trustees have a great deal of latitude in the use of foundation money. In each of these instances, there is the potential that the money will be channelled into the political arena.

Consistent with their views on policy organizations and think tanks, pluralists view foundations as simply one voice among many, and a weak voice at that. Pluralist Arnold Rose (1967), for example, argues that foundations lack power and influence in society. Commenting on the United States specifically, Rose says that public criticism has made foundations cautious when choosing funding recipients. If they were to appear politically biased, they would risk losing their tax-exempt status. Therefore, Rose claims, they confine their contributions to education and scientific research. True though these arguments are, they ignore the fact that donations are in themselves political because foundations can back whatever specific educational and scientific ventures they chose. When a multi-million dollar foundation decides to throw its weight behind one cause rather than another, this is a political choice with political implications. Furthermore, Rose overlooked the large amounts of money given to influential organizations like the Council on Foreign Relations, the Brookings Institution and the Committee for Economic Development (Domhoff 1970). According to Domhoff, these contributions are one of the central ways that foundations influence the political process. As noted earlier, policy groups bring together members of the elite and provide a setting in which differences on various issues can be reconciled and the views of various experts heard. In this way, foundations facilitate the development and implementation of general policies important to the interests of the elite. By the same token, their financial support of particular groups allows for the dissemination of elite ideologies, which affects the wider political culture. Jorge Niosi (1982: 133) contends that the presence of business leaders on foundations' boards of trustees has nothing to do with "honorifics," but "stems from their concern to shape the executive personnel of which they have need and thus to guarantee their own continuity as a class."

One must question the motivations behind foundations' activities, including those that appear to be goodwill gestures. Milton Friedman, for one, argues that philanthropy is a form of lobbying and, therefore, should not be tax-deductible. John Kenneth Galbraith is also skeptical. He believes that corporations should not be allowed to make contributions, because such contributions provide them with too much opportunity to exercise influence (cited in Neiheisel 1994: 24). From these perspectives, donations by means of corporate or family foundations are little different than direct patronage.

In her extensive study of the relationships between foundations, policy organizations and think tanks in the United States, sociologist Mary Anna Culleton Colwell (1980) found evidence of an inner circle within the foundation network. Specifically, she looked at the twenty largest foundations that conferred at least 5 percent of their total donations to public policy purposes. Of their 225 trustees, 124 also served as trustees in 120 other foundations. In addition, ten of the twenty foundations had direct interlocks with eighteen policy organizations and think tanks (419–421). In a subsequent study, Colwell (1993) draws the same conclusion, stressing the existence of an inner circle or interconnected foundation club. These results lend credence to the notion that career mobility in the philanthropic world parallels that in the corporate world. Both represent a progression toward the inner social circles, providing more contact with influential members of the economic elite.

There is also evidence from the 1970s that corporate philanthropy is controlled by inner circle business leaders. Useem (1984: 81-82), for example, notes that a select group of individuals collectively decides on the recipients and issues deemed worthy of funding. Looking at participation rates in the governance of philanthropic foundations in the U.S., Useem found that multiple directors were much more likely to oversee their activities than directors who reside on only one corporate board. Specifically, 18 percent of single directors were involved in foundation governance, compared with 42 percent who held two directorships and over 50 percent who held three or more directorship positions. It would appear that companies whose officers are well connected to corporate networks are considered a better source of trustees than those without such connections.

Furthermore, class-wide political criteria are often as important as company considerations in deciding what to support and how much to give. For example, corporate contributions to "the arts" are more than just a public relations exercise or an attempt at good corporate citizenship. For some inner circle business leaders, this kind of philanthropy has an "overarching corporate purpose," promoting a culture more conducive to the prosperity of the capitalist system (Useem 1984: 124). According to one business executive interviewed by Useem, a privately sponsored arts sector can "limit the power of government" and "enlarge the definition of freedom in art and commerce." Says another, "It's in our best interests to postpone the revolution," referring to the reduction of political tensions brought on by community arts programs and events (cited in Useem 1984: 124). Through contribution programs, then, single firms can enhance the public image of the entire business community and mitigate the dangers of unwanted policy initiatives.

Some Canadian foundations make their intentions well known. For example, according to the Canadian Centre for Philanthropy (2003), the purpose of the John Dobson Foundation is "to educate the public with respect to the free enterprise system and entrepreneurial activities in Canada" (310). The "current strategic priority" of the Max Bell Foundation is to "support projects which educate Canadians about public policy alternatives" (126). To help accomplish this, the Max Bell foundation gave a combined total of over $450,000 to the Fraser Institute, CDHI and AIMS in 2000.

Think Tanks as Foundation Recipients

Hundreds of organizations receive foundation grants in Canada, and they use the money in a multitude of ways. When measured in terms of public policy influence, the most significant foundation activity is funding think tanks. These grants are given with the expectation that state officials and political parties will seriously consider policy recommendations delivered by think tanks.

As recipient organizations, think tanks are heavily dependent upon foundation support. To illustrate, foundations make up only 2 percent of all members of the Fraser Institute, yet their donations account for 63 percent of all monetary contributions to it (Fraser Institute: 2002 Annual Report). This dependence helps to ensure that think tanks will focus much of their research on issues important to their rich benefactors. Given these structural arrangements, it is not surprising that private foundation funding does not generally go to groups or researchers who challenge current political and economic arrangements. To cite just one example, the Ford Foundation in the United States refused to consider applications from C. Wright Mills after he wrote *The Power Elite*; instead, the foundation actively promoted the work of pluralist scholars (Colwell 1993: 36).

There is good reason to believe that the activities of think tanks and other foundation recipients are restricted and channelled by the foundations who fund them. In some instances, there will be no need for foundation trustees to define directly the limits of acceptable research. In others, such as when there is a difference in political or economic orientation between foundation and recipient, the restrictions can be made more explicit and a

Table 6.2: Foundation Grants to Advocacy Think Tanks (over $1000)

Foundation[1]	Think Tank	Grant Amount[2]
Donner Canadian Foundation (2002)	Fraser Institute	$536,407
	C.D. Howe Institute	$318,391
	AIMS[3]	$300,000
The John Dobson Foundation (2000)	Fraser Institute	$111,954
	AIMS	$62,500
	C.D. Howe Institute	$10,000
Max Bell Foundation (2000)	C.D. Howe Institute	$50,000
	AIMS	$124,500
The W. Garfield Weston Foundation (2000)	Fraser Institute	$140,450
Carthy Foundation (2001)	Fraser Institute	$95,000
	AIMS	$10,000
Vancouver Foundation (2000)	Fraser Institute	$97,702
RBC[4] Foundation (2000)	C.D. Howe Institute	$52,575
	AIMS	$10,000
The Pirie Foundation (2000)	Fraser Institute	$45,000
	AIMS	$2,500
	C.D. Howe Institute	$2,000
Peter and Joanne Brown Foundation (2000)	Fraser Institute	$30,000
The Jarislowsky Foundation (2000)	C.D. Howe Institute	$30,000
The Morrison Foundation(2000)	Fraser Institute	$15,000
H. W. Siebens Charitable Foundation (2001)	AIMS	$15,000
Hunter Family Foundation (2000)	Fraser Institute	$10,000
The Edper Foundation (2000)	C.D. Howe Institute	$10,000
The William Nancy Turner Foundation (2000)	C.D. Howe Institute	$4,000
Birks Family Foundation (2000)	Fraser Institute	$2,000
	C.D. Howe Institute	$1,500
C.M. Harding Foundation (2000)	C.D. Howe Institute	$1,100

1 All amounts are from the most current fiscal information—the fiscal year is indicated in parentheses.
2 Grant amount represents the *total* given by the organization throughout the course of the year.
3 Atlantic Institute for Market Studies
4 Merges the formal Royal Bank of Canada Charitable Foundation and the RBC Dominion Securities Foundation

Source: Adapted from Canadian Centre for Philanthropy (2003)

negotiation of some sort must be undertaken. Foundations, of course, also do some of this kind of policy work themselves, functioning much like a think tank when working on a particular issue.

A significant number of Canadian think tanks have been created and/ or maintained largely through foundation grants. A few examples include the North-South Institute, the Mackenzie Institute, the Canada West Foundation and the Caledon Institute of Social Policy. Perhaps most notably, three of the advocacy think tanks discussed in Chapter Five—the Fraser Institute, C.D. Howe Institute and Atlantic Institute for Market Studies—have received generous financial support from foundations.[1] Table 6.2 contains a list of recent grants to these three organizations. The Fraser Institute is the one Canadian think tank that has managed to obtain a stable influx of money from American foundations and, though we can't be sure, likely from American corporations as well. One of its most consistent supporters has been the Lynde and Harry Bradley Foundation, whose express purpose is to support projects which "reflect the assumption that free men and women are ... able to run their daily affairs without the intrusive therapies of the bureaucratic, social service state" (Canadian Centre for Philanthropy 2003: 1101). From 1986 to 2001, it contributed $85,000 to the Institute. Another firm ally has been the Sarah Scaife Foundation, which donated $150,000 between 1998 and 2000 alone. Other American supporters include the Carthage Foundation, the Charles G. Koch Charitable Foundation, and the John M. Olin Foundation (Media Transparency 2003). The American foundation Liberty Fund has also provided money for the Institute's work on its Economic Freedom Index.

THE DONNER CANADIAN FOUNDATION

In terms of total dollar contributions, the Donner Canadian Foundation (DCF) is in a class by itself, donating well over $1 million to the three think tanks in 2002. Created in 1950 by American steel tycoon William Henry Donner,[2] the DCF has tried for most of its history to remain ideologically "neutral," and could have been located in the area of "middle-of-the-road Canadian liberalism" (Rau 1996: 12). But this changed dramatically when the foundation was taken over by conservative Donner family members and when, in 1993, American Devon Cross became president. One of Cross's goals was to "create a national network of new conservatives in Canada" (Rau 1996: 11).

Following the lead of its partner foundation in the U.S., the Canadian Donner also began to distribute money to conservative and corporate causes. The changes in political orientation were immediately apparent in the DCF's funding choices for 1994. According to Rau (1996: 16), the foundation announced that it would be providing the Fraser Institute with $450,000 over three years to monitor public debt and recommend ways to control government spending. The University of New Brunswick was given $450,000 over three years for the establishment of the AIMS, which would "investigate the role private enterprise and educational reform may play in revitalizing Atlantic Canada's economy." Not to be left out, the C.D. Howe Institute received $46,000 for a book entitled *False Premise: Canada, the Market and the Americans*, which dealt with the history of government intervention in Canada and the United States. The foundation also provided the right-wing Mackenzie Institute with $43,318 to study the impact of gun control legislation on Canada's underground arms market. These four grants are just a portion of the over $2 million the Donner Canadian Foundation dispensed in 1994. A more recent breakdown (2002) of contributions to the Fraser Institute, the CDHI, and the AIMS is provided in Table 6.3.

The funding of right-wing groups and projects was only part of the new Donner's agenda. Since 1993, the organization has initiated a number of its own projects. In 1994, it used $1.4 million to establish *The Next City*, a highly conservative Toronto-based magazine. According to Dobbin (1998: 211–212), since 1995 the magazine's writers have "celebrated Latin American Shantytowns, portrayed beggars as scam artists, and declared that poverty is a matter of personal choice." In the years following its inception, staff at *The Next City* had a very close relationship with "the Donner people" who met with them after every issue to discuss stories (Rau 1996: 12). The foundation also helped to launch another right-wing publication in 1995 by giving a $390,000 grant to conservative Garrick Mason to transform his newsletter *Gravitas* into a quarterly magazine. *Gravitas*, which specializes in Canadian foreign and trade policy, has published a number of articles by members of the Fraser Institute and AIMS. A more recent initiative is the Donner Awards for Excellence in the Delivery of Social Services. The evaluation protocol for the Donner Awards was developed in 1997 with the help of the Fraser Institute and with input from the Canadian Centre for Philanthropy, the Canadian Cancer Society, the Trillium foundation and Family Service Canada. The Fraser Institute administers the awards on behalf of the foundation.

The Donner Foundation ranks among the top ten family foundations in Canada (see Table 6.1) and yields considerable influence. It is but one of the private foundations that enhance the power of the economic elite in Canadian society. As noted earlier, foundations are an often overlooked component of the policy-formation network—a dangerous oversight. As governments continue to eliminate their own public policy research operations, opportunities abound for private foundations to shape Canada's political climate. Foundations are yet another way that corporations and members of the elite are able to exercise their influence and solidify a consensus. Clearly, policy groups, think tanks and foundations are all individually important for the elite. But it is important to remember that,

Table 6.3: Donner Canadian Foundation Grants to Advocacy Think Tanks 2002

Institute	Grant Amount	Project
Fraser Institute	$198,667	W.H. Donner Awards for Excellence in the Delivery of Social Services
	$100,000	CanStats
	$75,000	Centre for Globalization Studies/ Economic Freedom Index
	$50,000	Donner Leadership Program 2002
	$40,000	Economic Freedom Index/Cuba
	$30,000	Immigration Issues
	$22,740	"The Skeptical Environmentalist"— The Bjorn Lomborg Public Lecture
	$20,000	Teachers Workshop on Economic Principles in Ontario
C.D. Howe Institute	$171,491	The Border Papers
	$75,000	Improving Productivity and the Public Sector: A Comparative Analysis of Business Costs
	$50,000	Interpretation of Elementary Test Results
	$21,900	Examining Canada's Immigration Policy
Atlantic Institute for Market Studies (AIMS)	$150,000	Canada Cities and a National Urban Strategy
	$150,000	Atlantica: Creating the International Northeast Economic Region and the Fishery of the Future

Source: Adapted from: Canadian Centre for Philanthropy (2003: 312–316)

in terms of both common directors and funding, all three are heavily interlocked with each other and with the corporate community. The network as a whole integrates the elite and shapes policy issues, with different groups playing different roles depending on the task at hand.

CORPORATE SOCIAL RESPONSIBILITY:
A NEW ELITE CONSENSUS?

In addition to political influence, some foundation activity is aimed at providing corporations with a favourable public image. This is just one aspect of a growing trend towards corporate social responsibility. Many elites have come to realize that an important part of sound corporate governance is the appearance of compromise, compassion and responsibility to people and communities. Recently in New York, a hundred CEOs from the world's biggest corporations met with representatives from Greenpeace and Amnesty International to sign a promise to act in accordance with the U.N. Universal Declaration of Human Rights (Bakan 2004: 33). Likewise TNCs (under U.N. guidance) have constructed a "global compact," which commits them, in principle, to fair labour and human rights practices and environmental sustainability.

Some corporations have established entire departments to deal with social and environmental initiatives. Indeed, corporations now openly boast about their capacity to act in a socially responsible manner. Business schools have launched new courses on responsible corporate behaviour. According to Bakan (2004: 32), corporate social responsibility is now discussed wherever business leaders meet, whether in be the World Economic Forum in Switzerland, meetings of the World Trade Organization, corporate conferences or international trade summits.

Writing in the March 2004 *Report on Business* magazine, David Macfarlane asks the question, why now? Why are elites now encouraging business to take on a more socially responsible role? Macfarlane suggests that corporate social responsibility stems from

> a rational response on the part of the business community to the fact that on the very issue of survivability, time is running out. It may be that it has become apparent to even the most narrowly focused laissez-faire capitalist that on critical social and environmental issues, the business community has to take a leadership role, if only to ensure a future for itself. (Macfarlane 2004: 45)

A survey conducted by GlobeScan, a firm specializing in corporate issues, indicates that Macfarlane may have it right. The survey found that 83 percent of Canadians believe that corporations should "go beyond" their conventional economic role, and 51 percent said that they have punished a socially irresponsible company sometime in the past year (Macfarlane 2004).

Just as the corporate world recognized the threat posed by social movements in the 1960s and 70s, they are now increasingly aware that their conduct and activities are under a microscope. Today, there is widespread and growing opposition to the inherent inequities and injustices of the world economic system. Individuals and groups who oppose corporate domination are joining together at the national and international levels in networks of solidarity and activism. To be sure, these challenges are recognized and feared by business leaders. They have witnessed first-hand the unwavering resistance to the international corporate order, symbolized perhaps most dramatically by the "battle in Seattle" that raged around the WTO's 1999 ministerial meetings. Similar mass protests have greeted meetings of the International Monetary Fund, the World Bank, and other forums of elite rule. Anti-globalization and other recent social movements are focusing squarely on corporate power as a primary cause of social disintegration and injustice. Notably, even former advocates of the global economic system, like financier George Soros and World Bank economist Joseph Stiglitz, are calling for regulatory reforms and a more equitable distribution of wealth and power.

Many elites believe that a more concerted corporate effort towards social responsibility will tame concerns about corporate power. In a sense, this is a rational response to a changing market. Today, companies have little choice but to appear socially accountable if they are to grow and prosper. Of course, many within the business world challenge this view. Renowned economist Milton Friedman, for example, sees corporate social responsibility as immoral. Because corporate executives are bound to make as much money as possible for their shareholders, those who choose to pursue social or environmental goals at the expense of profits are acting immorally. These goals *are* acceptable, however, if the executive treats them as a means to maximize shareholders' wealth and not as ends in themselves. Thus, to people like Friedman, corporate social responsibility can be tolerated only when it is insincere (Bakan 2004: 34). Others go further, arguing that corporate social responsibility is punishable by law. The law compels executives to place the fiscal interests of the corporation and its owners above all else, and forbids them from acting in the interests of workers or improving the environment if these acts interfere with this legal requirement.

Nevertheless, many of today's largest corporations have, at least rhetorically, committed to higher values and moral behaviour. While some executives are undoubtedly genuine in their motives, the key purpose for most is improving the tarnished image of corporations and international financial institutions. There is, for example, no provision to monitor the performance of those corporations who signed on to the U.N. global compact and little expectation that they will abide by these promises. According to Maria Livianos Cattui, secretary general of the International Chamber of Commerce, "the global compact is a joint commitment to shared values, not a qualification to be met. It must not be a vehicle for governments to burden business with prescriptive regulations" (cited in

Korten 2001: 294). Among the first participants in the compact were companies like Nike, Shell and Rio Tinto, all of which are known for human rights abuses and environmental ruin. Furthermore, corporations have no incentive to reveal breaches of the compact to the United Nations or the public, and the NGOs who monitor these companies lack the resources and the legal authority to compel such disclosure. However self-gratifying the motives may be, the move toward greater corporate responsibility should be treated as no small victory for today's social movements. As William Greider explains,

> social change nearly always begins in hypocrisy. First, the powerful are persuaded to say the appropriate words, that is, to sign a commitment to higher and decent behaviour. The social activists must spend the next ten years pounding on them, trying to make them live up to their promises.... In the long struggle for global rules and accountability, this new phase may be understood as essential foreplay. (cited in Barlow and Clarke 2001: 179)

WHAT'S NEXT FOR THE POLICY-FORMATION NETWORK? THE DEEP INTEGRATION INITIATIVE

Many of the same economic and political elites that came together to push for the free trade agreement are now pursuing a new initiative, one that could have far-reaching implications. This is the plan for "deep integration" with the United States, a process that more often resembles assimilation than integration. Deep integration has been given different names by the players involved. The C.D. Howe Institute refers to it as the next "Big Idea." The Canadian Council of Chief Executives uses a more sophisticated term, calling it the North American Security and Prosperity Initiative. Whatever label it is given, the plan is the same: to integrate Canada-U.S. relations.

The initiative itself is predicated on fear. Deep integrationists believe that the U.S. will eventually put severe pressure on Canada in two major areas: resources and security. As Barlow (2004: 4) explains, "the Bush administration has made it clear that any independent foreign policy stance on the part of Canada is unwelcome and that the price of friendship is the further harmonization of Canada's foreign, security and energy policies with U.S. demands." Instead of waiting for this pressure to come, the policy formation network is arguing that Canada should anticipate U.S. demands. Wendy Dobson (2002) of the C.D Howe Institute, for instance, puts it this way: Canada needs to "initiate a Big Idea that serves the major interests of its partner, while channelling action in ways that best serve its own interests." Dobson goes on to say that to get the attention of U.S. elites, the process should begin with the handing over of Canada's energy resources as a kind of initial sacrifice. Following this, a resource security pact would be created based on open markets and the compatibility of regulatory frameworks. In effect, Canada would be forced to give up "all remaining regulatory mechanisms under which it claims sovereignty to its oil, natural gas, electricity, coal, uranium, primary metals, forest products, water and agriculture" (Barlow 2004: 10). In other words, Canada would surrender control over all its major resources.

Another facet of deep integration is to align Canada's foreign policy more closely with that of the United States and to further Canada's commitment to the "war on terror." This commitment would involve supporting the U.S. missile defence system (Star Wars II), integrating border controls, and integrating command for homeland security. In connection with these policies, Canada would have to agree to further integrate the Canadian and U.S. armed forces. In order to help pay the costs of these measures, Canada would also need to massively increase its military spending. Of course, under these arrangements, Canada would have very little say in military or security decisions. What would Canada receive in return? If by Canada one means the Canadian public—very little. Canada would be granted increased access security for Canadian goods, services and "knowledge workers" in the U.S., as well as full American citizenship for Canadian investors.

Long-term plans for deep integration include the establishment of a customs union, a common market and even a common currency. A customs union, the next step beyond a free trade agreement, would involve a common trade policy and common external tariff, which would apply to all countries not part of the free trade bloc. The plan to establish a common market goes even further, allowing for the free movement of all factors of production (including people, capital and technology) across national borders. For Canadians, a common market would also entail the harmonization of regulations, standards and other economic and social policies with the United States (Lee 2004: 6–7). To top things off, Canada would adopt the U.S. currency as its own. These long-term measures would undoubtedly lead to comprehensive social policy convergence between the two countries, including the possibility of a U.S.-style health care system in Canada. Although a customs union and a common market are unlikely in the near future, the resource and security measures noted above are very real short-term possibilities.

Many of the prominent players in the policy formation network have been actively involved in the deep integration initiative. Among the most vocal is the C.D. Howe Institute. It has produced a wide range of commentary and analysis, largely through a series of reports called *The Border Papers*. As we saw earlier in the chapter, the Donner Canadian Foundation gave the Institute over $170,000 in 2002 to help finance these reports (see Table 6.3). Not surprisingly, the Fraser Institute has also been highly supportive, advocating for the plan's most extreme measures. In line with other parts of the network, The Canadian Council of Chief Executives has been front and centre in the crusade. It has formed an action group of thirty CEOs to promote deep integration, including representatives of the banking, energy and defence industries (Barlow 2004: 9–10). In a recent report produced by the Council on "Canada-U.S. partnerships," Tom d'Aquino (2003) expresses the CCCE's position, "Canada should take the lead by articulating a vision for closer North American security and economic cooperation. It should then propose to the United States Administration the elements of a strategy for a new Canada–United States partnership within a common North American vision." He goes further, stating that "the first priority of the Council must be to develop a strong consensus among us around the principles and strategies [of deep integration].... As we work to build consensus, it is important that we engage the political leadership and key decision-makers in Canada." These comments by d'Aquino are reminiscent of the Council's actions in support of free trade. In April 2004, d'Aquino led a group of hundred CEOs to Washington. Their goal was to petition U.S. law-makers to implement the proposal as quickly as possible. Deep integration supporters have also sponsored a series of high profile conferences called Borderlines, organized by Canada's advocacy think tanks and funded by free enterprise foundations (Dobbin 2003b: 28).

Given the ramifications of the types of changes involved in deep integration, it is crucial that the issue stimulate strong public debate. It remains to be seen whether Paul Martin and the Liberals will endorse these proposals, but there are reasons for concern. Martin has made it clear that one of his priorities as prime minister would be repairing relations with the United States, and he chairs a new Cabinet committee on Canada-U.S. relations. Martin has also promised to increase military spending considerably and has come out in support of the Bush administration's missile defence system, both of which are key features of the plan. Much like free trade did years ago, deep integration represents a threat to Canadian sovereignty and to Canadians' quality of life. The record of the last fifteen years should be enough to dissuade us from taking another "leap of faith."

NOTES

1. Recall that the CDHI was formed through a merger of the Private Planning Association of Canada and the C.D. Howe Memorial Foundation. Also, the AIMS was founded in 1994 with a three-year start-up grant from the Donner Canadian Foundation.
2. In 1962, an American operation was established. The American foundation was administered by the Canadian operation until 1982 when it was decided that it was big enough to operate independently. It was also around this time that the American organization began to move in a decidedly conservative direction.

7. INTERPERSONAL, SOCIAL AND POLITICAL TIES

THE ROLE OF STATES IN THE ERA OF GLOBALIZATION

Over the past few decades, the relationship between nation-states and economic institutions has changed. One manifestation of this change is that national economies have been reorganized and more tightly integrated into the global economic system. Consequently, national networks have become increasingly fragmented and the number of linkages between elites within nations has declined.[1] While nationally organized capitalism has declined, however, this does not mean that the actions of states are now meaningless or ineffective. States do not impede globalization as much as they facilitate it, by providing a vital power base and set of organizing tools for TNCs.

In recent writings, it has been argued that the nation-state is redundant in the era of globalization. For example, though he is careful to point out that states have not become completely irrelevant, Robinson (2004: 88-89) maintains that "nation-states are no longer appropriate units of analysis.... We need to make a break with nation-state-centred analysis if we are to understand the twenty-first century world." Others go further, arguing that national governments have been overwhelmed by market forces and rendered powerless to set national policy. According to Susan Strange (1996: 4), "where states were once the masters of markets, now it is the markets which, on many crucial issues, are the masters over the governments of states." Media and politicians have also done their part to popularize the notion that states are unable to make real policy choices and have lost their ability to govern. The state's role is now confined to developing and maintaining a favourable investment climate for business.

Based on these interpretations, some might argue that investigations of national elite networks need to be re-conceptualized. Others argue otherwise, maintaining that the nation-state, while affected by globalizing pressures, has not been rendered powerless. And, far from being passive victims, states have been active participants in constructing corporate-led globalization. Kees van der Pijl (2001: 492), for one, argues that "the real-life ruling class cannot dispense with the national foundation of its power," even if it fully embraces globalization in principle. He goes on to argue that regardless of the nation in question, the nature of elite rule "will be decided in their respective countries and not in the Alpine winter resort of Davos [home to the meetings of the World Economic Forum], however much the national representatives may bask in the light of transnational brotherhood" (497). To highlight the sovereignty of nation states, van der Pijl uses the examples of contemporary Japan and South Korea, whose state-directed economies have provided them with a "buffer" to withstand the impact of globalization.

This point is echoed by Chomsky, who notes that Japan has a particularly efficient system of state-coordination, directed by the Ministry of International Trade and Industry (MITI). But he also stresses that *every* industrialized country continues to have a state-coordinated economy in which taxpayers are made to subsidize corporations, protecting such corporations from global competition (cited in Chomsky et al. 2002: 240). In a similar vein, Dobbin (1998: 84) says that "transnational corporations don't want the state to disappear because they could not operate for a week without it. But they do want to put in place appropriate state institutions that serve their particular global agenda." That corporations remain heavily dependent on nation-states for support is plainly illustrated in a recent study of transnationals. The study found that in 1993 virtually all of the world's largest firms had benefited substantially from state intervention on their behalf. Even more strikingly, no fewer than twenty of the top hundred global corporations were saved from complete collapse by state bailouts or takeovers (Chomsky 1999: 38). Although they do not typically like to admit it, "global" corporations from every nation are dependent on state industrial policies for their prosperity. Once again, we can see that the notion of a "free-market" is highly misleading. It does not fit with the reality of today's global economy.

Though the nature of state intervention has changed, the role of the state has not been reduced. Put simply, the state is being restructured in order to facilitate corporate-led globalization. As Bakan (2004: 154) makes clear, "it is a mistake to believe that because corporations are now strong, the state has become weak.... The state's power has not been reduced. It has been redistributed, more tightly connected to the needs and interests of corporations and less so to the public interest." The extent to which individual states have been restructured to support corporate interests varies across nations. Gregg Olsen's (2002) comparative analysis illustrates, for example, that despite a convergence in the pressures welfare states face, nations still vary considerably.[2] While globalization pressures do exist, the way states respond to them is, at least to some degree, a matter of choice rather than necessity. Clearly, then, the many ties which connect national corporate classes to their respective state leaders continue to be a relevant area of empirical investigation.

Pluralists argue that business does not and cannot dominate the state and politics. According to the pluralist model, no single group or association is capable of such influence, largely because power is widely distributed throughout society. From this perspective, the state is neutral: it mediates between the demands of different interest groups, which have highly diverse and often conflicting priorities. This dispersal of power also holds for the political system. Although resources are not equally shared among social groups, all have the opportunity to influence the political system. Pluralists contend that multiple channels exist through which citizens can shape the outcome of public policy and influence political leaders. The most important of these channels is voting. Free elections guarantee that citizens can exercise their civil liberties and participate in the political process. Further, elections and political competition greatly expand the number and variety of groups whose interests must be taken into account by those seeking office. Most pluralists acknowledge, however, that not all groups have equal power and influence in the political system. For pluralists, the size of interest groups is what is important to governments and political parties, as it indicates how closely they must attend to each group's demands. Crucially, though, they understand size and influence in terms of potential voting power, not as financial leverage or control over economic resources (Dunleavy and O'Leary 1987). For pluralists, then, political power resides with voters.

The significance of the enormous financial resources controlled by business (and their mobilization toward political ends) is passed over in silence by many pluralist scholars. Moreover, pluralists tend to downplay the organizational linkages between big business, the state and government. So while pluralists are correct to say that multiple channels of political influence exist, they err in saying that these exist primarily for the public. These connections provide an avenue whereby the economic elite can transfer their policy consensus to the state and political system. Indeed, ties and linkages among economic, state and political elites are unifying mechanisms in their own right.

ELITE CONNECTIONS AND OVERLAP: INTERPERSONAL TIES

One of the most direct forms of corporate domination is the degree of interlocking that results when members of the economic elite assume positions in state and political institutions. When they do so, members of the economic elite do not necessarily think of themselves as representatives of business. This is partly because many of the links do not involve simultaneous membership in corporations and the state and/or government. For example, cabinet members may have been or may become business executives, but they cannot be executives while in office.[3] Nevertheless, the disjuncture does not mean that these business leaders are more likely to support policies that run counter to the interests of capital. As Miliband

(1969: 55) notes, "It is much easier for [business leaders], when required, to divest themselves of stocks and shares as a kind of *rite de passage* into government service than to divest themselves of a particular view of the world, and of the place of business in it." Following this, there is little reason to believe, as Block (1977: 13) does, that "ruling class members who devote substantial energy to policy formation become atypical of their class, since they are forced to look at the world from the perspective of state managers."

While business leaders certainly do not occupy the majority of positions within the state, they are well represented. The interchangeability between state service and business is characteristic of a new breed of "technocrats" who wield power in a variety of departments, planning groups and regulatory boards. These people belong to both the world of business and the world of state power, and move fairly easily between the two. Some of these individuals possess the necessary aptitudes and vision to articulate the long-term interests of the elite.

Strong business connections are also typical within the upper levels of Canada's political system. While in government, corporate officials are given a temporary release from the concerns of their companies or industries. Politicians are often required to place their assets in a trust that would either maintain these assets as they were before the politicians entered office or administer them on a blind basis so politicians cannot (or at least should not) know what transactions are taking place. Ministers may also be forbidden to act on behalf of a corporation for a short period after leaving office. But this separation may not give them the time or propensity to become fully independent of the corporate community or to develop a perspective that includes the interests of other classes. What this implies is that the neutrality of these individuals should be taken with the proverbial "grain of salt." Indeed, Canada's highest political office is no exception. Apart from being surrounded with business-laden cabinets, Canadian prime ministers have had many direct and family links to the economic elite. Richard Bennett, for one, was prime minister from 1930 to 1935 and later became president of Calgary Power, owner of the E.B. Eddy Match Company, and a director of Imperial Oil and the Royal Bank (Clement 1983: 90-91).

A much more recent example is Brian Mulroney, whose extensive business connections have become legendary. According to Peter Newman (1998: 153), Mulroney had "one of the highest-quality business networks on the continent. He was a Canadian business titan before the category existed, and he went into politics very much as their ambassador." Mulroney had given up practising law seven years before he became the Conservative leader and in that time he ran the Iron Ore Company of Canada. Only a year before his transition to politics he was a director of ten major companies, including Conrad Black's Standard Broadcasting, the Canadian

Imperial Bank of Commerce and the Ritz-Carlton Hotel Company of Montreal. While in office, Mulroney quickly became recognized as Canada's version of Ronald Reagan or Margaret Thatcher. With one of its own at the helm, the economic elite was in a solid position to set Ottawa's political agenda directly. Newman (1998: 154) notes that this was "the mildest *coup d'etat* in history, dealing as it did with a compliant political authority and a prime minister who was its unindicted co-conspirator." Mulroney was rewarded for his loyalty. Upon leaving office, he was showered with directorships, stock options and speaking engagements. In 2004, Mulroney sat on sixteen corporate or international advisory boards (Yakabuski 2004: 39–40). The latter included J.P. Morgan Chase, the second-largest U.S. bank; Power Corporation of Canada; Magna International; General Enterprise Management Services, a Hong Kong-based investment fund; and China International Trust and Investment Corporation, a large state-owned conglomerate.

Recent prime minister Jean Chrétien offers another example. Before coming to power, Chrétien sat on a number of corporate boards including the Toronto-Dominion bank. Dobbin (1998: 175) tells us that Chrétien "had impeccable corporate credentials and his previous cabinet posts—finance; national revenue; industry, trade, and commerce; energy and mines; and Treasury Board—had brought him into contact with the most powerful business sectors in the country." He was particularly close to Quebec power broker Paul Desmarais, who presided over the huge conglomerate, Power Corporation. Chrétien sat on the board of Power Corporation until he ran for leadership of the federal Liberal party in 1990. Graciously, Desmarais offered his services as chief fundraiser for the campaign and today is the father-in-law of Chrétien's daughter.[4] Dobbin (1998: 175) believes that "the most dramatic demonstration that business was back and firmly in control, and that the elite consensus was solidified, was the cabinet choices Chrétien made upon achieving power."

Some business leaders merely take sabbaticals for stints in the state or government, then return home to the corporate world (sometimes with the added benefit of business-friendly policies they helped to put in place). Still others join the business world as a result of their participation in public service. It is quite common for high-ranking politicians and bureaucrats to join the ranks of the economic elite after they leave office. In fact, it has almost become a tradition. Examples abound of Canadian politicians who have successfully moved to the private sector. Peter Lougheed, former premier of Alberta, was especially active. He served as a director of seventeen boards, including Bombardier, Canadian Pacific, Noranda and the Royal Bank of Canada. One-time premier of Ontario William Davis became a director of fifteen companies, including the Canadian Imperial Bank of Commerce and Seagram Co. Ltd (McQueen, 2000: 43). In 2002, former New Brunswick premier Frank McKenna sat on the boards of about a dozen companies including CanWest Global, the Bank of Montreal, Noranda and General Motors of Canada. Donald Mazankowski, past deputy prime minister and federal finance minister, also directed companies such as Investors Group, Shaw Communications and Power Corporation of Canada in 2002. Canada's largest banks seem to be particularly interested in courting ex-politicians to their boards, as the examples above demonstrate. Another example is provided by John Robarts, who after stepping down as premier of Ontario was sought by all five big banks; he eventually chose the CIBC (McQueen 2000: 43). Recruiting ex-politicians makes good sense for business. In return for huge salaries, companies then benefit from the valuable knowledge and connections of a political insider.

Paul Martin

The issue of whether or not politicians can ever really act independently of their connections to business has recently complicated the political career of former federal finance minister and new prime minister Paul Martin. When Martin became finance minister in 1993, he signed an obligatory blind management agreement to avoid a potential conflict of interest. Under the agreement, interim managers were appointed to assume operational control of Martin's companies. One of these was Canada Steamship Lines (CSL), which he purchased with a friend in 1981 from Power Corporation. CSL, a major Great Lakes and international shipping line, whose parent company, the CSL Group, is headquartered in Montreal, controls assets worth upwards of $700 million. Martin and his wife Sheila also own 50 percent of CSL Equity Investments. Early in 2003, the opposition parties attacked Martin for allegedly ignoring his blind management agreement; they charged that Martin was receiving updates on his companies while serving time in office. In response, Martin announced that he would hand over control of his business holdings to his three sons and completely sever all ties with CSL. Obviously, many question why he did not sever this connection by divesting his holdings to a non-related third party. With Martin assuming the position of prime minister, these conflicts of interest will likely resurface in the months and years ahead.

Paul Martin has always had very close ties to the economic elite. After graduating from law school in 1966, Martin joined Power Corporation. Like Trudeau, Mulroney and Chrétien, Martin was "groomed for power" by the head of Power Corporation, billionaire Paul Desmarais. According to Murray Dobbin (2003a: 11), "being mentored by Paul Desmarais means that you are being prepared for public office whether or not you choose to go that route. Desmarais runs a virtual training ground for prime ministers and premiers in Canada."

Given his elite business background and ex-CEO status, it should not be surprising that while in office Martin has been a committed advocate of big business interests. In 1994, for example, the BCNI presented Martin (then finance minister) with "A Ten-Point Growth and Employment Strategy for Canada." The strategy included the familiar list of elite policy prescriptions: reducing corporate taxes, cutting unemployment insurance, expanding privatization and deregulation, downsizing government, encouraging non-inflationary growth, eliminating the deficit and cutting social programs. Paul Martin delivered in fine fashion, implementing every one of the BCNI's demands. Indeed, Martin took over the deficit hysteria developed during the Mulroney years with a vengeance, slashing Canada's social safety net in the process. His 1995 budget would prove to be one of the most far-reaching in Canada's history, going well beyond anything put in place by Mulroney's Conservative government. It was at this time that Martin introduced the *Canada Health and Social Transfer Act* (CHST). which, in effect, over a three-year period cut a staggering 40 percent out of federal transfer payments to the provinces for social assistance, health care, and education. The CHST replaced the Established Programs Financing (EPF) initiative and the Canada Assistance Plan (CAP) with a single block of money to the provinces—with few strings attached. This struck a major blow against the principle of universality, a cornerstone of Canadian social democracy, as provincial governments were now essentially free to run many phases of health, education and welfare programs as they saw fit. "The ultimate result," writes Linda McQuaig,

> apart from great hardship for many who lost their jobs, was a shrinking of the public sphere. All the programs and facilities in the public domain—universities, schools, libraries, hospitals, community centres, parks, museums, transportation facilities, the arts—were left scrambling to make up for lost funding, reduced to begging for donations from the corporate sector. (1998: 100)

Martin continued to dutifully serve the interests of corporate Canada into the late 1990s and beyond. In 2000, he spearheaded a record-breaking program of tax cuts, cuts which would radically reduce much-needed revenue for future social programs and help to lock in those program cuts already in place. Whether Paul Martin the prime minister will be any different than Martin the finance minister remains to be seen. Judging by his previous record and sturdy commitment to the corporate agenda, a different agenda is unlikely.

Many years ago, Leo Panitch (1977: 11) noted "a particularly striking characteristic of the Canadian state—its very close personal ties to the bourgeoisie." Since that time, the Canadian situation has not changed a great deal. While it is at least possible to argue that the economic elite has so much structural power that it need not involve itself in the state or government, it is clear that business leaders do not want to take the risk of finding out.

CLASS BACKGROUND OF THE ELITE: SOCIAL TIES

The colonization of state institutions and political parties by members of the economic elite is merely one weapon in corporate Canada's arsenal. Another important series of ties involves the social composition of the elite, that is, there is a marked similarity in the class backgrounds of state, corporate and political elites. Because a shared social class background often correlates with a similarity in values and ideological positions, it helps to facilitate agreement on the goals and purposes of public policy and to limit disagreement about ways of achieving them.

Typically, members of Canada's political elite are not among the very wealthy. Nevertheless, Dennis Olsen (1980: 29) found that a number of the provincial premiers and federal cabinet ministers in his study had substantial inherited wealth (e.g., former prime minister Pierre Trudeau) or had access to family fortunes through marriage (e.g., former Liberal leader John Turner). Although not excluded from power, the working class is significantly underrepresented within the major institutional offices of the Canadian government (Williams 1987: 12). As well, Williams contends that the frequency of kinship ties among elites suggests a network of relations much more extensive than can be documented. More recent data indicate that of a total of thirty-nine federal cabinet members, thirty-two had careers in law, business or academics (Fleming 1991: 439–445). While the wealthy do not constitute the norm in Canadian politics, their numbers are sufficient to suggest that political institutions do not offer equal opportunity. In other words, governmental leadership positions do not exclude those with roots in the working class, but they are disproportionately populated by individuals with more privileged backgrounds.

The same is true of the economic elite. Hierarchies within dominant corporations create positions of power to which social classes are differentially recruited. In the 1970s, of 673 Canadian-born members of the economic elite (of which 667 were men), Clement (1986: 192) found that 59 percent were of upper-class origin, 35 percent were of middle-class origin, and only 6 percent were of working-class origin. He further broke the group down into the top hundred Canadian capitalists and separated out those elites who held multiple directorship positions in major corporations. For multiple directorship holders, 73 percent were of upper-class origin, 22 percent of middle-class origin, and 5 percent of working-class origin (216).

These figures suggest that access to Canada's top corporate positions is by no means equal. A look at the family origins of the elite is a good starting point to explain why access is so heavily skewed in favour of the upper classes. Clement (1986: 183) shows that of the 673 economic elites he studied, 133 gained access to the elite through family firms and had spent the majority of their business careers in a corporation where their fathers (or in five cases maternal grandfathers) held key corporate positions.

Within these family firms there were twenty-four father/son combinations, and thirty-two members were brothers with someone else in the company. A total of 247 members embarked on their careers with the initial advantage of having elite connections. Another sixty-eight had fathers in businesses that were not dominant but of sufficient size to provide an avenue into big business. By providing historical continuity and a structure of stable linkages, social background and kinship relations unify elite networks.

Educational background, one of the many indicators of class background, is especially important in shaping the parameters of elite group membership. Evidence suggests that many members of the elite enjoy a virtually separate educational system. Such isolationism can easily produce a distinct set of attitudes and lifestyles and thus facilitate group cohesion. From kindergarten through university, schooling often takes on a different character for those of privileged backgrounds, providing the peer networks that sustain them throughout their lives. Although they are educational institutions, private schools can also be seen as class institutions designed to create elite associations and maintain class values both by exclusion and socialization (Clement 1983: 49). The private schools of eastern Canada, like Upper Canada College, founded in 1929, and Trinity College School, founded in 1865, have socialized many generations of Canada's elite.

Williams (1987: 13–14) found that approximately one in four state leaders, including a third of federal civil servants, attended private school. According to Fleming (1991: 439–444), 41 percent of his sample of federal cabinet ministers attended private schools, 89 percent had some post-secondary education, and 30 percent completed at least one post-graduate degree. In a sample of federal deputy ministers, he found that 31 percent attended private school, all had some post-graduate training, and 59 percent completed at least one post-graduate degree. These rates are far greater than among the general public.

The educational experiences of Canada's economic elite are very similar. Clement (1986: 244) reports that nearly 40 percent of the elites he studied attended private school. Moreover, no less than 65 percent of those with careers in family firms went to private schools (185). Similarly, Williams (1987: 13) notes that more than one in four business executives in his sample reported private school attendance. Fleming (1991: 448–450) found that of the corporate elites he studied, 37 percent attended private school, 92 percent had some post-secondary education, 30 percent obtained post-graduate degrees, and 50 percent held professional degrees (most frequently in law). Thus, in marked similarity to Canada's state and political elite, schooling for the economic elite is very different than the education received by the vast majority of Canadian citizens.[5]

Social background characteristics of the elite are important but should not be over-emphasized. As Miliband (1977: 71) points out, "the class bias of the state is not determined, or at least not decisively and conclusively determined, by the social origins of its leading personnel." In addition to class background, one must consider institutional roles and requirements. Clearly, although some members of the middle and working classes do make it into positions of power, this does not in any real sense democratize these institutions. While the state is potentially accountable to a range of class interests, its internal bureaucracy is another matter. As people become entrenched in structures within which they move to positions of higher power and authority, a system-preserving dynamic will typically overtake their "intentions." To operate outside of these institutional parameters is to increase the danger of a limited or terminated career. This is key in understanding why most state officials, including those who are not members of the economic elite, accept the capitalist context in which they operate. Knowing what is expected of them in ideological and political terms, new managers demonstrate their loyalty to senior management by attitudes and behaviour that fit within the desired spectrum.

In short, a series of filters effectively weed out those who do not conform to the values and ideologies of these institutions. This process is not monolithic but it is, nonetheless, extremely effective. Senior managers and leaders determine the values, attitudes and behaviours required, and recruit those who already possess the "correct" attitudes. This pre-selection of right-thinking individuals accounts for much of the class bias that exists within Canada's major institutions.

FUNDING OF POLITICAL PARTIES: POLITICAL TIES

Corporate ties to Canada's political parties are well documented. The major federal parties in Canada—with the exception of the New Democratic Party—have long been partly financed by big business and contained representatives from elite business ranks. The membership of these parties is drawn from a wide cross-section of the population, but the leading figures of these parties come largely from the upper and middle classes and include a substantial proportion of business leaders.

Corporate political contributions are not simply the result of company rationality but produce payoffs similar to those reaped through corporate philanthropy. In other words, factors beyond a company's immediate welfare influence funding decisions. By company logic, money should be channeled to candidates who are friendly to the particular firm, "but by classwide logic, money should be directed at candidates who are known defenders of free enterprise, regardless of their record on more specific matters" (Useem 1984: 140). The overall interests of big business are often taken into consideration by corporate managers attuned to the more general concerns of the broader business community. Consequently, corporations "with managements attached to the transcorporate network and its overarching political interests are more often found at the forefront of political contributors than firms whose management is less broadminded" (Useem 1984: 132).

Thus, it is not surprising that the leading corporate donors are typically the largest financial institutions and industrial corporations. In 1997, for example, corporations who gave money to all three of the Conservative, Liberal and Reform parties were some of the central players within Canada's interlocking directorate network (Carroll 2004: 175–177). Moreover, the leading donors were predominantly under the control of Canadian capitalists; foreign-controlled firms have tended to remain disengaged from Canadian federal politics, a disengagement that parallels their marginal status within the directorate network. The Liberal and Conservative parties are prime examples of the known defenders of free enterprise. Historically, many large corporations have split their generosity between the two, thereby applying the class-wide logic. An exception to this trend can be found in the period leading up to the 1988 free-trade election, when corporate Canada rallied behind the Conservative Party, showering it with donations and largely abandoning the nominally anti-free trade Liberals.

Political donations help politicians run more extensive electoral campaigns and ensure that they are well organized at all levels for the pursuit of year-round political activities. Providing a large amount of start-up money and other forms of political support affords the economic elite a very direct role in the political process and provides its members with personal access to politicians. Even if they rarely—or never—tie specific demands to the money, they are able to ensure a hearing for their views and to work against those candidates who they do not consider approachable. Although the open exchange of donations for political favours is illegal, contributions confer benefits for the elite in the form of access. Access to parties and politicians provides ample opportunity to exercise political influence. Unlike charitable contributions, few among the general population (or the elite for that matter) view political donations as altruism or as part of corporate social responsibility. On the contrary, it is widely recognized that corporations expect general policy returns on their donations. This is evidenced by the fact that the top donors are often those with the greatest stake in the political process, such as government contractors, recipients of government subsidies and firms in highly regulated industries.

In the past, fundraising loopholes at the federal level have allowed secret donations of virtually any amount. For instance, candidates in the political party leadership races have not been required to disclose their donors or donation amounts, nor have MPs between elections. In addition, there have been no limits on the quantity of donations made, and donations did not have to be disclosed until up to eighteen months after they were made (Canadian Centre for Policy Alternatives 2001: 12). Had more

Table 7.1: Ten Biggest Contributions Received by the Federal Liberal Party, 2001

Name of Contributor	Amount of Contribution $
Bombardier Inc.	142,504
Bank of Montreal	83,801
Power Corporation of Canada	74,346
Shire BioChem Inc.	56,536
Bank of Nova Scotia	55,707
Nexen Inc.	52,507
Rogers Group of Companies	49,883
Bell Canada	49,047
Telus Corporation	49,017
Canwest Global Communications Corporation	46,603

Source: Elections Canada (2004)

stringent financing laws been in place, Dobbin (1998: 27) argues that "it would have prevented the most powerful corporations in the country from engaging in an unprecedented $19-million propaganda campaign to subvert the 1988 election, in which free trade was the central issue." This weak regulation and secrecy of third party spending has raised alarming questions about whether money is coming from corporations that ministers regulate in their portfolios and shows contempt for the public's right to know who is financing their "representatives."

Although the Liberals fell out of favour with corporate donors during the 1988 election, the party quickly regained its privileged position. In the 1990s, the Liberals were, once again, the leading recipient of party donations. After coming to power, Jean Chrétien managed to raise over $30 million from fundraising dinners alone, with 90 percent of the money donated by corporations (Thompson and Missio 2003). According to Elections Canada (2004), the 2001 federal Liberal Party collected nearly $12.5 million in political contributions, $6.4 million of which came from big business. Some of the largest donations came from corporations that received lucrative federal contracts and subsidies, such as their largest donor Bombardier (see Table 7.1). In fact, seventeen of the top twenty-five government contractors gave over $210,000 to the Liberals in 2001. By comparison, these same companies gave just $31,600 to all of the other parties combined (Stanbury 2003). Banks and other financial institutions have always been amongst the most prominent contributors, and 2001 was no exception: they donated well over $200,000 to the Liberals. Many business associations, such as the Canadian Association of Petroleum Producers, the Canadian Bankers Association and the Canadian Drug Manufacturers Association, also gave generously. These large corporate donations are not surprising, given that the Liberals are held in such high

Table 7.2: Contributions to Registered Political Parties, by Donor Category, 2001

Donor Category	Number of Contributions	Value of Contributions ($)
Canadian Reform Conservative Alliance		
Individuals	48,589	2,940,918
Businesses, Commercial Organizations	504	873,989
Electoral District Association	261	973,958
Total	49,354	4,788,864
Liberal Party of Canada		
Individuals	3,873	2,384,538
Businesses, Commercial Organizations	2,307	6,411,391
Governments	15	19,074
Trade Unions	17	40,481
Unincorporated Organizations of Associations	96	239,151
Electoral District Association	228	3,374,764
Total	6,536	12,469,399
Progressive Conservative Party of Canada		
Individuals	12,109	2,192,748
Businesses, Commercial Organizations	1,232	1,457,507
Governments	4	174
Trade Unions	3	6,061
Unincorporated Organizations of Associations	26	14,706
Party Trust Fund	1	4,243,584
Electoral District Association	17	56,562
Total	13,392	7,971,342

Source: Elections Canada (2004)

regard by Canada's business community. Although all three business parties received generous individual and corporate donations in 2001, the Liberals received considerably more corporate patronage (see Table 7.2). By contrast, in the same year the NDP received just $97,000 (out of a total of more than $5 million) from businesses.

The rules governing political party financing in Canada, however, are undergoing considerable change. On June 11, 2003, Bill C-24, proposing to alter political financing, passed in the House of Commons by a vote of 172 to 62. The NDP and Bloc Québécois supported the bill, while the Canadian Alliance and Conservatives were opposed. Also opposed to the bill was Liberal Paul Martin, who has been criticized in recent years for his heavy reliance on corporate donations. In May 2003, for example, Martin disclosed that since October 2002, in his campaign for Liberal party leader he had raised $4.3 million (Thompson and Missio 2003). The new legislation limits the political donations of corporations, unions and unincorporated organizations to a maximum of $1,000 per year. Further, these donations can be made only to candidates, nomination contestants or electoral district associations, and not directly to federal parties. The act also places a limit of $5,000 on individual donations. To make up for party revenue losses, new public financing provisions will provide parties with an annual subsidy of $1.50 per vote received in the previous election. The new federal legislation is similar to the rules already operating in Manitoba and Quebec, both of which limit public donations to political parties and completely ban financing by corporations and labour unions.

Over the course of the next few years, it will be interesting to watch how Canadian elites respond to the new rules. It will no longer be legal for large companies to donate tens or hundreds of thousands of dollars to the mainstream parties, a change which should narrow the large disparities in political contributions. Whether or not this new law will restrict their direct political influence is still unclear. One way to get around the limitation is using individual donations by corporate executives, business associates and donors' family members. As well, instead of providing a large donation to one candidate, money could be dispersed in smaller donations to a number of business-friendly political figures.

Corporate lobbying efforts might also increase. Since the 1970s, lobbying expenditures by corporations have increased enormously, so that they are now considerably larger than the value of contributions. It is very likely that corporate executives will funnel even more money into the lobbying process in order to maintain their high degree of influence in the political sphere.

Interpersonal, social and political ties are an important element of elite unity and power. These ties, separately and in combination, provide Canada's economic elite with an enormous degree of political influence. Insofar as there is a division of labour among different elite segments that dominate economic and political life, the shared framework of assumptions and political goals generated by business ties to other social institutions represents a clear context within which elite unity can be forged.

As the above arguments make clear, there are numerous means not available to other classes through which the elite can influence the state and politicians. While these means exert strong pressures on the state to defend capitalist class interests, it should be noted that they in no way ensure that the state will support elite interests in all instances. Ultimately, the state is a contested terrain on which struggles for democracy and social rights take place. In this way, the state has the potential to respond to the interests and challenges of a broad range of social groups, including those from more marginalized classes. Once again, the slogan of rural Brazilian workers—"expanding the floor of the cage"—is useful for conceptualizing this contested terrain. It should never be doubted that popular organizations and social activism from below can significantly influence the organization, structure and policies of the state in capitalist society.

NOTES

1. Some characterize this process as "the end of organized capitalism," which involves "the uneven transition in the world economic system's centre from a capitalism more or less structured around national corporate economies regulated by nation states to a more globalized capitalism subject to less effective national regulation" (Lash and Urry 1987).
2. Power Resources Theory has shown that the character and impact of social policies vary significantly across nations, depending on the balance of power between capital and labour. It highlights critical differences among nations with respect to social inequality and working-class strength, and stresses the central role that organized working classes have played in reducing inequality and promoting welfare programs. See O'Connor and Olsen (1998) and Olsen (2002).
3. Thomas R. Dye (1995) distinguishes between *concurrent* interlocking, where individuals hold more than one institutional post at one time, and *sequential* interlocking, where individuals hold a number of leadership positions over their lifetime, often alternating between state and corporate positions. Today, concurrent interlocks involving state and corporate positions held simultaneously are illegal in most advanced capitalist nations while sequential interlocks are quite common. Concurrent interlocks are more common within the economic elite (as in the case of interlocking directorates).
4. Not surprisingly, Desmarais was also close to Brian Mulroney, hiring him as a negotiator during a labour dispute in 1972 and backing his leadership bid in 1976. Mulroney returned the favours some years later when he appointed Desmarias' brother-in-law to the senate in 1990 and his brother to the senate in 1993 (Hackett and Gruneau 2000: 131–132).
5. Up-to-date research in these areas is sorely needed.

8. CHALLENGING CORPORATE RULE

In general, it is safe to say that there is a considerable degree of social unity and political consensus among the Canadian economic elite. The evidence presented throughout this book strongly supports the position of unity theorists: the Canadian economic elite constitute a highly unified and class conscious group that is able to overcome differences in perspectives and promote policies that secure their position of dominance.

In Canada, and to varying degrees in nations throughout the world, the economy, state and political system have been largely influenced—and in some cases taken over—by institutions of private power. These institutions (and the elites who run them) remain mostly unaccountable to people and communities. The Canadian economic elite advance policies that serve corporate interests and, at the same time, undermine the foundations of democracy and ultimately lead to widespread social inequalities. What is more, elites have led us to believe that unfettered (global) capitalism is inevitable and ultimately beneficial. The workings of the global economic system, they say, is the result of economic and technological forces that have naturally evolved over decades to their present form. Some even go so far as to label contemporary capitalism as "the end of history."

Given the overarching structure and unprecedented degree of corporate power, both within nations and globally, it is not surprising that many people feel powerless to reorder this state of affairs. The challenges on the horizon can, at times, appear formidable, even overwhelming. Indeed modern life is so dominated by corporations that it is difficult to imagine a world without them. But the reality is that none of this is inevitable. The rise of corporate power was initially made possible through the actions of courts and lawyers, and it has since been supported by conscious and well planned social and economic policy initiatives. Corporate domination is not the culmination of a natural, evolutionary process; rather, it was crafted by human beings with very specific agendas. There is no reason to consider these power structures any more permanent than those which existed in the past.

The idea that private power controls some of the most important aspects of our lives is for many citizens beyond comprehension. As Ed Finn (2000: 160) points out, "the corporate coup d'état has been so insidious, so cleverly concealed behind the facade of democracy, that it remains undetected by [most people]." Yet hundreds of thousands of people are aware of corporate rule and, more importantly, have come together in recent years to challenge corporate power. Growing levels of inequality and poverty, declining living conditions, mass social dislocations, rampant unemployment and deteriorating working conditions have been met by popular resistance movements all over the world. A diverse range of community and citizen-based groups have challenged the elite consensus, with varying degrees of success.

ANTI-CORPORATE AND CIVIL SOCIETY MOVEMENTS

Currently, the worldwide anti-globalization—more properly called the anti-corporate movement—is the most visible form of active resistance. The movement has organized protests and demonstrations wherever global elites congregate, at meetings of the World Trade Organization (WTO), of the International Monetary Fund (IMF) and of the World Bank. The most dramatic example was the "battle in Seattle," which erupted around the WTO's Ministerial meetings in 1999. Large demonstrations followed in Washington, DC, Melbourne, Prague, Quebec City and Genoa. These mass protests were especially prominent because they were captured by the mainstream media; however, similar actions have taken place in coun tries all over the world, including many developing nations. In the year 2000, for example, over 7.2 million Argentinian workers supported a general strike in defiance of IMF prescribed labour laws. In Columbia, workers numbering in the thousands rallied against IMF loan conditions dealing with economic restructuring and cuts to social provisions and jobs. In Costa Rica, 10,000 people gathered against privatization initiatives, while some 40,000 indigenous people in Equador marched against IMF reforms. Also in 2000, more than a million electricity workers protested World Bank prescriptions to privatize the power sector in India. Such protests have been only the most visible forms of resistance. Their success has depended on the millions of others who have been working to rebuild their communities and local economies in the face of powerful obstacles.

Some of today's most vibrant resistance activities and organizing efforts are happening in Latin America. For years, neoliberalism—the corporate ideology—in Latin America was a virtually impregnable paradigm, guarded forcefully by its corporate ideologues and, when necessary, by military might. The region has been subjected to the same patented formula as many other regions around the world: demands for wholesale privatization, deregulation, trade liberalization and financial integration. These policies have resulted in deep economic depression, the escalation of foreign dependency and the impoverishment and social exclusion of huge sectors of the population. Despite these obstacles, the legitimacy of the neoliberalist ethos continues to be challenged. The people of Latin America are firmly committed to change, and social movements are developing on a massive scale.

Workers in Chile, for example, have actively resisted the exploitation of their resources by foreign mining corporations. A coalition of Chilean environmental groups is fighting to reverse free market economic policies and reassert democratic control over national resources. Likewise, the Piquetero movement in Argentina has successfully organized the non-working poor into democratic and non-hierarchical assemblies to oppose neoliberal policies. Specifically, the assemblies coordinate resistance activities and develop workable, community-based solutions to economic problems. The Piquetero movement has been so successful, in fact, that a poll in 2002 found that half of Buenos Aires residents believed that the assemblies "would produce a new political leadership for the country" (cited in Kline 2003).

In Venezuela, the Bolivarian Circles, with 2.2 million members, form the backbone of popular movements and grassroots organizing. To encourage participation in the democratic process, the Bolivarian Circles educate people and communities to take control of their lives, and they assist with the formation of cooperatives, non-profit corporations and other economic projects.

The Movimento Sem Terra (MST)—Landless Workers' Movement—in Brazil is one of the largest social movements in the world. The key role of the MST is to organize and mobilize the poorest sectors of Brazilian society. For years, it has been fighting for agrarian reform through direct action and providing social services to those most in need. In an effort to pull all of the sectors of Brazilian society into the democratic process, the people are experimenting with various forms of direct democracy and participatory decision-making (Rocha and Branford 2003).

Massive social uprisings have also swept through Bolivia, with the population issuing a clear message that they want to be in charge of their own livelihoods. In 2000, a coalition of Bolivian peasants and workers successfully blocked the privatization of their water resources. The same groups are now active in the fight to assert control over the country's natural gas reserves.

In Canada, anti-corporate social movements have grown in size and scope. Their efforts have targeted the privatization of health care and the country's fresh water resources, trade agreements, the concentration of media ownership, job layoffs, cuts to social programs, the war in Iraq and environmental destruction.[1] Policy and political organizations like the Council of Canadians (COC) (with over 100,000 members), the Canadian Centre for Policy Alternatives (CCPA) and the Polaris Institute have actively opposed the agenda of corporate Canada and worked to develop alternative economic policies and strategies. Their top priorities include educating the Canadian public and building awareness about the threats that corporate power poses to Canadian citizens. Presently, these organizations are attempting to prevent a deep integration initiative (discussed in Chapter Six) that would dramatically change Canada-U.S. relations by allowing U.S. business open access to Canada's resources. Deep integration would also align Canada's foreign and military policies with those of George W. Bush's unilateralist regime.

Canadian organizations have joined forces to oppose corporate power on many issues. A few years ago, for example, the Council of Canadians allied with the Canadian Labour Congress and dozens of other groups to form the Common Front on the WTO (CF-WTO). According to Maude Barlow (head of the COC) and Tony Clarke (head of the Polaris Institute), many of the same organizations in the CF-WTO were also members of Common Frontiers, a coalition targeting the Free Trade Agreement of the Americas, and the Halifax Initiative, which concentrates on debt relief for poor countries and the effects of IMF/World Bank structural adjustment programs (Barlow and Clarke 2001: 214).

In addition to encouraging Canadian citizens to challenge corporate power, Canada's activist community has engaged in developing alternative economic proposals. Each year the CCPA, with input from many community groups and policy specialists, develops an Alternative Federal Budget (see, for example, CCPA 2003, 2004). Provincial Alternative Budgets are also done by regional CCPA offices in Manitoba, British Columbia, Saskatchewan and Nova Scotia. These initiatives offer citizens the opportunity to participate in the development of public policy and make choices about spending priorities, based on their own values and interests. Coordinated grassroots efforts such as the Alternative Budget are critical for educating citizens and for demonstrating, in very concrete ways, that there are workable, efficient and humane alternatives to the corporate policy consensus (see Loxley 2002 for a detailed discussion of the Alternative Budget process).

The power of Canada's economic elite to shape the policy agenda is certainly formidable, but it is not insurmountable. In December 2002, the House of Commons voted to endorse Canada's ratification of the Kyoto Protocol on climate change. In the years prior to this, Canadian business, led by the oil and gas sector in a coalition with other manufacturing and resource sectors and Canadian policy organizations, had "mounted its largest effort to date" to influence the Federal Government's environmental policy. Indeed, it had "conducted an all-out campaign to prevent ratification" (MacDonald 2003: 4). The three policy organizations involved in the effort were familiar ones: the Canadian Council of Chief Executives, Canadian Manufacturers and Exporters, and the Canadian Chamber of Commerce. In spite of the united front, Canadian business ultimately lost the battle and the agreement was signed (it has, of course, been trying to undo the agreement ever since). There is little doubt that a key reason for this outcome was the collective stance assumed by the "other side"— represented by the environmental movement, organized labour, church groups, globalization activists and a legion of concerned citizens.

INTERNATIONAL COALITIONS

In contrast to the unity of the economic elite, diversity has marked its opposition: The social movements that oppose corporate rule are not nearly as well organized or financed, and they lack the institutional structures and concrete venues available to the elite. Yet, as solidarity among transnational corporations and global elites continues to grow, civil society movements have started to come together, aided by advances in telecommunication technologies such as email and the Internet. At the same time, networks have been established to unite civil society organizations. One example is the People's Global Action (PGA) network, a worldwide alliance of organizations and grassroots movements which grew out of the international Zapatista gatherings in the late 1990s. For years, the PGA has mobilized activists from different countries around the meetings of international financial institutions like the IMF, World Bank and WTO (see Peoples' Global Action 2004). Another example is the International Forum on Globalization (IFG), formed in 1994, which represents an alliance of social activists, economists, researchers and writers from sixty organizations and twenty-five different countries. The IFG constructs viable alternatives to corporate-led globalization and builds public awareness of its consequences (see Cavanagh et al. 2002).

The creation of the World Social Forum (WSF) in 2001 is an especially compelling example of international civic mobilization. Each year, tens of thousands of representatives from organizations all over the world gather at the WSF to organize resistance strategies, develop alternative economic proposals and strengthen alliances among diverse movements. WSF discussions, forums and workshops are guided by the principles of participatory or direct democracy, encouraging input and active participation from all of those in attendance.[2] Building on the success of the WSF, similar kinds of meetings have been planned worldwide. International resistance activities have also created a space for governments of developing nations to express opposition to the policy prescriptions of the World Bank, the IMF and the rich and powerful states.

One of the first truly international coalitions was the mobilization that occurred around the proposed Multilateral Agreement on Investment (MAI), discussed in Chapter Four. The MAI amounts to an international charter of investors' rights (misleadingly called a free trade agreement). If the MAI were realized, it would severely restrict the capacity of any government to impose regulatory measures on capital, such as labour or environmental standards. The elites who designed the MAI attempted to keep the proposed agreement a secret and push it through without public knowledge. When concerned members of the public learned of the plan, they quickly assembled an international coalition of NGOs, public interest groups and other organizations to oppose it. In part, the failure of the MAI resulted from internal disputes among participating governments; there were concerns about cultural autonomy, economic sovereignty and U.S. power. But an even more important problem for global elites was the massive and rapid public opposition. Largely as a result of this mobilization, the deal was never ratified. For activists around the world, this outcome represents an extremely important victory over "a consolidated power of a kind that you can't find in history" (Chomsky and Barsamian 2001: 5). Chomsky summarizes the significance of the victory this way:

> A lot of people feel that we can't do anything, that prospects are gloomy. I don't think that's true at all. This is a rather dramatic illustration of the opposite. Against tremendous odds, confronting the most concentrated power in the world, the richest, most powerful countries, transnational corporations, international financial institutions, and close to total control of the media ... grassroots activism was able to stop it. (cited in Chomsky and Barsamian 2001: 5)

Of course, such a victory does not mean that elites will give up on the MAI or similar investment regimes. Negotiations will continue within a more secretive framework, meaning that concerned citizens must continue their efforts to expose what is happening behind closed doors. After the collapse of the MAI, activists in Canada (brought together by the Council of Canadians) started to build on the victory by organizing a series of hearings in cities across the country. They called the series "The MAI Inquiry: A Citizens' Search for Alternatives." The activists solicited input from hundreds of community-based organizations and thousands of concerned citizens on ways to transform social and economic structures in Canada and abroad. "The final report of the Citizens' Inquiry demonstrated," according to Barlow and Clarke (2001: 164), that "there is certainly no shortage of creative imagination when it comes to proposing ways of reorganizing the global economy to serve the democratic rights of people and to ensure the survival of the planet. Through the Citizens' Inquiry, the groundwork was laid for reclaiming democracy and the commons."[3]

THE CORPORATE RESPONSE

To be sure, elites are aware that—for the first time since the 1970s—opposition to the current political and economic order is widespread and growing. As a result, the celebrations emanating from elite forums and ideological institutions have quieted in recent years. The protests in Seattle and those that followed delivered a strong message that the public could no longer be ignored. It should come as no surprise, then, that many elites either strongly condemned the protestors or dismissed them as irrelevant. Following their lead, the corporate media pronounced judgement. For example, *The Wall Street Journal* referred to the Seattle protestors as "global village idiots." Thomas Friedman of the *New York Times* denounced them as a "Noah's ark of flat earth advocates, protectionist trade unions, and yuppies looking for their 1960s fix." Other media pundits characterized the demonstrators as "ignorant protectionists," claiming they were ill-informed about the issues and offered no credible alternatives.

Within the media, the complex nature of the issues was often reduced to a contest between "openness" and "protectionism," or between those who were "pro-trade" and "anti-trade." However, according to researchers from the International Forum on Globalization, these allegations are contradicted by a quick look at the proposals and platforms of those involved (see, for example, Feffer 2002). They write, "Anyone who makes even the smallest effort to find out why millions of people from virtually every nation and walk of life have taken to the streets finds these simplistic characterizations to be untrue." In reality, "the resistance is grounded in a sophisticated, well-developed critique set forth in countless publications and public presentations." In the opinion of the IFG, civil society groups offer "a wealth of alternatives with a striking convergence in their beliefs about the underlying values human society should serve" (Cavanagh et al. 2002: 3). In the opinion of David MaNally (2002), the sharp and heated response of the elite media is evidence that the resistance efforts had a major impact.

In related attempts to discredit and minimize their opponents, elites and the corporate media have repeatedly claimed that the opposition to corporate globalization has no centre, core ideology or overall vision. Resistance movements have been portrayed as scattered and diffuse, lacking clear goals and alternatives. Acts of resistance against environmental destruction, "free trade," growing poverty and inequality, privatization, unemployment, urban decay and the elimination of social services have been treated as if they were unrelated. Contrary to this elite perspective, however, many of today's social movements are united around an opposition to corporate rule and its devastating effects on democracy and the distribution of resources. It has become increasingly obvious to those taking part in resistance movements that all of these social problems are part of the same multi-faceted process. As Barlow and Clarke (2001: 125) point out, "from Birmingham to Geneva, Cologne to Seattle, and Washington to Prague, the corporate hijacking of democracy and the commons has been the principal target of mass demonstrations."

In recent years, international campaigns have been launched against corporations such as Nike for using sweatshop labour; against Shell Oil for environmental pollution and its role in human rights abuses; and against Monsanto and other agribusiness giants for their attacks on biodiversity and millions of small farmers. When today's activists target particular corporations like these, they are not limiting their critiques to particular corporations or to the harm that these corporations do—they are targeting "the corporation" itself. More precisely, they are challenging those features of the corporation that make corporate rule possible. Speaking of the new breed of activists, Lasn and Liacas note:

> [They] want to go back to the beginning, back to the laws and legal precedents that gave birth to the corporate 'I.' They want to tinker with the corporate genetic code, to change the laws under which charters are granted and revoked, the laws that protect investors from even the foulest taint of their investments, and the rules and regulations under which corporations operate from the local to the international level. (Lasn and Liacas 2000)

Not surprisingly, elites (often through government representatives) have mobilized against the emerging opposition, just as they did after the uprisings of the 1960s and 1970s. Not long after Seattle, the powerful public relations firm Burson Marsteller published a "Guide to the Seattle Meltdown," in which they listed many of the groups that took part in the demonstrations, along with their addresses and websites. The report was distributed to corporate clients so that they could "defend" themselves against protestors (Barlow and Clarke 2001: 46). The FBI and other law enforcement agencies in the United States have recently shifted their attention to the threats posed by new global movements. The change actually came shortly before Seattle, when word of the upcoming protests was discovered on the Internet. Similar developments are occurring in Canada. In 2000, the Canadian Security Intelligence Service (CSIS), Canada's "spy agency," released a study called *Anti-Globalization—A Spreading Phenomenon*, which essentially equated protestors with "terrorists" (Barlow and Clarke 2001: 48).

In an effort to placate resistance movements around the world, some elites have opted for an appeasement strategy. As noted in Chapter Six, a selection of corporate leaders have issued promises to be socially responsible, in an attempt to alleviate fears about the destructive effects of corporate behaviour. Under U.N. guidance, a group of transnational corporations have constructed a "global compact," which constitutes a pledge to follow certain guidelines dealing with labour standards, human rights standards and environmental sustainability (though these codes of conduct remain voluntary). Along the same lines, corporate and government officials have "extended a hand" to civil society groups, promising to establish a dialogue to address their concerns. According to Barlow and Clarke (2001: 221), "while not all 'dialogue' initiatives are necessarily meant to derail civil society groups, the strategic aim is clearly to facilitate a relegitimization of these dominant institutions." Related to this, the authors add, are divide-and-conquer strategies designed to disrupt the unity of the movement: "Blatant attempts have been made to label civil society organizations as either 'good' or 'bad,' depending on whether they accept or reject the basic corporate-state agenda for the global economy and on whether or not they engage in direct action tactics" (2001: 221). Corporate social responsibility and dialogue initiatives tend to serve merely as pretexts for modest reforms, whereas today's activists seek much more: a massive overhaul of the global economic system, the replacement of autocratic institutions of corporate rule with democratic ones (see Albert 2000, 2003). Indeed, the terms of the struggle have shifted from keeping up with or adapting to capitalism, to mobilizing against it. If the various counter-measures that exemplify this mobilization are not enough to quell the rising tide of opposition, citizens should expect a much more concerted elite offensive in the years to come.

Elite backlash against today's social movements has found a new stronghold in the aftermath of 9/11. Around the world, elite groups have used—and continue to use—the horrible attacks of September 11th 2001 to pursue their agendas more relentlessly. Military spending (along with support of corporations that produce military goods) has increased, while the funding of social programs has declined. Protestors have been commonly equated with terrorists. New laws have been passed allowing governments to repress resistance activities and infiltrate activist organizations. Not surprisingly, these activities have slowed, at least temporarily, the progress of global civil society movements.

Another alarming development of the post-9/11 period concerns the foreign policy agenda of the United States. The U.S. has served notice that its own unilateral objectives will take precedence over multilateral agreements, international law and the United Nations, except when the latter correspond with the global ambitions of the United States. In late 2002, the U.S. formally announced its new National Security Strategy, whereby it declared, in effect, the right to use military force to quash any perceived challenge to U.S. global domination. The goal of the strategy, according to John Ikenberry (2002), is to maintain "a unipolar world in which the United States has no peer competitor ... [so that] no state or coalition could ever challenge [the US] as global leader, protector, and enforcer." As the self-appointed leader of the "war on terror," the Bush administration has indicated to the rest of the world that any and all defiance of U.S. objectives will not be tolerated. The administration has also flagrantly undermined international efforts to reduce threats to the environment, a matter of no small significance.

These brazen declarations by U.S. leaders have been met with anger and hostility around the world. While there was a general expression of solidarity with the United States after 9/11, this sentiment has largely given way to fear and distrust—and rightly so. In the eyes of much of the world the Bush administration represents the single greatest threat to world peace. This was the opinion of 80 percent of Europeans, according to an informal poll conducted by *Time* magazine. A similar poll in Canada found that over 36 percent of Canadians viewed the United States as the world's largest threat to world peace, compared to 21 percent who chose Al Qaeda and 17 percent who named Iraq (Chomsky 2003: 41). Global elites are also concerned. At a recent meeting of the World Economic Forum in Switzerland, discussions were dominated by the then impending U.S. war in Iraq. According to the *Wall Street Journal*, "a chorus of international complaints about the American march toward war with Iraq [reached] a crescendo at this gathering of some 2,000 corporate executives, politicians and academics" (cited in Chomsky 2003: 40). The tens if not hundreds of thousands of innocent people killed in the most recent round of U.S. militarism in Iraq has brought the reality of these fears to the fore. In response, social activists in Canada and elsewhere have begun to integrate an opposition to war and imperialism with their resistance to corporate-led globalization. In future years, Canadians will also be pressed to consider the moral and political implications of "deep integration" proposals to align our foreign policy and our armed forces more closely with those of the Bush regime.

To oppose corporate rule effectively, we need to understand the nature and conditions of elite dominance; that is, how the elite exert their influence over the economic, social and political spheres. The primary purpose of this book is to contribute to this endeavour. The millions of people suffering around the world and the scarcity of national or global principles to address this catastrophe demand public attention. The acts of resistance discussed above are symptomatic of the growing awareness of and dissatisfaction with the gap between those at the commanding heights of the economy and the vast majority of the world's population. Such acts of resistance also offer a verifiable challenge to agreements that ensure such inequality, many of which are proposed, negotiated and ratified without public consultation and enforced by perimeters of armed forces, police pepper spray, jail cells and in some cases death for those who do not passively accept the current state of affairs.

In what promises to be a long battle for social justice, a distinction has to be made between short-term goals and long-term visions. Recent resistance movements offer much hope and inspiration but have yet to challenge the foundations of the institutional structures of corporate power. Speaking of Seattle, Ed Finn (2000: 178) notes that "their success in preventing the rich and powerful from agreeing on how they could become even more rich and powerful—as laudable as it undeniably was—still leaves an already brutal and barbaric system intact."

Given this, it would be a tactical error for social movements to abandon engaging the state. At present, the state is the only institution large enough to act as a counterweight to corporate power; therefore, short-term goals should involve defending, even strengthening, those elements of the state that are accountable to public input (which are the ones constantly under attack by private power). Opening up the state to democratic participation and improving the effectiveness and accountability of state regulation are the most realistic interim strategies for dealing with the corporate threat and the practical problems of tomorrow—problems on which people's lives often depend. In the short-term, then, political activism that directly targets corporate power should be complemented by efforts to re-democratize the state and government. In the long-term, the inherent injustices of the centralized state system need to be challenged and ultimately dismantled. If the diverse array of today's social movements were to come together—and further align themselves toward common goals—the possibilities for meaningful social change would be endless. They could very well change the course of modern history.

NOTES

1. For discussion of anti-corporate movements in Ontario, see Conway (2004).
2. For more information on the WSF, see Houtart and Polet (2001). For discussion of social and economic alternatives developed at the WSF, see Fisher and Ponniah (2004).
3. For more information on reorganizing the global economy, see Bello (2003) and Shutt (2001).

REFERENCES

Abelson, Donald E. 2002. *Do Think Tanks Matter? Assessing the Impact of Public Policy Institutes*. Montreal: McGill-Queen's University Press.

Abelson, Donald, and Christine Carberry. 1998. "Following Suit or Falling Behind?: A Comparative Analysis of Think Tanks in Canada and the United States." *Canadian Journal of Political Science* 31, 3.

Abelson, Donald and Evert Lindquist. 2000. "Think Tanks in North America." In J. McGann and K. Weaver (eds.), *Think Tanks and Civil Societies: Catalysts for Ideas and Action*. New Brunswick, NJ: Transaction Publishers.

Albert, Michael. 2000. *Moving Forward: Program for a Participatory Economy*. London: AK Press.

_____. 2003. *Parecon: Life After Capitalism*. London: Verso Books.

Anderson, Sarah, and John Cavanagh. 2000. *Top 200: The Rise of Corporate Global Power*. Baltimore: Institute for Policy Studies.

Archer, Simon. 1997. "Export, Eh? Canada Dismantles Its Social Programs." Available at www.zmag.org/ZMag/articles/archerjuly97.html (accessed on July 15, 2003).

Bagdikian, Ben. 2000. *The Media Monopoly*. Boston: Beacon Press.

Bakan, Joel. 2004. *The Corporation: The Pathological Pursuit of Profit and Power*. New York: Free Press.

Baldwin, John, Desmond Beckstead, Guy Gellatly and Alice Peters. 2000. "Patterns of Corporate Diversification in Canada: An Empirical Analysis." *Analytical Studies Branch—Research Paper Series*. Ottawa: Statistics Canada No. 11F0019MpE No. 150.

Barlow, Maude. 1990. *Parcel of Rogues: How Free Trade is Failing Canada*. Toronto: Key Porter Books.

_____. 1999. "Citizens vs. Corporate Canada." *Multinational Monitor* 20.

_____. 2004. "The Canada We Want: A Citizens' Alternative to Deep Integration." Available at www.holycrossjustice.org/pdf/TCWW_eng.pdf (accessed on May 23, 2004).

Barlow, Maude, and Bruce Campbell. 1995. *Straight Through the Heart: How the Liberals Abandoned the Just Society*. Toronto: Harper Collins.

Barlow, Maude, and Tony Clarke. 2001. *Global Showdown*. Toronto: Stoddard Publishing.

Barlow, Maude, and Heather-Jane Robertson. 1994. *Class Warfare: The Assault on Canada's Schools*. Toronto: Key Porter Books.

Barrow, Clyde W. 1993. *Political Theories of the State*. Madison: University of Wisconsin Press.

Bell, Daniel. 1971. "The Corporation and Society in the 1970s." *The Public Interest* 24 (Summer).

Bello, Walden. 2003. *Deglobalization: Ideas for a New World Economy*. Black Point, NS: Fernwood Books.

Block, Fred. 1977. "The Ruling Class Does Not Rule: Notes on the Marxist Theory of the State." *Socialist Revolution* 31.

_____. 1980. "Beyond Relative Autonomy: State Managers as Historical Subjects." In R. Miliband and J. Saville (eds.), *The Socialist Register*. London: Merlin Press.

Bradford, Neil. 2000. "The Policy Influence of Economic Ideas: Interests, Institutions and Innovation in Canada." In M. Burke, C. Moores and J. Shields (eds.), *Restructuring and Resistance. Canadian Public Policy in an Age of Global Capitalism*. Halifax: Fernwood Publishing.

Brym, Robert. 1989. "Canada." In T. Bottomore and R. Brym (eds.), *The Capitalist Class*. New York: New York University Press.

Burris, Val. 1991. "Director Interlocks and the Political Behavior of Corporations and Corporate Elites." *Social Science Quarterly* 72, 3.

Business Council on National Issues (BCNI). 1986. *BCNI Issues, 1976-1986*. Ottawa: BCNI.

_____. 2000. *Marching Towards Prosperity*. Ottawa: BCNI.

Cameron, Duncan. 1988. "The Dealers." *This Magazine* 21, 8.

_____. 1997. "Selling the House to Pay the Mortgage: What is Behind Privatization?" *Studies in Political Economy* 53.

Campbell, Bruce, and David Macdonald. 2003. "Straight Talk: Big Business and the Canada-US Free Trade Agreement Fifteen Years Later." *Canadian Centre for Policy Alternatives*. Available at www.policyalternatives.ca/publications/btn5-2.pdf (accessed on June 3, 2004).

Canadian Centre for Philanthropy. 2003. *Canadian Directory to Foundations and Grants*, Seventeenth edition. (volume one). Toronto: Canadian Centre for Philanthropy.

Canadian Centre for Policy Alternatives (CCPA). 1996. *Challenging Free Trade in Canada: The Real Story*. Ottawa: CCPA.

_____. 2000. "Farmers are Victims of Market Failure, Not EU Subsidies." *CCPA Monitor* 7, 1.

_____. 2001. "Election Fund Loopholes Need to be Closed." *CCPA Monitor* 8, 5.

_____. 2003. *Alternative Federal Budget 2003: The Cure for the Common Budget*. Ottawa: CCPA.

_____. 2004. *Alternative Federal Budget 2004: Rebuilding the Foundations*. Ottawa: CCPA.

Canadian Chamber of Commerce. "Canadian Chamber Profile." Available at www.chamber.ca/article.asp?id=139 (accessed on March 13, 2003).

Canadian Council of Chief Executives (CCCE). "History and Background." Available at www.ceocouncil.ca/en/about/history.php. (accessed on April 4, 2004).

Canadian Federation of Independent Business. "CFIB Vision." Available at www.cfib.ca/ info/vision_e.asp (accessed on March 13, 2003).

CanWest Global Communications. "Overview." Available at www.canwestglobal.com/ overview.html (accessed on March 23, 2004).

Carnoy, Martin. 1984. *The State and Political Theory*. Princton: Princeton University Press.

Carroll, William. 1986. *Corporate Power and Canadian Capitalism*. Vancouver:

University of British Columbia Press.

_____. 1989. "Neoliberalism and the Recomposition of Finance Capital in Canada." *Capital and Class* 38.

_____. 2001. "Westward Ho? The Shifting Geography of Corporate Power in Canada." *Journal of Canadian Studies* 36, 4.

_____. 2004. *Corporate Power in a Globalizing World: A Study in Elite Social Organization.* Toronto: Oxford University Press.

Carroll, William, and Malcolm Alexander. 1999. "Finance Capital and Capitalist Class Integration in the 1990s: Networks of Interlocking Directorships in Canada and Australia." *Canadian Review of Sociology and Anthropology* 36, 3.

Carroll, William, and Colin Carson. 2003. "The Network of Global Corporations and Policy Groups: A Structure for Transnational Capitalist Class Formation?" *Global Networks* 3, 1.

Carroll, William and Meindert Fennema. 2002. "Is There a Transnational Business Community?," *International Sociology* 17, 3.

Carroll, William, and Scott Lewis. 1991. "Restructuring Finance Capital: Changes in the Canadian Corporate Network 1976-1986." *Sociology* 25, 3.

Carroll, William, and Murray Shaw. 2001. "Consolidating a Neoliberal Policy Bloc in Canada, 1976-1996." *Canadian Public Policy* 27, 2.

Cavanagh, John, et al. 2002. "Alternatives to Economic Globalization." *A Report of the International Forum on Globalization.* San Francisco: Berrett-Koehler Publishers.

Chen, Jennifer, and Gary Graves. 2002. "Media Ownership in Canada." Available at cbc. ca/news/indepth/background/mediaownership/html (accessed on May 12, 2003).

Chomsky, Noam. 1989. *Necessary Illusions: Thought Control in Democratic Societies.* Toronto: Anansi.

_____. 1999. *Profit Over People: Neoliberalism and Global Order.* Toronto: Seven Stories Press.

_____. 2003. *Hegemony or Survival: America's Quest for Global Dominance.* New York: Metropolitan Books.

Chomsky, Noam, and David Barsamian. 1997. *Class Warfare.* Vancouver: New Star Books.

_____. 2001. *Propaganda and the Public Mind.* Cambridge, MA: South End Press.

Chomsky, Noam, and Heinz Dieterich. 1999. *Latin America: From Colonization to Globalization.* Melbourne, Australia: Ocean Press.

Chomsky, Noam, Peter Mitchell and John Schoeffel. 2002. *Understanding Power.* New York: The New Press.

Chomsky, Noam, and Arthur Naiman. 1998. *The Common Good.* California: Odonian Press.

Clarke, Tony. 1997. *Silent Coup: Confronting the Big Business Takeover of Canada.* Ottawa: Canadian Centre for Policy Alternatives.

Clement, Wallace. 1983. *Class, Power and Prosperity.* Toronto: Methuen Publications.

_____. 1986. *The Canadian Corporate Elite: An Analysis of Economic Power.* Ottawa: Carleton University Press.

Coburn, Elaine. 2003. "Interrogating Globalization: Emerging Contradictions and Conflicts." In Y. Atasoy and W. Carroll (eds.), *Global Shaping and Its Alternatives.* West Hartford: Kumarian Press.

Cohen, Marjorie. 1995. "Neo-Cons on Campus: How the Fraser Institute Captured the Hearts and Minds of Students While the Left Stood by and Did Nothing." *This Magazine* 29.

Colwell, Mary Anna Culleton. 1980. "The Foundation Connection: Links Among Foundations and Recipient Organizations." In R. Arnove (ed.), *Philanthropy and Cultural Imperialism*. Boston: Hall.

_____. 1993. *Private Foundations and Public Policy. The Political Role of Philanthropy*. New York: Garland Publishing.

Conway, Janet. 2004. *Identity, Place, Knowledge: Social Movements Contesting Globalization*. Black Point, NS: Fernwood Publishing.

Crozier, Michel, Samuel Huntington and Joji Watanuki. 1975. *The Crisis of Democracy: Report on the Governability of Democracies to the Trilateral Commission*. New York: New York University Press.

d'Aquino, Thomas. 2000. "How to Become a Beacon of Irresistible Opportunity." *Canadian Business Economics* 8, 2.

_____. 2003. *Security and Prosperity: The Dynamics of a New Canada-United States Partnership in North America*. Toronto: Canadian Council of Chief Executives.

Dahl, Robert. 1958. "A Critique of the Ruling Elite Model." *American Political Science Review* 53.

_____. 1961. *Who Governs?* New Haven: Yale University Press.

_____. 1967. *Pluralist Democracy in the United States*. Chicago: Rand McNally.

Davies, Charles. 1977. "The Origins of the BCNI." *Board of Trade Journal* April.

_____. 2002. "New York State of Mind." *National Post Business* May.

Derber, Charles. 2002. *People Before Profit*. New York: St. Martin's Press.

Dobbin, Murray. 1992. "Thomas d'Aquino: The De Facto PM." *Canadian Forum* November.

_____. 1998. *The Myth of the Good Corporate Citizen: Democracy Under the Rule of Big Business*. New York: Stoddart Publishing.

_____. 2000. "Medicare Benefits Business, So Why Aren't CEOs Defending It?" *The CCPA Monitor* 7, 3: 22.

_____. 2003a. *Paul Martin: CEO for Canada?* Toronto: James Lorimer and Company.

_____. 2003b. "Our Elites Pushing Hard for Canada to Become a U.S. Colony." *The CCPA Monitor* 9, 8.

_____. 2003c. *The Myth of the Good Corporate Citizen: Canada and Democracy in the Age of Globalization* (2nd edition). Toronto: Lorimer.

Dobson, Wendy. 2002. *Shaping the Future of the North American Economic Space: A Framework for Action*. Toronto: C.D. Howe Institute.

Doern, G. Bruce, and Brian Tomlin. 1991. *Faith and Fear*. Toronto: Stoddard Publishing.

Domhoff, G. William. 1970. *The Higher Circles: The Governing Class in America*. New York: Random House.

_____. 1974. *The Bohemian Grove and Other Retreats: A Study in Ruling Class Cohesiveness*. First edition. New York: Harper and Row.

_____. 1978. *The Powers That Be*. New York: Vintage Books.

_____. 1983. *Who Rules America Now? A View for the 80's*. Englewood Cliffs: Prentice Hall.

_____. 1987. "Where do Government Experts Come From? The CEA and the Policy-Planning Network." In G.W. Domhoff and T. Dye (eds.), *Power Elites and Organizations*. London: Sage Publications.

_____. 1998. *Who Rules America? Power and Politics in the Year 2000*. Mountain View,

CA: Mayfield Publishing.

Draffan, George. 2000. "The Corporate Consensus: A Guide to the Institutions of Global Power." Available at www.endgame.org/corpcon1.html (accessed on February 27, 2004).

Dreiling. Michael. 2000. "The Class Embeddedness of Corporate Political Action: Leadership in Defense of the NAFTA." *Social Problems* 47, 1.

Dunleavy, Patrick, and Brendan O'Leary. 1987. *Theories of the State: The Politics of Liberal Democracies*. London: Macmillan.

Dye, Thomas. 1995. *Who's Running America? The Clinton Years*. Prentice Hall.

Economic Policy Institute. 2001. "NAFTA at Seven." Available at www.epinet.org/briefingpapers/nafta01/nafta-at-7.pdf (accessed on October 13, 2004).

Ekos Research Associates. 1995. "Rethinking Government." Ottawa: Ekos Research Associates.

Elections Canada. 2004. "Political Parties' Financial Reports." Available at www.elections.ca /scripts/ecfiscals2/Default.asp?L=E&Page=Welcome (accessed on June 2, 2004).

Ernst, Alan. 1992. "From Liberal Continentalism to Neoconservatism: North American Free Trade and the Politics of the C.D. Howe Institute." *Studies in Political Economy* 39.

Erosion, Technology and Concentration (ETC) Group. 2001. "Concentration in Corporate Power: The Unmentioned Agenda." Available at www.etcgroup.org/documents/comglobilization.pdf (accessed on January 30, 2002).

_____. 2003. "Oligopoly, Inc." Available at www.etcgroup.org/documents/Comm82OligopNovDec03.pdf (accessed on October 22, 2004).

Evans, Peter, Dietrich Rueschemeyer and Theda Skocpol. 1985. *Bringing the State Back In*. Cambridge: Cambridge University Press.

Feffer, John. 2002. *Living in Hope: People Challenging Globalization*. London: Zed Books.

Finn, Ed. 2000. *Who Do We Try To Rescue Today?* Ottawa: Canadian Centre for Policy Alternatives.

Fisher, William, and Thomas Ponniah. 2004. *Another World is Possible: Popular Alternatives to Globalization at the World Social Forum*. Black Point, NS: Fernwood Publishing.

Fleming, James. 1991. *Circles of Power*. Toronto: Doubleday Canada.

Fox, John and Michael Ornstein. 1986. "The Canadian State and Corporate Elites in the Post-War Period." *Canadian Review of Sociology and Anthropology* 23, 4.

Fraser Institute. "2002 Financial Statements." Available at www.fraserinstitute.ca/pdf/Statements02.pdf (accessed on August 15, 2003).

_____. "*2002 Annual Report*." Available at www.fraserinstitute.ca/pdf/annualreports/AR2002.pdf (accessed on March 17, 2003).

Gabel, Medard, and Henry Bruner. 2003. *Global Inc.: An Atlas of the Multinational Corporation*. New York: The New Press.

Gallup Canada. 1995. "Increased Concern Over Government Deficits, Debt." The Gallup Polls: 55, 10. Toronto: Gallup Canada Inc.

Gaughan, Patrick. 2002. *Mergers, Acquisitions, and Corporate Restructurings*. New York: John Wiley and Sons.

Grace, Kevin Michael. 2001. "Welcome to AsperLand." *Newsmagazine* (Alberta Edition) 28, 10.

Gramsci, Antonio. 1971. *Selections from the Prison Notebooks of Antonio Gramsci*. New

York: International Publishers.

Green, Milford, and Rod McNaughton. 2003. "Changes in Inter-Corporate Ownership and Aggregate Industry Diversification in the Canadian Economy 1976-1995." Available at publish.uwo.ca/-mbgreen/control.pdf (accessed on August 29, 2003).

Grubb, Thomas, and Robert Lamb. 2000. *Capitalize on Merger Chaos. Six Ways to Profit from Your Competitors' Consolidation—And Your Own.* Toronto: The Free Press.

Gutstein, Donald. 2000. "Papers Favour Right-Wing Think Tanks Over Left, 4 to 1." *Canadian Centre for Policy Alternatives News Watch Monitor* 3, 1.

Hackett, Robert A., and Richard Gruneau. 2000. *The Missing News. Filters and Blind Spots in Canada's Press.* Ottawa: Canadian Centre for Policy Alternatives/ Garamond Press.

Hackett, Robert, and Yuezhi Zhao. 1998. *Sustaining Democracy? Journalism and the Politics of Objectivity.* Toronto: Garamond Press.

Haddow, Rodney. 1994. "Canadian Organized Labour and the Guaranteed Annual Income." In A. Johnson, S. McBride and P. Smith (eds.), *Continuities and Discontinuities: The Political Economy of Social Welfare and Labour Market Policy in Canada.* Toronto: University of Toronto Press.

Herman, Edward, and Noam Chomsky. 1988. *Manufacturing Consent.* New York: Pantheon Books.

Houtart, Francois, and Francois Polet. 2001. *The Other Davos: The Globalization of Resistance to the World Economic System.* London: Zed Books.

Hurtig, Mel. 2002. *The Vanishing Country: Is it Too Late to Save Canada?* Toronto: McClelland and Stewart.

Ikenberry, John. 2002. "America's Political Ambition." *Foreign Affairs* September/ October.

Kang, Nam-Hoon, and Sara Johansson. 2000. *Cross-Border Mergers and Acquisitions: Their Role in Industrial Globalization.* STI Working Papers 2000/1. Paris: Organization for Economic Cooperation and Development.

Kerstetter, Steve. 2003. *Rags and Riches: Wealth Inequality in Canada.* Ottawa: Canadian Centre for Policy Alternatives.

Klein, Naomi. 2003. "Elections and Democracy in Argentina." *The Nation,* May 14.

Knox, Paul. 2002. "Not In the Newsroom ... Free Expression and Media Concentration in Canada: The Case of CanWest Global." *The Round Table* 366.

Knuttila, Murray, and Wendee Kubik. 2000. *State Theories: Classical, Global, and Feminist Perspectives.* Third edition. Halifax: Fernwood Publishing.

Koenig, Thomas, Robert Gogel and John Sonquist. 1979. "Models of the Significance of Interlocking Corporate Directorates." *American Journal of Economics and Sociology* 38.

Kome, Penny. 2002. "Double Standard for Charity Status Benefits Right Wing Think Tanks." *Straight Goods News,* September 10. Available at www.straightgoods.ca/ ViewFeature/cfm?REF=623 (accessed on January 3, 2003).

Korten, David. 2001. *When Corporations Rule the World.* West Hartford: Kumarian Press.

Krause, William, and Jack Lothian. 1989. "Measurement of Canada's Level of Corporate Concentration." *Canadian Economic Observer* 3.

Langille, David. 1987. "The Business Council on National Issues and the Canadian

State." *Studies in Political Economy* 24.

Lash, Scott, and John Urry. 1987. *The End of Organized Capitalism*. Cambridge: Polity Press.

Lasn, Kalle, and Tom Liacas. 2000. "The Crackdown." *Adbusters* August-September.

Lee, Marc. 2004. "Indecent Proposal: The Case Against a Canada-U.S. Customs Union." Available at www.policyalternatives.ca/publications/customs-union.pdf (accessed on May 21, 2004).

Lindquist, Evert. 1993. "Think Tanks or Clubs? Assessing the Influence and Roles of Canadian Policy Institutes." *Canadian Public Administration* 36, 4.

_____. 1998. "A Quarter Century of Canadian Think Tanks: Evolving Institutions, Conditions and Strategies." In D. Stone, A. Denham and M.Garnett (eds.), *Think Tanks Across Nations: A Comparative Approach*. New York: Manchester University Press.

Loxley, Jon. 2002. *Alternative Budgets: Budgeting as if People Mattered*. Black Point, NS: Fernwood Publishing.

MacDonald, Douglas. 2003. "The Business Campaign to Prevent Kyoto Ratification." Paper Presented at the Annual Meeting of the Canadian Political Science Association, Dalhousie University. Available at www.cpsa-acsp.ca/paper-2003/macdonald.pdf (accessed on July 18, 2003).

Macfarlane, David. 2004. "Why Now?" *Globe and Mail Report on Business* 20, 9.

Macklem, Katherine. 2002. "Can the Aspers Do It?" *Macleans*, April 8.

McBride, Stephen. 2001. *Paradigm Shift: Globalization and the Canadian State*. Halifax: Fernwood Publishing.

McBride, Stephen, and John Shields. 1993. *Dismantling a Nation: Canada and the New World Order*. Halifax: Fernwood Publishing.

McChesney, Robert. 2000. *Rich Media, Poor Democracy: Communication Politics in Dubious Times*. New York: The New Press.

McNally, David. 2002. *Another World is Possible: Globalization and Anti-Capitalism*. Winnipeg: Arbeiter Ring Publishing.

McQuaig, Linda. 1991. *The Quick and the Dead: Brian Mulroney, Big Business and the Seduction of Canada*. Toronto: Penguin Books.

_____. 1995. *Shooting the Hippo: Death by Deficit and Other Canadian Myths*. Toronto: Viking.

_____. 1998. *The Cult of Impotence: Selling the Myth of Powerlessness in the Global Economy*. Toronto: Penguin Books.

McQueen, Rod. 2000. "Forget Cronyism." *National Post Business*, April.

Media Transparency: Searchable Database. Available at www.mediatransparency.org/advanced_search.php (accessed on June 30, 2003).

Miliband, Ralph. 1969. *The State in Capitalist Society*. London: Quartet Books.

_____. 1970. "The Capitalist State—Reply to Nicos Poulantzas." *New Left Review* 59.

_____. 1977. *Marxism and Politics*. London: Oxford University Press.

Mills, C. Wright. 1956. *The Power Elite*. New York: Oxford University Press.

Minister of Supply and Services Canada. 1978. *Report of the Royal Commission on Corporate Concentration*. Ottawa.

Mintz, Beth, and Michael Schwartz. 1985. *The Power Structure of American Business*. Chicago: University of Chicago Press.

Mizruchi, Mark S. 1992. *The Structure of Corporate Political Action. Interfirm Relations and their Consequences*. London: Harvard University Press.

_____. 1996. "What Do Interlocks Do? An Analysis, Critique, and Assessment of Research on Interlocking Directorates." *Annual Review of Sociology* 22.

Morck, Randall, David Strangeland and Bernard Yeung. 2000. "Inherited Wealth, Corporate Control, and Economic Growth—The Canadian Disease?" In R. Morck (ed.), *Concentrated Corporate Ownership*. National Bureau of Economic Research Conference Volume: University of Chicago Press.

National Post Business. 2002. *Financial Post 500*, Thirty-eighth edition. Toronto: Financial Post Data Group.

_____. 2003. *Financial Post Directory of Directors*, Fifty-sixth edition. Toronto: Financial Post Data Group.

Neiheisel, Steven R. 1994. *Corporate Strategy and Politics of Goodwill. A Political Analysis of Corporate Philanthropy in America*. New York: Peter Lang Publishing.

Newman, Peter 1975. *The Canadian Establishment*. Toronto: McClelland and Stewart.

_____. 1981. *The Acquisitors*. Toronto: McClelland and Stewart.

_____. 1998. *Titans: How the New Canadian Establishment Seized Power*. Toronto: Penguin Books.

Niosi, Jorge. 1982. *The Economy of Canada: Who Controls It?* Montreal: Black Rose Books.

_____. 1985. "Continental Nationalism: The Strategy of the Canadian Bourgeoisie." In R. Brym (ed.), *The Structure of the Canadian Capitalist Class*. Toronto: Garamond Press.

O'Connor, Julia, and Gregg Olsen (eds.). 1998. *Power Resources Theory and the Welfare State*. Toronto: University of Toronto Press.

Olsen, Dennis. 1980. *The State Elite*. Toronto: McClelland and Stewart.

Olsen, Gregg. 1991. "Labour Mobilization and the Strength of Capital: The Rise and Stall of Economic Democracy in Sweden." *Studies in Political Economy* 34.

_____. 2002. *The Politics of the Welfare State: Canada, Sweden and the United States*. Toronto: Oxford University Press.

Olsen, Gregg, and Julia S. O'Connor. 1998. "Understanding the Welfare State: Power Resources Theory and Its Critics." In J. O'Connor and G. Olsen (eds.), *Power Resources Theory and the Welfare State*. Toronto: University of Toronto Press.

Ornstein, Michael. 1980. "Assessing the Meaning of Corporate Interlocks: Canadian Evidence." *Social Science Research* 9.

_____. 1982a. *Political Cleavages in the Canadian Capitalist Class*. Downsview, ON: Institute for Behavioural Research.

_____. 1982b. *Capital and the Canadian State*. Downsview, ON: Institute for Behavioural Research.

_____. 1984. "Interlocking Directorates in Canada: Intercorporate or Class Alliance." *Administrative Science Quarterly* 29.

_____. 1989. "The Social Organization of the Canadian Capitalist Class in Comparative Perspective." *Canadian Review of Sociology and Anthropology* 26, 1.

_____. 1998. "Three Decades of Elite Research in Canada: John Porter's Unfulfilled Legacy." In R. Helmes-Hayes and J. Curtis (eds.), *The Vertical Mosaic Revisited*. Toronto: University of Toronto Press.

Ornstein, Michael, and H. Michael Stevenson. 1999. *Politics and Ideology in Canada: Elite and Public Opinion in the Transformation of a Welfare State*. Montreal: McGill-Queen's University Press.

Palmer, Donald. 1983. "Broken Ties: Interlocking Directorates and Intercorporate Coordination." *Administrative Science Quarterly* 28.

Panitch, Leo. 1977. "The Role and Nature of the Canadian State." In Leo Panitch (ed.), *The Canadian State: Political Economy and Political Power.* Toronto: University of Toronto Press.

_____. 1994. "Globalisation and the State." In R. Miliband and L. Panitch (eds.), *Socialist Register: Between Globalism and Nationalism.* London: Merlin Press.

Peoples' Global Action (PGA). 2004. Available at www.nadir.org/nadir/initiativ/agp/en/index.html (accessed on October 15, 2004).

Porter, John. 1965. *The Vertical Mosaic: An Analysis of Social Class and Power in Canada.* Toronto: University of Toronto Press.

Poulantzas, Nicos. 1969. "The Problem of the Capitalist State." *New Left Review* 58.

_____. 1975a. *Political Power and Social Classes.* London: NLB.

_____. 1975b. *Classes in Contemporary Capitalism.* London: NLB.

Rau, Krishna. 1996. "A Million For Your Thoughts." *Canadian Forum* 75 (851).

Richardson, Jack. 1992. "Free Trade: Why Did it Happen?" *Canadian Review of Sociology and Anthropology* 29, 3.

Robinson, William. 2004. *A Theory of Global Capitalism: Production, Class, and State in a Transnational World.* Baltimore: Johns Hopkins University Press.

Robinson, William, and Jerry Harris. 2000. "Towards a Global Ruling Class? Globalization and the Transnational Capitalist Class." *Science and Society* 64, 1.

Rocha, Jan, and Sue Branford. 2003. *Cutting the Wise: The Struggle of the Landless Movement in Brazil.* London: Latin American Bureau.

Rose, Arnold. 1967. *The Power Structure.* New York: Oxford University Press.

Shutt, Harry. 2001. *A New Democracy: Alternatives to a Bankrupt World Order.* Black Point, NS: Fernwood Publishing.

Sklair, Leslie. 2001. *The Transnational Capitalist Class.* Oxford: Blackwell Publishers.

Skocpol, Theda. 1985. "Bringing the State Back In: Strategies and Analysis in Current Research." In P. Evans, D. Rueschemeyer and T. Skocpol (eds.) *Bringing the State Back In.* Cambridge: Cambridge University Press.

Smith, Doug. 2002. *How to Tax a Billionaire: Project Loophole and the Campaign for Tax Fairness.* Winnipeg: Arbeiter Ring Publishing.

Smith, Mark. 2000. *American Business and Political Power: Public Opinion, Elections and Democracy.* Chicago: The University of Chicago Press.

Smith, Martin. 1990. "Pluralism, Reformed Pluralism and Neopluralism: The Role of Pressure Groups in Policy-Making." *Political Studies* 38.

Stanbury, W.T. 2003. "Low-Down and Dirty on Big Political Donations." Available at www.thehilltimes.ca (accessed on June 13, 2004).

Stanford, Jim. 2001. "The Economic and Social Consequences of Fiscal Retrenchment in Canada in the 1990's." In K. Banting, A. Sharpe and F. St-Hilaire (eds.), *The Review of Economic and Social Progress: The Longest Decade, Canada in the 1990's.* Volume 1. Available at www.csls.ca/repsp/repsp1.asp (accessed on April 24, 2004).

Steinmo, Sven, Kathleen Thelen and Frank Longstreth. 1992. *Structuring Politics: Historical Institutionalism in Comparative Perspective.* Cambridge: Cambridge University Press.

Stokman, Frans, Rolf Zieger and John Scott. 1985. *Networks of Corporate Power.* Cambridge: Polity Press.

Stone, Diane. 1996. *Capturing the Political Imagination. Think Tanks and the Policy*

Process. London: Frank Cass and Company.

Strange, Susan. 1996. *The Retreat of the State: The Diffusion of Power in the World Economy*. Cambridge: Cambridge University Press.

Taras, David. 1999. *Power and Betrayal in the Canadian Media*. Peterborough, ON: Broadview Press.

Teeple, Gary. 2000. *Globalization and the Decline of Social Reform*. Second Edition. Toronto: Garamond Press.

Thompson, Justin, and Erik Missio. 2003. "Chrétien's Plan for Reform." *CBC News Online*, July 9, 2003. Available at www/cbc.ca/nwes/features/campaign_contribut ions030128.html (accessed on July 10, 2003).

Thunderbird Online Magazine. 2001. "A Lot of Noise But Just a Few Voices: Media Ownership in Canada." Available at www.journalism.ubc.ca/thunderbird/ archives/2001.12/canmedia.html (accessed on April 14, 2003).

Useem, Michael. 1979. "The Social Organization of the American Business Elite and Participation of Corporation Directors in the Governance of American Institutions." *American Sociological Review* 44.

_____. 1982. "Classwide Rationality in the Politics of Managers and Directors of Large Corporations in the United States and Great Britain." *Administrative Science Quarterly* 27.

_____. 1984. *The Inner Circle. Large Corporations and the Rise of Business Political Activity in the U.S. and the U.K.* New York: Oxford University Press.

van der Pijl, Kees. 2001. "Globalization or Class Society in Transition." *Science and Society* 65, 4.

Veltmeyer, Henry. 1987. *Canadian Corporate Power*. Toronto: Garamond Press.

Watson, Thomas. 2002. "Flacks in the Box." *Canadian Business*, November 11.

Watson, William, John Richards and David Brown. 1994. *The Case for Change: Reinventing the Welfare State*. Toronto: C.D. Howe Institute.

Whitt, Allen. 1980. "Can Capitalists Organize Themselves." *Insurgent Sociologist* 9.

Williams, Paul. 1982. *Elite Attitudes Toward Canadian Social Welfare Policy*. Downsview, ON: Institute for Behavioural Research.

_____. 1987. *Social Background and Socialization: Canadian Elites and the Politics of the Welfare State*. Downsview, ON: Institute for Social Research.

Wilson, Kevin. 2002. *Spinning Competition: Convergence, Concentration and Public Policy in Canada's New Media/Communications Landscape*. Available at www.er.uqam.ca/nobel/gricis/actes/bogues/Wilson.pdf (accessed on December 30, 2002).

Winter, James. 1990. *The Silent Revolution: Media, Democracy, and the Free Trade Debate*. Ottawa: University of Ottawa Press.

_____. 1997. *Democracy's Oxygen: How Corporations Control the News*. Montreal: Black Rose.

_____. 2002. "Canada's Media Monopoly." Available at www.fair.org/extra/0205/ canwest.html (accessed on February 12, 2003).

Yakabuski, Konrad. 2004. "The Prime of Brian Mulroney." *Globe and Mail Report on Business* 20, 11.

APPENDIX A: MEDIA—CORPORATE DIRECTOR BOARD INTERLOCKS

QUEBECOR

2001 Revenues—$11,633,300,000; 2001 Assets—$19,513,200,000

Érik Péladeau—The Jean Coutu Group Inc.

Alain Bouchard—CEO of Alimentation Couche-Tard Inc., RONA Inc.

Robert R. Dutton—CEO of RONA Inc.

Pierre Laurin—Microcell Telecommunications Inc.

Brian Mulroney—Barrick Gold Corporation, COGNICASE Inc., TrizecHahn Corporation

ROGERS COMMUNICATIONS INC

2001 Revenues—$3,912,656,000; 2001 Assets—$8,960,708,000

Edward Samual (Ted) Rogers—The Toronto-Dominion Bank

H. Garfield Emerson—CAE Inc.

Philip B. Lind—Brascan Corporation

Ronald D. Besse—C.I. Fund Management Inc.

Albert Gnat—Vitran Corporation Inc., AXA Insurance (subsidiary of AXA Canada inc.), CLL Industries Inc., Slater Steel Inc., MDC Corporation Inc.

Robert W. Korthals—Co-Steel Inc., Cognos Inc., Suncor Energy Inc.

Alexander Mikalachki—The Independent Order of Foresters

David R. Peterson—Industrial-Alliance Life Insurance Company, Ivanhoe Cambridge Inc., SMX Speedy International Inc. (subsidiary of Goldfarb), Tesma International Inc. (subsidiary of Magna International Inc.), Vector aerospace Corporation

John A. Tory—Abitibi-Consolidated Inc., The Thomson Corporation

W. David Wilson—The Bank of Nova Scotia

CANWEST GLOBAL COMMUNICATIONS CORPORATION

2001 Revenues—$1,944,775,000; 2001 Assets—$6,299,220,000

Gail S. Asper—Great-West Lifeco Inc. (subsidiary of Power Corporation)

Lloyd I. Barber—Bank of Nova Scotia, Molson Inc., Teck Cominco Ltd.

Jalynn H. Bennett—Bombardier Inc., Canadian Imperial Bank of
Commerce, Sears Canada Inc., Ontario Power Generation
Inc. (crown corporation)

Lord Conrad Black—CEO of Hollinger Inc., Brascan Corporation,
Canadian Imperial Bank of Commerce

Frank J. McKenna Jr.—Acier Leroux Inc./Leroux Steel Inc., Bank
of Montreal, General Motors of Canada Ltd., Noranda Inc.,
Shoppers Drug Mart Corporation

F. David Radler—Hollinger Inc., West Fraser Timber Co. Ltd.

SHAW COMMUNICATIONS INC

2001 Revenues—$1,571,953,000; 2001 Assets—$8,787,956,000

J.R. Shaw—Suncor Energy Inc.

Leslie Earl Shaw—ShawCor Ltd.

James Francis Dinning—Finning International Inc.

Ronald V. Joyce—Sobeys Inc. (subsidiary of Empire Co. Ltd.)

Donald Mazankowski—ATCO Ltd., Conoco Canada Resources Ltd.,
Weyerhaeuser Company, Power Corporation of Canada

BELL GLOBEMEDIA

2001 Revenues—$1,203,000,000; 2001 Assets—not available

W. Geoffrey Beattie—Thomson Corporation (owns 20 percent of
Bell Globemedia), Hydro One Inc., Royal Bank of Canada

Donna Soble Kaufman—Hudson's Bay Company, TransAlta Corporation

Brian M. Levitt—Alcan Inc., Domtar Inc., Fednav Ltd

David K.R. Thomson—Thomson Corporation

Peter J. Thomson—Thomson Corporation

TRANSCONTINENTAL INC.

2001 Revenues—$1,779,377,000; 2001 Assets—$1,340,720,000

Rémi Marcoux—Canadian Tire Corporation Ltd., MAXX Inc.

Pierre Brunet—National Bank of Canada, METRO Inc., Slater Steel
Inc.

Robert Chevrier—Bank of Montreal

Gail C.A. Cook-Bennett—Manulife Financial Corporation, Petro-
Canada

J.V. Raymond Cyr—Air Canada, COGNICASE Inc., Canadian National Railway Company, TransCanada PipeLines Investments
Inc.

Harold P. Gordon—Dundee Bancorp Inc.

Hubert T. Lacroix—Zarlink Semiconductor Inc.

Monique Lefebvre—COGNICASE Inc.

HOLLINGER INC.

2001 Revenues—$1,822,060,000; 2001 Assets—$3,689,559,000

Lord Conrad Black—CanWest Global Communications, Brascan Corporation, Canadian Imperial Bank of Commerce

F. David Radler—CanWest Global Communications, West Fraser Timber Co. Ltd.

Peter Y. Atkinson—Canadian Tire Corporation Ltd., Toronto Hydro Corporation (crown corporation)

Fredrik Stefan Eaton—Masonite International Corporation

R. Donald Fullerton—Canadian Imperial Bank of Commerce, George Weston Ltd.

Henry H. Ketcham III—CEO of West Fraser Timber Co. Ltd., Toronto-Dominion Bank

Maureen J. Sabia—Canadian Tire Corporation Ltd.

Peter G. White—Cinram International Inc., Transat A.T. Inc.

APPENDIX B: THINK TANKS—CORPORATE DIRECTOR BOARD INTERLOCKS FOR 2003

FRASER INSTITUTE

Brandt C Louie—Slocan Forest Products Ltd., Royal Bank of Canada

Gwyn Morgan—CEO of Encana Corporation., HSBC Bank Canada

Phillips Roger—Canadian Pacific Railway Ltd., Fording Inc., Imperial Oil Ltd., Toronto-Dominion Bank

David Radler—Hollinger Inc., CanWest Global Communications Corporation, West Fraser Timber Company Ltd.

William W. Siebens—Petro-Canada

P.G. White—Cinram International Inc., Transat A.T. Inc., Hollinger Inc.

C.D. HOWE INSTITUTE

André Bérard—National Bank of Canada, Groupe BMTC Inc., Noranda Inc., Saputo Inc.

William Black—CEO of Maritime Life Assurance Company

Jack L. Cockwell—Brascan Corporation, Astral Media Inc., Brookfield Properties Corporation, Nexfor Inc., Noranda Inc.

F. Anthony Comper—CEO of Bank of Montreal

Peter W. Currie—Royal Bank of Canada

Jim Dinning—Finning International Inc., Shaw Communications Inc.

N. Murray Edwards—CEO of Magellan Aerospace Corporation, Ensign Resource Service Group Inc., Penn West Petroleum Ltd., Business Development Bank of Canada (crown corporation), Canadian Natural Resources Ltd., Rio Alto Exploration Ltd.

John T. Ferguson—TransAlta Corporation, Royal Bank of Canada, Suncor Energy

Kerry L. Hawkins—CEO of Cargill Ltd., Hudson's Bay Company, NOVA Chemicals Corporation, Shell Canada Ltd., TransCanada PipeLines Ltd.

Stephen Jarislowsky—Goodfellow Inc., Slocan Forest Products Ltd., Velan Inc.

David W. Kerr—Noranda Inc., Brascan Corporation, Canada Life Financial Corporation, Ontario Power Generation Inc. (crown corporation)

The Hon. Frank McKenna Jr.—Acier Leroux Inc./Leroux Steel Inc., CanWest Global Communications Corporation, Bank of Montreal, General Motors of Canada Ltd., Noranda Inc., Shoppers Drug Mart Corporation

John T. McLennan—CEO of AT&T Canada Inc., Hummingbird Ltd.

Jack M. Mintz—Brascan Corporation

William Morneau Jr.—AGF Management Ltd.

Peter J. Nicholson—Aliant Inc. (Subsidiary of Bell Canada, which is a subsidiary of BCE Inc.), Stelco Inc.

David P. O'Brien—Air Canada, Fairmont Hotels and Resorts Inc., Inco Ltd., Molson Inc., Royal Bank of Canada, TransCanada PipeLines Ltd.

Sheila H. O'Brien—CFM Corporation

Ronald Osborne—CEO of Ontario Power Generation Inc. (crown corporation), Air Canada, Shell Canada Ltd., Sun Life Financial Services of Canada

Michael E.J. Phelps—Canadian Imperial Bank of Commerce, Canadian Pacific Railway Ltd., Canfor Corporation

Roger Phillips—Canadian Pacific Railway Ltd., Fording Inc., Imperial Oil Ltd., Toronto-Dominion Bank

Charlotte A. Robb—NAV CANADA

Joseph L. Rotman—Bank of Montreal, Barrick Gold Corporation, Masonite International Corporation

ATLANTIC INSTITUTE FOR MARKET STUDIES

Purdy Crawford—AT&T Canada, Canadian National Railway Company, Emera Inc., Maple Leaf Foods Inc., Petro-Canada

Hon. John C. Crosbie—Bell Canada International Inc. (subsidiary of BCE Inc.), FPI Ltd.

Peter C. Godsoe—CEO of Bank of Nova Scotia, Empire Company Ltd.

John T. McLennon—CEO of AT&T Canada, Hummingbird Ltd.

J.W.E. Mingo—Onex Corporation

Peter J.M. Nicholson—Aliant Inc. (subsidiary of Bell Canada, which is a subsidiary of BCE Inc.), Stelco Inc.

James S. Palmer—Canadian Broadcasting Corporation (crown corporation), Canadian Natural Resources Ltd., Magellan Aerospace Corporation

Derrick Rowe—CEO of FPI Ltd.

Paul D. Sobey—CEO of Empire Company Ltd., Bank of Nova Scotia, Emera Inc., Wajax Ltd.

Harry R. Steele—CHC Helicopter Corporation, Dundee Bancorp

Inc., Hollinger Canadian Newspapers, LP (subsidiary of Hollinger Inc.)

THE CONFERENCE BOARD

Robert M. Astley—Sun Life Financial Services of Canada

Eleanor R. Clitheroe—Dofasco Inc., Inco Ltd., Toronto-Dominion Bank

Patrick Daniel—CEO of Enbridge Inc., Enerflex Systems Ltd.

Marcel Dutil—CEO of The Canam Manac Group Inc., Acier Leroux Inc./Leroux Steel Inc., The Jean Coutu Group (PJC) Inc., MAXX Inc., National Bank of Canada

David L. Emerson—CEO of Canfor Corporation, British Columbia Ferry Corporation (crown corporation), BC Gas Inc., Royal and SunAlliance Canada

William C. Fraser—CEO of Manitoba Telecom Services Inc.

Christina A. Gold—Torstar Corporation

John S. Hunkin—CEO of Canadian Imperial Bank of Commerce

Peter S. Janson— DuPont Canada Inc.

Jacques Lamarre—CEO of SNC-Lavalin Group Inc., Canadian Pacific Railway Ltd.

Pierre Lortie—The Canam Manac Group Inc.

David McD. Mann—CEO of Emera Inc.

Lorna R. Marsden—Manulife Financial Corporation

H. Stanley Marshall—CEO of Fortis Inc., Toromont Industries Ltd.

Gilles P. Ouimet—Pratt and Whitney Canada Corporation

Madeleine Paquin—Canadian Pacific Railway Ltd., Sun Life Financial Services of Canada

Réal Raymond—CEO of National Bank of Canada, COGNICASE Inc.

Raymond Royer—CEO of Domtar Inc., Power Financial Corporation (subsidiary of Power Corporation), Shell Canada Ltd.

John W. Sheridan—Bell Canada (subsidiary of BCE Inc.), Manitoba Telecom Services Inc.

Stephen G. Snyder—CEO of TransAlta Corporation, Canadian Imperial Bank of Commerce

John H. Tory—CEO of Rogers Cable Inc., Rogers Media (both subsidiaries of Rogers Communications Inc.), Cara Operations Ltd.

John M. Van Brunt—CEO of Agrium Inc., Canpotex Ltd.

Michel Vennat—CEO of Business Development Bank of Canada (crown corporation), NAV CANADA

Douglas W. G. Whitehead—CEO of Finning International Inc., BC Gas Inc.